PRAISE FOR THE MARKE

"Karen Reyburn has always been my go-to person for firms to gain that deep understanding of digital marketing that delivers a constant flow of their dream customers. There's no hype or BS with Karen. Just a structured approach built on robust, timeless principles that are easy to understand and adopt. This book provides very generous insights from the industry's leading marketing expert that will challenge, illuminate, and ultimately . . . deliver results."

JAMES ASHFORD, BESTSELLING AUTHOR
OF *SELLING TO SERVE*

"...takes the mystery out of marketing and turns it into a step-by-step process for us to follow. Highly recommended for any accountant starting, or during, their marketing journey."

CHERYL SHARP, OWNER & FOUNDER,
PINK PIG FINANCIALS

"If you want to grow your accounting business this is a must-read. Karen guides you to better understand your firm, who you want to work with, and how to find them. When it comes to your clients, the amount of money doesn't matter; what matters is who's behind the money. We used to feel obligated: they need help, so we have to help them. Now, we know we get to choose."

GEORGI ROLLINGS, OWNER, STARFISH
ACCOUNTING

"It takes twenty years to write a book like this. I love the practicality of the chapters and the deep how-to that she covers all the way through. Embrace the truth that you as an accountant are creative, and you will begin to change the world with this book as your field guide!"

JASON M. BLUMER, CPA , FOUNDER/CEO,
THRIVEAL CPA COMMUNITY NETWORK

"...Karen reminds us that great marketing isn't for you; it's for your audience, your clients. As part of this, her book helps us find our unique 'cornerstone,' showing clients how we do things so they can feel comfortable signing up. *The Accountant Marketer* is an essential read for any accounting firm leader who wants to stand apart and effectively reach their target audience."

IAN VACIN, CO-FOUNDER, KARBON

"I used to think marketing was an investment in ads, something that didn't deliver on promises. Now I understand that marketing is everything you do, and we have almost no "bad" clients! This book will give you all the tools you need to attract the clients you so desperately need and deserve. Karen and her book have transformed the whole view of marketing for me."

ALEXANDER MALMSTROM, DIGIM

THE ACCOUNTANT MARKETER

THE ACCOUNTANT MARKETER

THE STRUCTURED APPROACH ANY ACCOUNTANT CAN FOLLOW TO ATTRACT CLIENTS THEY LOVE

KAREN L. REYBURN, CPA

To Lauren,

who knows we are all creative, including accountants!

Keep On
Publishing

Keep On
Publishing

Keep On Publishing
Manchester, UK

Onboarding Graphic Copyright © 2023 by Raedan
Financial Maturity Graphic Copyright © 2023 by MAP

First Edition

Paperback: 978-1-7394117-0-1
Ebook: 978-1-7394117-1-8
KDP: 978-1-7394117-3-2
Audiobook: 978-1-7394117-2-5

Edited by Intrepid Literary
Cover design by The Book Designers

To my dad, who always cheered me on.

And for every accountant who is capable of more than you know. I'm cheering YOU on.

CONTENTS

FOREWORD

While I am never short on ideas, I am short on the time and skill required to produce compelling content that captures the attention of the right people.

Most accounting professionals could say the same. We already have the knowledge and experience necessary to create great content, but the time and resources needed to share them are limited. By partnering with marketing experts, we can overcome those obstacles and help others in a deep and meaningful way.

I was fortunate that Karen showed me how to leverage the diverse skills of a network of marketers in order to transform my ideas into professional-looking content that gets results. She helped me understand our ideal client, their issues, and, ultimately, how to communicate our proposition to them.

My firm, MAP, is a UK accountancy firm with a niche focus on the digital agency sector. We work with 120 UK digital agencies by providing them with an outsourced finance function using Xero and other connected apps. We want to be seen as the go-to firm for this sector by using our brand and marketing to stand out and give value. The assets that we have built up in MAP over the years—blogs, graphics, brochures, guides, social posts, website, and more—have become timeless lead-generation and brand-awareness tools.

Marketing is becoming more complex with so many channels and tactics to keep up with. Yet the ability to find and retain the right customers is as important as ever. That is why marketing remains so important and why you need to partner with the experts. It's too intrinsic to your business for you to abdicate responsibility of it. Success comes from combining your knowledge and experience with theirs.

The methodology shared within this book provides the framework for working through your marketing in an approachable and effective way.

If you are looking for instant results, this book is not for you. If you are ready to build a meaningful brand that your clients love, use this book as your guide and you will steadily improve your firm's ability to attract your ideal clients.

As the famous saying goes, we often overestimate what we can achieve in the short term and yet underestimate what we can achieve in the long term. By following the practical framework outlined in this book, you will build long-term value in your brand and be seen as a trusted advisor to your clients.

Paul Barnes, Owner and Managing Director, MAP

THINGS YOU NEED TO KNOW FIRST:

CHAPTER 0

"I AM AN ACCOUNTANT, NOT A MARKETER," you say.

What if you not only are a marketer, but you actually have what you need to be quite a good one? What if all you need is a little direction and training?

Marketing doesn't stand alone: it's integral to your firm

As an accountant, you're good at what you do. You've trained and even qualified in it, you feel comfortable with it, and you have the experience and stories to prove it. Marketing, on the other hand, feels less familiar. You know your firm needs it, but you figure if you stay focused on serving your clients well, the leads will come. A few tactics, some things you saw worked for other accountants, and (you believe) you'll be good to go.

You're used to going straight to the numbers. The data. The quick wins, the instant return on investment (ROI). You want to spend a little, get more in return, and be confident you are not wasting a single moment doing what won't work.

However, when you approach marketing from that angle only, eventually you will struggle. Your tendency will be to focus on those same numbers and depend on them to fix the problem.

"I just need more leads," you think. "Got to fill that funnel." But what if simply getting more—more numbers, more leads, more clients—isn't the best solution? What if you get those numbers, get the clients, and then discover new problems with the type of clients you're getting?

I've been helping accountants with their marketing for over twenty years, and the things holding you back in marketing aren't the things you think they are. The single biggest roadblock to creating and delivering great marketing isn't knowing the tips and tricks, the tactics, or the actions to take to deliver a great ROI. It's the mindset you hold about yourself, your responsibilities, and your ideal clients which will change everything.

When you take a step back and look at the structure of marketing—where leads come from, who marketing is for, and what to create in what order—marketing begins to look a lot different. Instead of putting the burden on more numbers, more successes, more quick wins, you take the responsibility to heart and look at what it is you really want from your marketing. And it goes far beyond "more clients" or "more profit."

Marketing is not one solo part of your business, something you put in a nice, tidy category or delegate to someone else. You can delegate marketing tasks, hire a marketing agency, build a marketing team, and even outsource your marketing department. But for marketing to work the way you've always wanted it to, you, the accountant, must understand how and why it works and where all the elements of marketing intersect. Your marketing is a reflection of you and your accounting business, and therefore it is entirely your responsibility.

Being a good accountant allows you to run an excellent accounting firm and truly help people in their businesses. But if the story your marketing is telling doesn't fully reflect the amazing accountant you are or the firm you're part of, it's your responsibility to fix it. Those gaps in your marketing will get wider and wider over time until your marketing is actively turning away the very clients you wish you were getting more of. It might succeed in bringing in a few ideal clients every once in a while, but it will bring many who aren't a good fit. Clients who aren't the right type of person or business for your firm to work with and don't have the same values as you do.

This book is your progressive plan to make marketing work *for* you as an accountant. You may even be surprised to discover . . .

. . . you don't hate it and aren't bad at it.

. . . maybe you actually quite like it.

. . . maybe you're even pretty good at it.

. . . maybe you enjoy it.

. . . maybe you can come to love it!

When you understand and love marketing, you accept your role as an Accountant Marketer, and marketing ceases to be an obligation weighing on your shoulders. It becomes your helper, something you never imagined marketing could be: an integrated part of your business contributing to a drip feed of the kind of prospects you love to hear from and who then become the clients you love to work with every day.

Start small, start safe

The first time I went snowboarding, I spent almost the entire day on the learner slopes. The "bunny slopes," they called them, to make sure I, a newbie, understood my low and weak position compared to the adventurers, the wildcats, the mavericks of the black runs. As much as I loved the idea of me swooping down the slopes like an Olympian, wild and daring and fearless, I recognised I wasn't even able to get both feet locked onto the snowboard without falling over, so the bunny slopes it was for me.

The ski resort suggested taking a lesson first thing, before we learned any bad habits. For forty-five minutes, we'd get direction and guidance with all our falling over, and then we'd be released to fall over all by ourselves.

I saw the value of this. I'd tried skiing before, and although I was hardly flying down the black runs, skiing made sense to me. I fell once or twice, but I did some flying and turning and felt very Olympian—at least in my own mind.

Snowboarding was not like that. At all. Snowboarding is like surfing or skateboarding, neither of which I have mastered in any way, shape, or form. The difference with snowboarding is your feet are locked onto the board itself so when you fall it comes with you. And when you fall, you land in soft snow, so it's not as harsh as concrete or as spluttery as seawater.

Falling was the lesson of not only the forty-five-minute training session but also the next eight hours. My instructor told me, "You'll basically fall a lot, so it's important to fall right." I thought he was exaggerating, but after an hour or so, I realised he was correct. (Though maybe "constantly" was more accurate than "a lot.") I got up and fell. I shifted my weight and fell. I leaned back and fell. I leaned forward and fell. The instructor showed me how to lean, how to fall, and what to do after I fell in order to get up quickly and try again. I spent the entire day falling . . . and yet I found myself really enjoying it. I loved the challenge, and I kept trying.

By the end of the day, something finally clicked, and I was actually snowboarding. I was moving—fast. I was lifting the board, and my whole body came with it. I was turning, landing, and moving again. I loved it. I was bruised all over (and knew there were more bruises coming), and I couldn't wait to do it all over again the next time.

As an accountant, marketing is going to be for you like skiing and snowboarding were for me. It may be like me and skiing: something you think you understand pretty well, and you pick it up fairly quickly without much training or practice. You point your marketing in the direction you want to go, and it more or less takes you there, so you want to get better at it. Or maybe it's like me and snowboarding: something you don't understand at all. Things don't work too well, you try things and don't see a return, and you fall a lot. (And then you love it.)

This book is for both kinds of accountants. Those of you who have picked it up fairly quickly can unlearn bad habits picked up from doing marketing on your own. If you're just getting started, this is your chance to get it right before you even get going, before you learn those bad habits.

To all of you, I say: start small, start safe. Your goal is not to be an Olympian marketer, much less become one by the time you're done reading this book for the first time. It's about doing marketing in a way that makes sense both to you and the clients who are drawn to your firm. It's about falling—a lot—but doing so because you are actually trying and are directly involved. It's about falling in a way which hurts you less and teaches you more. And it's about actually enjoying marketing and discovering to your surprise you are pretty good at it too.

This isn't a marketing instruction manual with a list of actions guaranteed to deliver results. Every accountant is a different human with different skills, talents, and tendencies. Your firm is different from others because of who you are as a human, because of all the humans who work for and with you, and because of the humans who pay for your accounting services. You're learning to snowboard, and how you do that will vary from how others learn. You get some direction, strap your feet in, wobble a bit, fall, and ultimately move in the direction you want to go, tackling the run you want to be on at the speed you feel comfortable with.

Marketing isn't a dry, emotionless list of actions which works for everyone; it's a process of telling stories. Your firm has a story. Your clients have stories to tell. Think of marketing as your storybook, and this book as your guideline to follow so the story gets told well to the people who need to hear it.

"Start small, start safe" means you get to choose how quickly you move, how much you spend, and what you try. It means growth or success will look different for you than it will for others, and you don't have to do what others are doing (and indeed I'd recommend you don't focus on that). This opens up potential for you, including:

Not having to choose an exclusive niche straight away (or at all). You do need to identify the audience you want to work with, and this will get more specific over time. But you don't have to choose only one industry. You might not choose an industry as your audience at all. We'll talk more about your audience in the next chapter.

Doing a little bit of test marketing instead of going all-in straight away. You don't have to (and I would argue, please don't) create an entire brand with a new firm name and new website with its own domain straight away. If you're trying to reach a new audience or promote a new service or course, create one website page on your current site. Write a few blog posts and record a few videos. Follow your ideal audience on social media, make some connections, and see how it goes in a small way first.

Creating the kind of content which feels more comfortable to you at first. You may be more comfortable writing blog posts than recording videos, and that's okay—at first. Yes, you want some wins with marketing to keep yourself motivated; you also need wins to build confidence. You need to know you can do this. As we'll talk about in chapter 10, video will completely change the way you engage with your prospects, and it will help them make decisions faster as well as save you and your team time. But if video feels scary (or downright terrifying), start with what you can do. The blog posts you write could become scripts for videos in the future. You could record short screensharing videos for a client you love working with or for your team.

Trying something with no idea whether it will work or not. Falling doesn't mean you've failed and have to start thumping your way back to the ski lodge. It means you get back up and start again. Download a new social media platform and start using it. Write a few personal emails to specific clients. Start writing blog posts every week. Download and edit images on your phone to fit your firm's brand. Learn how captions work for videos. This turns your attention from asking "Will this one action deliver leads?" and helps you take another small step towards building your marketing toolkit.

Giving yourself permission to go at your own pace is the first step. Next, you need to hear that creativity is for accountants too. You're not held back because you're an accountant: your skills mean you are uniquely placed for great creativity in marketing.

Accountants, you are creative

As a part of starting small and safe, it's time to recognise that you, the accountant, are creative.

You personally are creative. Your team is creative. Your firm is creative. Creativity is a quality all humans innately have, regardless of our role or job or how we perceive our fit into society. Every human is designed to be creative, and we have these qualities long before we learn who we are as individuals. And yet the belief that "accountants aren't creative" is one you've heard, been told, or, worst of all, told yourself for most of your life. Ever since you decided to be an accountant or chose to work in accounting, there's a part of you that believes you are boring, the complete opposite of creative. What you do on a daily basis can reinforce this belief:

Following rules.

Ticking boxes.

Putting numbers in columns.

Telling people what they can't do, what's not allowed.

That's certainly how others perceive accountants. Even doing an image search for "accountants" brings up endless pictures of people in suits sitting at desks with calculators. But that isn't who you are, and it doesn't reflect how you help people.

For many of us, creativity brings up the idea of artists. Painters, writers, illustrators. We think the only people who are creative are those who . . . create things. Out of nothing. Ex nihilo. As an accountant, you don't do that. What you work with is presented to you. Sometimes it's a mess and you make sense of it, but you're not usually starting with a blank page or canvas.

The more time I spend with accountants, the more I see your creativity. I see you coming up with ideas, hesitantly sometimes, but still asking the creative question "What if we . . . ?" You explore how you can help your clients better and how to live out your culture and values better. You praise your clients for what they do well in marketing, social media, and video, then wonder, "Could we do something like that?" Yes, a creative team can take your idea and help bring it to life or turn it into something on-brand and visually impressive, but the core idea is yours. We are all being creative in our unique ways.

Defining creativity is hard. What *is* creativity, after all? How do we define it? How can you accept you are creative and notice it in your business and life?

Ed Catmull, computer scientist, cofounder of Pixar, and president of Walt Disney Animation Studios, said in his book *Creativity, Inc.: Overcoming the Unseen Forces That Stand in the Way of True Inspiration*, that he intentionally tried not to define the word "creativity," because that didn't seem useful. "I believe that we all have the potential to solve problems and express ourselves creatively," he said. "What stands in our way are these hidden barriers—the misconceptions and assumptions that impede us without knowing it."

Ultimately, creativity comes down to two things:

problem-solving

and

curiosity.

My agency, The Profitable Firm (known as PF) ran a series of "Accountants are Creative" events. For one of these events, I asked an accountant I know to speak about how he views creativity. He had shared with me how he believes it's about problem-solving and inviting other perspectives. He shared this at the event, showing how he and his firm have used creativity and an entrepreneurial mindset to work through the problems they faced. This included systemising communication so deadlines were always met and setting up the qualifying process so they only took on the very best clients (rather than just any client who might become troublesome later).

Every accountant present was spellbound. They had so many questions. They all wanted to talk systems and processes and how-tos, and for a moment, I thought, "No, this isn't what I meant for us to talk about. We're supposed to be talking about being creative!" Then I realised I was the one with the wrong perspective. Yes, creativity includes your marketing, your brand, and your events. It includes getting materials and websites designed and having printed banners and art. But it also includes solving problems and being curious. These two qualities lead to all kinds of creativity, whether it's a designed image for your marketing, a new onboarding system, or a better way to communicate with your clients.

Accountants, you are creative. And if you choose to believe you're not creative, it slows down or even shuts down the very qualities you need the most, the ones which help you, your firm, and your whole team. When you think about problem-solving and curiosity, it's a little easier to believe in your own creativity. You can say to yourself, "Okay, maybe I'm not much for drawing, painting, sketching, or even writing. I find it easier to send an email or work through a spreadsheet than try something new, like writing a blog post or recording a video. But what's the problem here I can work on solving? How can I have a curious, open mind to ask questions and see things differently? Who could I involve in this process to help me see new possibilities and remind me that, when it comes to creativity, there's no right answer?"

That's the real kicker with creativity, especially for accountants—there's no right answer. There are no debit and credit columns, always adding up. Creativity can be a bit of a mess, like a child with crayons going all over the page and outside the lines and maybe even onto the table (or wall). You try something. Maybe it works, and maybe it doesn't. Maybe it sort of works, but you need to tweak it a little. Maybe in the process of working on it, you realise what's not working. Maybe you struggle to figure it out, so you scrap the whole thing and try something else.

Yes, accounting follows rules, and you help your clients stay on the right side of those rules. But what you really love—what stirs you up, gets you motivated, and keeps you doing this work called accounting—is the conversations with your clients about their business problems. Whether it's a problem with their software, prices, products, taxes, or profits, you get to look at the pieces and help them consider what the possible solutions are. You and your client both get to stay curious, ask new questions, get excited, and find a new way (or an old way) that works. All of this is creativity. All of this is problem-solving, curiosity, and trying. You are creative. And your team is creative too.

Personal involvement makes your firm's marketing better

When you have team members, even if it's only one other person right now, get them involved with marketing too. The more involved they are, the more accurate your marketing is, the better reach you get, and the easier it is for people to see who your firm truly is. Marketing isn't words on a website page; it's telling people how things will be once they start working with you. What you say and share is meant to be lived out by people —you and the people who work with you.

One of the challenges with involving your team is understanding the level at which they want to be involved and how much you want them involved. After all, they've been hired as an accountant, bookkeeper, payroll specialist, or some other specific role. When we talk with accountants who have never had this conversation with their team, they often find their efforts to introduce marketing involvement meet with resistance. The team members don't want to do social media; they want to do accounting work. They don't want to record videos; they feel more comfortable sending emails. They don't want to write blog posts; they want to do the work they were hired to do.

In one sense, that's correct. You haven't hired them to be marketers, and one of the worst things you can do is place the burden of marketing responsibility on people who haven't been trained for it, don't understand it, and would be doing it on top of the job you originally hired them to do. However, just as you are reading this to discover how and why you need to be an Accountant Marketer, your team also needs to learn they will have some involvement in marketing too. Marketing isn't something set aside only for a marketing team to do in isolation. It must be connected to everything and everybody in the firm so it is more accurate and more authentic. Your marketing flows from the work you're actually doing with clients, and who is doing that work? The team. All of you need to understand the Concentric Circles of Team Involvement in Marketing.

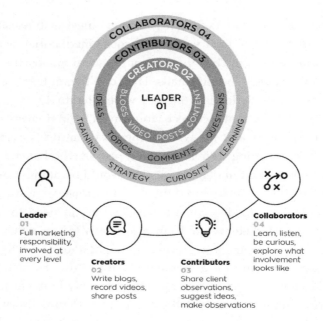

The Concentric Circles of Team Involvement recognises not every person in the team has the same responsibility or involvement in marketing, and that's okay. It also shows every person in the team does have *some* involvement and responsibility in marketing. Let's go through each of the levels:

Leader: That's you. Marketing is ultimately your responsibility, and you must own that. Reading this book may be one of your first steps towards understanding this. The buck stops with you. You don't abdicate responsibility for marketing; you delegate it. That means you're involved at the very heart of marketing. You care about it. You listen, suggest ideas, write blog posts, and record videos. You talk with your marketing manager and team. You review the numbers and discuss analytics for your firm. The responsibility for ROI is yours too. It's yours because the business is yours. We'll talk more about that in the final chapter of this book.

Creators: These are the people who are excited and willing to create content, which includes writing blog posts, recording videos, and sharing on social media. This could be one person or two people to start with, but eventually you do want more people moving from other circles into this one. However, this takes time. There's no race to push someone from thinking "I'm an accountant" to "I'm uniquely and daily involved in marketing" within moments. The kind of firm and brand you have will direct the level and speed to which this happens. If you have a fast-growing firm, changing often and quickly, you can introduce this concept right away and involve the team without delay. If your firm moves at a slower pace and change takes time, you can introduce this concept in stages and consider comfort levels of those you involve in marketing. It's your call. But at the beginning, you need at least one other person to join you in learning and applying marketing to your firm. This is particularly hard in larger firms where marketing is delegated to others and most of the team do "the accounting work." Maybe there's one director who has been tasked with marketing. Eventually, you need everybody collaborating in marketing; but if you have at least one other person alongside you from the start, you can make a lot of progress and start to see results. These results encourage others to move circles.

Contributors: These people are not actually creating the content yet, but they are actively contributing ideas, questions, and observations. When the firm posts a blog, they read and comment on it. When the new website is launched, they have ideas and observations to share. These are generally people who want to be Creators but don't have the confidence yet or aren't sure what kind of creating they want to do. Let them contribute, and listen to what they have to say. Encourage contribution by asking specific questions and holding meetings designed specifically for these team members. Give them training. Invite them to marketing meetings. Let them absorb, learn, and contribute.

Collaborators: This is everybody. Every single person who is part of the firm from the admin assistants to the payroll specialists, from the bookkeepers to the receptionist, and from the IT department to the partners and directors. Every single person in the firm needs to have some sense of what marketing you're doing, who your audience is, what the firm's brand is and why, and how they are a part of the whole marketing picture. Ideally, many people will be moving from Collaborators to a more active Contributor role, but it's okay if that takes time. Some people will never move out of this circle, and that's okay too, as long as it's the right place for them. You never want someone's motivation for leaving or staying in a circle to be fear or an unwillingness to change or try. Give them every opportunity, every training, every direction, and it will become clear which circle offers the best position for them to participate in the firm's marketing.

When I first created the Concentric Circles asset, I shared it as a sketch with owners and leaders of accounting firms and asked them to identify where they were on the graphic. One firm owner said, "I'm in that white area outside of the circles." I realised I'd been expecting leaders to see themselves within the diagram. I hadn't anticipated how much the feeling of barely getting started, not being organised or ready, or merely thinking about where to begin would impact where they saw themselves. I admired the honesty in that reply, and we agreed his first goal was to move into the Collaborator circle. We talked about the progression from one circle to the next, how long that might take, what he could do to make transitions more quickly, and where the rest of the team were.

The team will follow your leadership. If you, as the leader, hang about at the outer edges or in the white spaces, they will too. If you begin to move to the outermost circle, they will come a little closer. As you move deeper within, they will too. Your job as an Accountant Marketer is not only to be personally involved in marketing but also to encourage involvement from the rest of the team.

Most importantly, none of this will work unless your firm is a place of psychological safety. This means it is a safe place where people can live, work, and mess up sometimes. This is a place where . . .

. . . people can make mistakes and not be terrified about what will happen to them.

. . . people get praised when they do great work and held accountable when they do something not so great.

. . . everyone is human and admitting that isn't seen as weakness.

. . . people are allowed to be curious and get things wrong without being punished.

Otherwise, they'll try once and give up out of despair, and you'll be worse off than you ever were because they're not going to try anything, out of fear of reprisals.

A place of psychological safety is really tough to build. At PF, we've been consciously working on it for years. The most important factor of all is the leader is never the one who gets to say whether the workplace *is* safe or not. Only your team members and clients get to decide that. You can say you want your firm to be a safe place for people to work and live. You can say you're working towards it being a safe place and be open to listening when someone mentions (or hints) it's not. You can (and need to) work on your own transparency and vulnerability because that encourages others to do the same. You can take responsibility when you fail. You can share failures and learnings together, focusing on what the learnings tell you. Building your firm into a place of psychological safety is hard. It's personal. It's full of vulnerabilities, fears, and failings. But when the team feels safe, you know the company is safe with them. This includes your brand, social media, and marketing. When everyone who works in your company feels safe, they do their very best work and reflect the company well on social and elsewhere.

Accepting your responsibility in marketing and what you're learning as an Accountant Marketer is a good start towards building this place of safety. When you understand marketing is far more than a list of actions for one person or a small team to carry out, you may realise you have a lot of work to do when it comes to the culture of your firm. This is work related to your brand and values, how you hire, and the way you lead. It's how you help the team feel part of the firm you're building together. Recognising how marketing is connected to every single spoke of the accounting firm wheel is a first step. The spoke we'll talk about next is hiring new team members.

Marketing isn't only for attracting clients; it's also for attracting new team members

Marketing isn't only about reaching potential new clients. When you use content marketing to share who your firm truly is, it helps future team members see it is a place where they want to work. This is why all your marketing must be an accurate reflection of who you truly are. Often our clients ask, "Would it be okay for me to write about . . . ?" Often what they're asking about is a topic which seems to have nothing to do with accounting. It could be the new house they're building, social justice, women's rights, or environmental impact. I'll give you the answer I give them: if it's important to you, it will help your marketing attract the people you want, both clients and team members. If the environment or social justice are important to you, not only is it okay to write about those things but I'd argue you really must write about them. What you believe in affects the way you approach the world around you, how you deliver accounting services, and how you choose who to work with. You work with people who matter to you, whose businesses matter to you, and they need to know what this looks like for you.

Some businesses will literally work with anyone. I've known firm owners who will sign up a client they don't really like or believe in if the business is big, the fee is high, and the work falls within their expertise. That's a short-sighted way to do business. Inevitably, something will happen to make the relationship difficult. It's difficult for you to serve a business owner, helping them grow their sales and profits, if you don't believe what they're doing is good or worthwhile. It's hard to advise someone about their numbers, and ultimately their life, when their values aren't yours. They need to match.

The same applies to reaching potential new team members. Part of the impact of your marketing will be helping future team members understand who your firm is, how you do business, and what you care about. The more they understand your firm, the more likely they are to know whether this is the place for them before they start working there. The more they understand before they're hired, the more "on brand" they will be once they join because they won't have to learn a hidden culture, one which wasn't fully expressed online.

As we'll talk about in the first chapter, when you prepare marketing content, you start with your audience: who they are, how they feel, and what they're going through right now. Potential employees are an audience too. As you prepare career pages, role descriptions, and videos, think about how the person looking for a job is feeling. Most potential employees will be nervous, wondering if you really are who you say you are on the "About" page of your website. Before they apply, they'll read about your values, which likely sound admirable. They'll read the bios of your partners and team members, which seem interesting and share some personal quips or quotes. They'll explore your recent blogs, watch videos you and the team have created, and they'll read through your social media posts. But even when all of those feel like a match to them and show them how you approach accounting, business, and life, they may still feel unsure. What if it all seems great, and they leave their current job and come to you but within a few months realise it was all a show? What if it's all merely words, a facade of nice-sounding values covering over the same difficult work environment they left behind?

You can assuage those fears by showing the true heart of your firm in what you say, the things you post, the videos you record, and the way you interact with people on social media. Potential team members will notice. And if who you seem to be in your marketing is appealing but does not truly match the way the rest of the firm really behaves and does business, you've got some internal culture work to do.

ROI comes from following the twelve elements in order

Return on investment (ROI) may feel like the most important part of marketing. The twelve elements in the following chapters will help you discover how you get that return. I'll talk about the specific topic of ROI in the very last chapter, not because it's the least important but because you'll be tempted to make it your highest priority. Before you start looking at your audience, you'll be thinking, "But how will I get them to sign up?" Before you start thinking about the issues and feelings and problems they face, you'll be wondering, "But how many leads will I get?" When you focus on ROI alone, you miss out on the purpose and intention of marketing, which is to speak to your audience and help them. This in turn will help you.

The beauty of these twelve elements is how they help relieve the burdens you've been carrying. Marketing isn't meant to be a burden; it's meant to relieve your burdens. It helps the right kind of people to find you and delivers the very best clients to you on a drip feed. The great news is you don't have to put pressure on yourself, your marketing team, or even your prospects. Good marketing can handle the pressure when you let it do its job consistently and patiently in the same direction, tracking the numbers all the way.

When you are an Accountant Marketer, ROI is not someone else's responsibility; it's yours. You don't hand it off to someone else, shouting, "Show me the money!" or "Prove this works!" ROI doesn't belong to your marketing team, your business coach, the ads you run, or even this book you're reading. The responsibility for ROI belongs to you because the business is yours. The time you invest is yours. The team is yours. The money is yours. The ownership is yours. Yes, you need to see a return, and you will get that return when you follow the marketing map; apply the twelve elements of content marketing; and invest money, time, effort, partnership, and opinion. You will see your numbers improve, whether it's website numbers, social numbers, sales, or profits. But the credit for that doesn't sit with a marketing agency or with a coach. We aren't the ones who get the results for you. You're the one who makes it happen.

You're the one who identified your goals and shared your perspective, collaborating with others to connect those elements to marketing actions. You're the one who thought about your firm's values and shared what matters most to you in life. You're the one who hires the team, trains them, and helps them work with your clients. You and your team decide whether to take on a client or not. You decide to sack a client if they're not living your values and aren't a fit anymore.

A good marketing agency will take seriously your need to see ROI and help you understand what that looks like for your firm. They will also take responsibility to advise, direct, educate, and support. They'll share case studies. They'll rejoice and groan with you in appropriate measure. They'll celebrate the wins and work through the losses, looking for patterns and helping you see what can be hard to see because you're so deep in it. But the wins (and you will get them, and they will be big, and you'll be so excited) are all yours. A good marketing agency will be pleased with you, but *you* are the one who's done it. You're the one who got the ROI. You're the hero, not us. We're just the guide.

The same principle applies to the relationship I have with our own accountants. I meet with my client manager monthly to go through the accounts. We identify what numbers went up and which ones went down, and we discuss why. We celebrate when the profit percentage is rising, and we consider what to do if it's not. We meet annually to set budgets, targets, and goals. But when we have amazing results, he says, "Really good job. Well done to you and the team. *You* did this." I thank him and the whole firm for how they contributed and for being a calm voice of reason when we have fears. I thank them for helping us see what other agencies like ours were doing (or not doing) and how we can learn from that. We're grateful to have them there, supporting, advising, and guiding. But ultimately, we are the ones who got the profits within our business. We're the ones who got the ROI.

That's what I want for you in your marketing.

So before we look at the numbers and how to track them and look at getting new leads, let's turn our attention to the reason you're doing all this marketing: the people you most want to work with.

CHAPTER 1
AUDIENCE

When I started working in an accounting firm, I was asked to help with business development and marketing. Early on, we were talking about who their ideal client was and how we would decide which ones to choose. The partners laughed and said, "Really, it's anyone who will write us a cheque!"

Not every person who is ready to pay will be the right client for you

Time has moved on, and now it's bank payments and payment authorisation apps, but the principle is still there, and the joke isn't really a joke after all. It wasn't a joke in the firm I worked in, either; we really would take anyone who would pay us. The problems resulting from that were significant. We worked with clients who didn't pay their fees. Clients who brought their records in a day before the deadline, clients whose business we didn't fully understand, and clients who didn't understand what we were doing for them.

The "anyone who will pay" approach is old-school thinking, and it builds bad habits. The truth is you do *not* want anyone who will pay your fees. Simply because someone pays your fees doesn't mean they're the right client for you and your firm to work with. Are they your kind of person? Do they live out your values? Do you *like* working with them? Will you be able to get results for them, and will taking them on help you be a more profitable firm?

There's a big difference between good money and bad money. Good money is money paid to you from a client who is good *for you and your firm*.

Bad money is money from anyone else.

The amount doesn't matter. You know as well as I do what it's like to take on a client because they seem so attractive at first. They have three businesses! Their sales are growing every month! They're so keen and enthusiastic, and everything is a yes. And then over a period of weeks and months, you start to see this enthusiasm and energy means you're working with someone who continually changes their mind. Who will change accountants again, on the spur of the moment, like they did when they came to you. Whose moods change like the weather, and you find one of the team crying because of something the client said or how much pressure they were under. You can learn about setting expectations, creating good systems, being clear with boundaries, and helping the team do the same; but sometimes no matter what you do, no matter how much money a client is willing to pay you, it's still bad money.

Similarly, you could take on a client who is young and keen, listens to everything you say, works hard, and pays a very small monthly fee to start. The work is still profitable for you, but it's small in comparison to some of your larger fees, and it's certainly not the size of the fee you got all excited about with the client who had three businesses. But this other client paying you smaller fees is your kind of person. They listen to you, they value your advice, and the moment their business grows or they start diversifying or growing globally, they buy more and work more closely with you and continue listening. This is good money—they're a client who is a good fit for you.

Think about who a good client is for your firm. There's no such thing as "a good client" in the abstract. There is no objective ideal in marketing, because it's your marketing. All that matters is what fits for you.

And yet, oddly enough, the place we start is not with you. We start with them: the clients you want to work with. These are the people you want to discover your firm. This is your audience.

Good marketing makes your buyer say, "Oh, that's me!"

We start here because your marketing is not for you.

Your brand is not for you. Your website is not for you. The blogs, videos, content, and social posts you share are not for you. Your website, your emails, your social media posts, your team, your systems—none of them are for you. They all exist, as does your accounting firm, for the people and businesses you serve.

Yes, marketing needs to bring you a return. So does your entire accounting business. We'll talk more about how to track marketing return in a later chapter, but if you focus your thinking on you and what you get (even subconsciously), your marketing will reflect that, and your audience won't find it as appealing. When your intention in creating a website page is focused on "making more sales" rather than helping your audience to solve a problem, they won't feel heard or see the solution for what it is. When you choose a name or logo based on whether it is appealing to *you*, it won't be as appealing to the kind of people you want to work with. Because your logo is not for you. You are not the audience.

As business owner and author Donald Miller says, your client is the hero. You're the guide. You're still someone important—you're Dumbledore, you're Gandalf, you're Yoda. But every moment you spend thinking about how your marketing is going to help *you* is a moment you've lost which could have been turned to thinking about your clients. What do *they* want?

What do *they* need? Why *they* would read this email or sign up with you as their accountant?

Make everything about them, so much so that when they see your content, they think, "Oh! That's me!" You want to be so specific they're almost shocked. They say (or think) things like:

- "I didn't know it was possible to find an accountant who gets how I feel."
- "Wait—is this an accounting firm? They're so helpful and understanding. I didn't expect that."

It may be surprising to you how much emotion is involved in choosing an accountant; they need to *feel* (as well as believe) you can help them.

Accountants have historically been all things to all people. You do your accounting work and maybe some advisory and strategy for anyone who needs it. Maybe after a while you stopped working with smaller or start-up businesses or stopped doing tax returns only, but you still take anyone who wants to work with you or is ready to pay you money. And you're almost afraid of doing marketing which will send people away. However, the very best marketing *does* send people away. That's its job.

Good marketing divides.

It draws in the very best clients for you, and it is literally unappealing to the sort of clients you don't want. It sends them away. This doesn't mean they aren't lovely people with amazing businesses. But there will be people who think they want to work with you who are not *your* kind of clients, because they aren't the ones you know best or are best placed to help.

At PF, we've worked exclusively with accountants for over ten years. We also work with a particular kind of accountant we've defined as ambitious accountants, who serve with heart, who have ideas, and are willing to be involved in their own marketing. When they come to us, they're still getting the kind of clients they don't want or their prospects and clients are leading the marketing. This means they're waiting on the prospects, not taking the initiative. Your marketing doesn't have to work this way. You have two options:

- You can try to appeal to lots of people and market from a place of fear; or
- You can appeal to *only* those you absolutely want and no one else, and market from a place of confidence.

Your audience wants you to choose the second option. They want you to be confident. They want you to know who you serve. They want to feel they're critically important to you, that they're not simply another client. Once they sign up with you as their accountant, you are in a position of massive trust. That trust starts building long before they send an enquiry.

As an accountant, you're not selling stuff, a product they can buy from you or anywhere else. The work you do is deep. You're talking about families, money, and personal worries and fears. Some accountants tell me, "I think part of the accounting qualification needs to include training in psychology, therapy, and relationship counselling!" You know when your clients are getting divorced or thinking about it. You know the milestones of their lives and the names of their children and pets. Your client pops round, or you do, or you get together for drinks or dinner.

It's relational, not transactional.

You do want to sell services and make a profit, but that's because profits are what provide for you, your family, and your employees. They help deliver the life you've imagined, and they do that for your team as well. It's lovely when your clients' businesses become more profitable and they need more services from you, but ultimately you care about your clients and their successes. You're building relationship. It's relationship which will bring you both the returns you're looking for. When you think about your ROI, think beyond the monies, the services, and the leads. Think about the relationships you're building, and be someone who delivers a return on that relationship. Then it will deliver a return back to you.

You may want to know what marketing *stuff* you need to do. What actions work best? Which tools and apps do you use? What content do you write? What analytics do you track and when, and what do you keep doing or stop doing? As with all marketing questions, the answer is "it depends," and it depends on the kind of audience you're talking to and their preferences. Behind all this *stuff* are the people you want to work with and the messages they will understand and appreciate. They want to see you understand them and the problems they're facing on a day-to-day basis. This is a relationship you're building. And good relationships take time. Let's look at how that works from a buyer's perspective.

How your buyers buy: The Buyer Progression Model

Overheard in the pub: "Hey, you seem like a nice person. Want to get married?"

Actually, I haven't overheard that in the pub, but if I did, I would immediately know it was a bit odd and possibly creepy. What kind of person wants to leap from "I've never met you before" to "Let's build a lasting relationship"?

Unfortunately, for many accountants, this is what you're trying to do with your marketing. You want to move potential buyers from a place of never having heard of you before to a situation in which they are trusting you with their financial and personal information and a significant amount of money as well. Regardless of the type of relationship it is, building that relationship follows similar principles. Whether you're getting to know someone at the pub who seems like a pretty cool person or you're connecting with someone who could eventually become a client of your accountancy firm, you can't rush things. There's a process.

You want the drip feed of good clients. The magical place where people find you and come to you, slowly and steadily, and neither you nor they actually remember where the relationship began. Maybe you even build a waiting list because the drip feed is working so well. Content marketing delivers the drip feed and does it at a slow burn. You may have invested some time and money in this already. You've been blogging, sharing a few videos, being more visible on social media, and perhaps you've run an event or tried some social ads. But in spite of all your efforts, you're not getting that drip feed of enquiries you were hoping for.

Why? You're missing a few elements from your progression model.

Accountants are in a massive position of trust, and marketing is your opportunity to build trust with people who don't know you yet. The Buyer Progression Model helps you see the progress your buyer makes and helps you identify the type of marketing you need at each stage.

Each stage of this model varies depending on the type of person and audience. It may take days; it may take months or years. Depending on how they think and make decisions and how clear your marketing is, their progression time will vary. You can even begin tracking the numbers for each section of the progression model so you know what your buyer's progression is and plan your marketing accordingly. Here's how each section works.

Nothing

At this point, your prospect has never heard of you. They literally have no connection with you, they don't know you exist, or they may not even know accountants like you exist. They have concerns, fears, and issues, and those may be pushing them to take action. They might even be actively ignoring them. Your goal is to move them to awareness.

Awareness

Here, you want to appear on their radar from time to time. The more often you appear, the more likely they will move to the next step. The buyer reads website pages, follows you on social, reads and absorbs blog post content, and watches videos. This content you've created is answering the questions they have, teaching them about what confuses or bothers them, being helpful—and they notice it. Building awareness can be a short or a long process; it will vary depending on how much time and money you are ready to invest. If you throw yourself into this fully by trying things, being willing to fall or fail, involving your entire team, getting help, learning, and making it a part of your daily work, then you will build awareness more quickly. If you go a bit slower, the process will take longer. Either way, it will still happen, and small daily actions build on each other until one day you realise you have more people on your database, following you on social, or recognising your firm name.

Here are some of the ways you can build awareness of your firm and your expertise. If the suggested time frames feel too much to start with, start small and start safe. Do these activities once a month if you aren't ready to do once a week. But start, and keep going. Each of these are discussed in more detail in subsequent chapters.

Regular blog posts: I'd recommend writing one per week. Write them yourself, involve the team, or outsource the work (as long as the content is yours and unique to you). Building fresh content helps you get found.

Social media daily posting: Have a consistent presence on at least one of the basic social media platforms (i.e., Facebook, Twitter, LinkedIn, Instagram), and post on a daily basis. Ideally, you will be doing the posting personally, and your team will be involved as well. But you can also outsource some of this, so if you're busy or are away, you're still building social awareness for your firm.

Videos: This is the most powerful way to build trust and awareness at the same time. Prospects see you, they hear you, and they learn from you. They get familiar and comfortable with who you, your team, and your firm are. Start recording videos to answer the questions you get regularly from clients or prospects.

Connections: This means engaging with people as the real humans they are. You're not offering them a download or inviting them to an event; you're simply commenting on their post, asking a question, or sharing their content. Ideally, you and your team will do this on a daily basis. Even five minutes a day will help you be more present and build awareness.

At this stage, you are being the least "salesy" you could possibly be. Most accountants I talk to have a horror of being pushy in sales, and don't want to pressure people into something they don't want or need. Most of us also hate being on the receiving end of this type of approach. The Buyer Progression Model is about slowly sharing yourself and your content so the right people come when they are ready. Answer questions they can review when it feels right to them. They can go at their own pace. You can influence their progression and help them decide as quickly as they want to; but you're never pushing them faster than they actually want to go.

Free things

Now your potential buyer is aware of you, it's time to offer something helpful which requires no investment (and very little effort) on their part. They are still exploring whether you are trustworthy, so you build on their awareness level by being helpful in a practical way. The key at this stage is to be helpful simply because it's the right thing to do and because you have expertise people need. If you are being helpful purely to "monetise" your audience, this comes across in your marketing and prevents building trust. To avoid this pitfall, give away information and only charge for implementation.

When you create information applicable to anyone, give it away. Write a blog post, record a video, create a guide, and share it. When they need to talk about how this information applies to their situation, charge for that. The more free information you give away, the more chargeable work you can do. Instead of repeating the same types of things to every prospect in endless meetings, you only meet with those who are ready to receive a proposal. If they're not ready, the free content is there, quietly building trust.

The shiny object syndrome is classic for accountants when it comes to marketing. It's hard and discouraging to press on day after day writing blogs, attending events, sending emails, and being visible on social. You want *results*, and you want them *fast*. So when you notice something shiny and new in marketing, you want to try it now and have it start working now.

A firm owner I was speaking to once got all excited about Facebook ads. He said, "Someone in a group I'm in told me they did some Facebook ads, and they got two new leads per week! Let's do Facebook ads!"

The best kind of marketing places you in front of the highest quality prospects and leads. The problem is this kind always takes time. You can accelerate the process by spending more time or money, getting support, or involving more people, but at the end of the day, you are going to have to go through the hard slog for a little while.

Let's go back to the firm owner considering Facebook ads because he wanted to *get sales*. The first thing he did was link the ad for his firm to an enquiry form. This form asked for a name, company name, email address, phone number, and other information to arrange a meeting. Unsurprisingly, he got a grand sum of zero leads from that Facebook ads campaign. That's because he was trying to skip steps within the progression model. He was going from zero awareness ("I've never heard of this firm") to sharing personal information and pushing for a sale ("I'm ready to buy"). Back at the pub, it's like someone saying "Hey, I got you a drink," and before you can even take a sip, they've invited you back to their place. Bit creepy, mate. Think I'll go move over here.

What worked better for this firm owner was running a new Facebook ad, directing the visitor to a blog post. The firm chose a blog post they knew to be popular which had been shared with many clients and prospects. No personal information was required to access it. There was no investment at this stage, simply good content helping the visitor get to know the firm, spend a little time on the website, and create trust. The firm then retargeted those same people with another invitation, this time to a webinar on a similar topic as the ad they clicked. At that stage, the registration form asked for a name and email address. As a result of doing this, their retargeted group was sitting at eight hundred people instead of zero.

Here are types of free things you can share. You can mix and match these a bit; for example, you might include a link to a template in a blog post or include a video on a website landing page along with a PDF guide.

- PDF guide (industry guide, tips on a particular topic)
- Blog post (answering a question they have)
- Video (screenshare of how to do something)
- Unique landing page (specific to their industry or business)
- Downloadable template (a tool they can use straight away)
- Event (on a topic they care about)
- Webinar (providing specific tips and help)

You can also download the Buyer Progression Model guide for more ideas at wearepf.com/buyer. (See what I did there?)

By this stage, your prospect has gone from being unaware of

you to vaguely aware to building a little bit of confidence and trust. They've downloaded a few things, attended a webinar, registered for an event, and spent time on your website. You'll be tempted to rush it at this point, thinking, "Yay, they downloaded this PDF! That means they're ready for a meeting." That could be the case; but it's even more likely they're still gathering information. Let them go at the speed they want to. At this stage, your biggest mistake will be to try to skip stages again. Be ready with a small paid thing they can buy when they want to test the waters.

Small paid things

Let's go back to how this feels from the prospect's perspective. Back at the pub, you've been chatting with the same person for a few hours. You get on brilliantly, know all the same film quotes, and enjoy the same drink. You've let them buy you a drink or two. You're interested in moving on to something beyond the pub, but you're not at full relationship level yet. It's not time for them to break out the engagement ring. With a personal relationship, the growth in trust involves spending more time together, maybe going out on Saturday afternoon, hanging out with a group of friends, or getting dinner. You're committing to more time, trusting yourself with the other person in a small way.

As the firm owner, you follow a similar approach in your marketing by offering a small paid thing: a service or product. There's a little investment on the prospect's part, but they can still back out if they're not ready.

Few accountancy firms truly offer something at this stage. You want people to sign up for accountancy services with monthly payments, and some people will be ready for that. But what can you offer those who aren't quite sure yet?

A great example is a firm we worked with at PF. The owner wanted to run a free event. The owner's goal was to get more clients working with him on strategic advisory services, not just getting their accounts and taxes done. He did everything right when it came to content marketing; he created a website landing page, embedded a video, shared social media posts, sent emails, and made phone calls. He built awareness and then offered prospects something for free.

What he did next was go properly through the progression model. He didn't skip from the free event to asking people to sign up for a monthly retainer. He offered a small paid thing: a one-on-one planning session charged at £300. Out of the sixty-five people who attended the event, thirty-three of them signed up for the £300 paid session. It's very likely many of those thirty-three people will end up signing up for more services eventually. Some won't. But he's letting his prospects follow the progression model and sign up for what they want and when they feel comfortable. Here is a list of some small paid things you can offer:

- *A workshop or planning session:* This needs to be structured and clear with a defined deliverable. Your prospects need to feel confident you aren't simply having a chat; they're going to come away with something no matter what they end up doing next.
- *A paid event:* If you've invited them to a free event, the call to action (CTA) could be buying tickets for a follow-up event, one which is more intensive and focused. You could run a webinar about an online accounting app, then invite attendees to sign up for a training session to get the app set up for their business.
- *Consultative time for a niche:* If you have expertise in a particular area, open your calendar to a certain number of paid sessions with those who need advice relating to that area. This could be tax planning for property owners or a profit review for IT companies. If they won't pay for a small session, they may only be

looking for free advice, which is available in your free
content!

- *Online training or course:* This is often proclaimed to be
an easy way to make money. You take all the
knowledge you've been sharing for months or years,
combine it into a structured course, package it up on a
website, and voila! Instant leads and money flowing in
day by day. Before you go all in, keep it simple. Record
some videos, share them on a web page, and find out
if it actually helps people before you turn it into an
intensive course.

Now, at last, it's time for what you were hoping for from the
beginning: the monthly services, the annual accounts, the recur-
ring fees, the client relationship, or the big project. At this point,
the client can go either towards a project, a retainer, or both.
They might even go back and forth between them. Let's look at
the retainer first.

Monthly retainer

You're no longer in the pub. You've spent time together,
gotten to know each other, and it's clear something is really
happening here. The key at this stage is to continue to be patient
and not get lazy. It's exciting at the start of a relationship, and
you'll do anything for them and they for you. And then time
goes by, life happens, and things get a little harder. Maybe it's
not as exciting as it was in the early days, or communication
stalls a little.

You may feel like you've got this stage covered, and in terms
of delivering a great service, it's likely you have. But keep the
Buyer Progression Model in mind. As the buyer moves through
this stage, you must continue to be the person you were at the
beginning. Be helpful, be generous, look for ways to support
them, have a laugh, and enjoy their company. Go beyond the
basics every accountant provides and look for ways to help your
clients by providing events, training, advice, and helpful

resources. Offer more within the retainer services you're providing:

- *Bookkeeping, credit control, and payroll:* Make sure they're aware of every kind of service they need when they need it. They may only have one or two services to start, so schedule regular service reviews or experience reviews. As a side note, I don't recommend calling them "fee reviews" because if they do show up, they'll come expecting you to push them into services they don't want or need.
- *Masterclasses and coaching:* Offer high-level support and training so they are continually being educated and get accountability to implement true change in their business. These could be paid, free, or a combination, and your offering can move prospects slowly through its own progression model.
- *Community groups:* When you serve an industry niche or a group of like-minded business owners, you have the opportunity to connect them to each other. This could be a free thing, if you simply set up the group and let them network together. If you decide to charge for it, you could provide exclusive events, resources, and one-to-one meets.

At last . . . the wedding day has arrived.

Big project

You've gone from meeting a stranger down at the pub to being two people ready to trust each other with their lives. In the same way, your prospect has gone from someone who never knew your accountancy firm existed to a place where, no matter what happens in their business, you're the first one they come to. This includes mergers and acquisitions, legal support, investment and funding, building new systems, buying property, and major tax planning. Whatever they need, you're the one they'll come to for the rest of your business relationship and often for the life of their business.

This is where most accountants shine. You've already got the relationship, you talk to them regularly, and it's so easy to sell a big project because it's not even really selling. They mention a need, you tell them how you can help, and they buy. Job done.

But, as we talked about in the previous stage, don't get lazy. Because they may need . . .

More things

This stage brings them right back round to the beginning—to awareness. Instead of general awareness of your firm, they now need awareness of the other services you have so they ask about them when they need them. What new services are you continually offering? How are you changing the reports you create, the apps you recommend, or the specialists you connect them to? Do you have new team members with a particular area of expertise your clients need?

It's dangerous to leave clients to move along at a comfortable pace, doing what they've always done and getting what they've always gotten. It's even more dangerous to focus on the next shiny prospect and leave existing clients behind. Existing clients will buy more and faster because they trust you. Do you have a system for them to hear about what's available when it appears? Are you clear about what's included/involved? How can they sign up when they need it?

You can build awareness for your existing clients using the following methods:

- Sending emails specific to niche areas or demographics
- Running client-only events or sessions
- Providing extra resources and free things only your clients have access to
- Taking them to dinner, lunch, or a fun event

- Sending thoughtful gifts, something relevant to what they care about (not a generic mug or coaster)
- Creating a community group, channel, or forum
- Ringing them up to ask how they're doing, listening to the answer, and taking action afterwards
- Looking for businesses or people to refer to them

There you have it. The Buyer Progression Model, from nothing to everything, in all its stages. Let prospects go through the progression at their own pace. It is *their* model, *their* progression. Some will leap directly from awareness to a big project. Others will stay at the free things stage for years and years before they move on. It's their call. All you can do is influence and direct them so when they get to the point they need you or need more, enquiring and buying becomes the easiest thing in the world.

So who exactly are you talking to? Who is *your* buyer?

How do I define my audience?

The more specific you are about your audience, the better. Yes, I know it's a risk. You may be concerned about who you might lose. What if you're so specific that an amazing potential client never gets in touch because the message isn't specifically directed to them? What if the message is directed to someone else entirely?

The only way this will happen is when your message is still too broad, too generic. When your message has been crafted for the type of people you want to work with, the really amazing ones, it will *always* appeal to that audience. Your message could even say "accounting solutions only for dentists" and you'll still get a few people or businesses who say, "I know you say you work only with dentists, but I really love what you do and your style, and I wonder if you'd work with me?" (It happens to us at PF from time to time.)

Before you panic about sending people away, ask yourself if that could be a good thing.

I once spoke with the owner of a firm who wanted to get into content marketing and social media but felt he didn't have the budget. At the end of the conversation, he mentioned he was spending almost £1,000 per month on Google PPC ads (pay per click). He said he got a lot of leads from it, so I asked how many.

"About twenty or thirty per month," he said.

"And are they the best kind of the leads?" I asked. "The highest quality clients? People who like you and your firm and are ready to do work with you and pay you the money?"

"Probably one or two of them are that kind of client," he admitted.

If you're worried about sending people away, you're still accepting everyone. You're so open you get tons of leads, but they're not ready to buy from you yet. Wouldn't it be better to invest your marketing budget in a way that delivered three to four amazing leads every month who are ready to buy now rather than wasting your time on twenty to thirty leads who are not a good fit? Think about when a prospect turns out not to be the best fit for your firm. Think about all the time you invest in replying emails, setting up calls, having calls or meetings, sending proposals, and following up. Maybe they didn't realise the investment they'd need to make and what kind of value you're offering. Maybe they were just looking for free information.

Your specific, focused audience is like a bouncer. A security guard. Its job is to protect your business from the riffraff, the time wasters—anyone banging on the door and hoping to be let in but who will only bring chaos to you and your team. Let your marketing do its job and qualify people out for you while allowing the right ones to come at their own pace on their own time. This protects you from salesy marketing and helps the buyer to feel they have freedom of choice. Marketing flows like white water rapids; prospects have a lot to choose from, and they only notice so much. People don't read every piece of marketing material you share.

This is one of the biggest mistakes accountants make in marketing. You spend hours and hours on that blog post. You take and retake the video until it's absolutely perfect. You spend well over a year editing every tiny word and letter and colour on your new website. Then you publish. And you wait in eager anticipation. And you forget your amazing piece of content is simply one of a million messages zooming past your buyer in a day. Part of the river rapids.

They're flicking through these marketing rapids at top speeds on their phone, on the go, often doing six other things at the same time. They skim. They forget. They save information and never go back to it.

Don't panic so much about alienating prospects when your bigger concern is simply being seen.

Let your audience filter through what you share and see the big picture of who your firm is through your brand and style, your people, your niche (or focus areas). Then let them decide whether they want to work with you. Rather than worrying about turning people away, flip the question on its head. Ask yourself, "*How* will this alienate people? *Who* will this alienate?" Make sure your content alienates some people and wins over others. That's its job.

You cannot be all things to all people. No one is, and you won't succeed with that philosophy. Be who you are. Share what you want. Turn away the people you don't want and win over the ones you do. Let them decide if they like your firm or not. Your content and marketing do not have to be perfect. Embrace the imperfection with this mantra: "Not perfect but done."

Not perfect but good. Not perfect but visible. Get your content out there. Be seen, and let your audience decide.

When you think about defining your audience, perhaps you imagine a buyer persona. Sometimes this is called a client avatar. You create a list of all the qualities you want in the clients who come to you. You might even have this written down already. Perhaps you imagine a target with a literal bull's eye in the centre, and your "target audience" as one you shoot your marketing at, hoping it hits.

Perhaps you imagine a niche, an industry on which you'd focus all your efforts. You might feel nervous about this because you like the variety you have already, but there's a lot of advice out there saying a niche is the most profitable and you have to pick one. You wonder if it's true.

The simplest approach to identifying your audience is to be as specific as possible.

Review existing clients

If you have an existing bank of clients (at least fifty or one hundred), you've got a great starting point to review and look for patterns. If you're new or small and don't have a bank of clients yet, think about the qualities you *wish* your ideal client would have. Review your client list with these three questions in mind:

1. Do you *like* them?
2. Have you delivered great *results* for them?
3. Is this client *profitable* to you?

Let's look at each of these questions individually.

Likability: How much do you like this client? You could use a scale from one to five, one being "I wish they would go away tomorrow" and five being "I wish every client I had was like this one." Rank them for likeability because you want clients you enjoy working with. I'd even go so far as to say you need to *love* them, but let's start with at least liking every single client you work with.

Once you've ranked them on likeability, ask yourself: "Who's my favourite client right now?" Think of their first name and bring that particular person to mind. What is it you specifically like about them? The list can include the following:

- Personality traits
- Motivations
- Their way of doing business
- Communication
- How and when they pay
- Things you talk with them about

This is the start of your list of perfect clients, the audience you will be marketing to. You can make this list anywhere or use your Accountant Marketer workbook, shared at the end of this book. Add your list of perfect clients to this workbook.

Results: What level of results have you delivered for this client? While you want to like working with your chosen audience, you also want to be sure you are valuable to them. The more you can define the results you've helped deliver for a certain type of client, the more you have to share in your marketing which will appeal to that kind of client. As they review your marketing they will be wondering, "Could I work with this firm? Is it possible they could help me?" Think about profit increases, goals achieved, and tax savings. Consider companies you've helped with growth, scaling, pivoting, and retirement.

You can also ask yourself, "What characteristics does this client have which contributed to their achieving those results?" Are they particularly motivated to learn what their numbers mean? Do they have a particular kind of business, or are they in a certain age range? All this helps define your ideal client type.

If you want to focus on a new type of audience and you don't have results yet, make those results your highest priority. Work with one or two clients in the category you want to expand into, and help deliver results for them. Until you have results to share, it's going to be harder for this kind of audience to trust you.

Add these types of clients to your workbook.

Profit: How profitable is this client to you? Now we come to the third question, and you need all of these three questions to work together. It's not enough to merely find a client likeable; you can like a client you make no money from. It's not enough to get them great results if they don't do the same for you. Look at your client (or list of clients) and identify their profitability to the firm. You may need to ask a few questions:

- How do you calculate this profitability? Is it consistent? How often do you track it?
- What services do they receive from you?
- What services do they not receive? Are there any they need?
- How profitable are each of those services to you? Do you know?
- How profitable is this client's business to them? If it's not profitable, what makes that difficult? (i.e., what qualities do they have which make their business and profitability struggle?)
- If they are profitable (to themselves and to you), what qualities help that along?

Now you've done all this, it's time to look for patterns.

Look for patterns in the list

Review your client list, and look at all the qualities you've noted down. Pay particular attention to the clients you really like, got great results for, and are profitable to you. What patterns do you see? You could look for connections in the following categories:

- Industry
- Type of business
- Location
- Number of owners
- Number of employees
- Sales
- Product lines/complexity
- Qualities of owner

On the flip side, you can also ask yourself who you do *not* like. Go deeper than your gut feeling. Write down specific qualities, such as comments they make when you send a proposal or jokes you don't find funny. Consider anything you wish was different about them. How do they compare to the clients you love?

Once you've found patterns in all of the above qualities and characteristics, pull them together in a list.

Compile the very best qualities in a list

Now you have a list of client qualities. Choose the qualities on that list which represent the kind of clients you absolutely love, the ones you want more of or the ones you wish every client was like.

To streamline your list, you could play "winner stays on." This means you start with a full list of all the qualities you like or want in the clients you work with. Then look at the first two qualities on your list and ask, "If I could only have one of these, which one would I keep?" and strike out the other. Then take the winner (the one you chose), compare it with the next item on the list, and ask the same question. Once or twice, you will hit a point when you absolutely must keep both, in which case they both win. Do this all the way down the list until you are left with the very best list, the very best clients, the people you absolutely want to work with above all else.

This resulting list of qualities is sometimes called your ideal client, your avatar, or your buyer persona. It doesn't really matter what you call it. What matters is being absolutely specific about who you will work with and who you won't.

Compile the "other" qualities too

You can also have a list of the undesirables—qualities of people or types of clients you won't work with no matter what. If you don't feel strongly about this yet, you can simply create a list of qualities which aren't your favourite. It can take a while to create a list like this, and you may feel a little badly when putting it together. You may feel you're saying this is a terrible, horrible, no good, very bad person that every accountant, or every person, needs to stay away from. When someone is that terrible, there's no question about it. If you do have any of those, I'd expect you to be in the process of getting rid of them if you haven't already done it. What you're facing in this exercise is something much harder than identifying someone who is truly terrible. You are separating the "good for me" from the "not good for me." Maybe they are a good person or a good business. That doesn't mean they're good *for you*.

Your undesirable could be someone else's perfect client. All you're saying when you make this kind of call is you're choosing not to work with these kinds of clients. Whether this comes down to an industry, quality, or personality trait, it's entirely your call. You get to decide, and you get to change your mind too. If later you find out you were wrong, you can add them back to your list, although your list usually starts bigger and gets smaller and more specific rather than the other way round.

. . .

The more specific you are about your audience, the faster they buy

Being specific about your audience helps them as much as it helps you. The more specific you are, the easier it is for them to decide whether they are going to work with you. For those who already wanted to work with you, it hurries along the buying decision. For those who weren't sure, it helps them make the buying decision. And for those who were not a fit, they weren't going to work with you anyway (or would have been a very difficult client), so you've successfully helped them go on their merry way to find the firm who is right for them.

When you are all things to all people, being very broad in your marketing, it takes longer for the potential buyer to make a decision. It's also more likely you'll take on difficult clients who take time, energy, and money from your team, which makes marketing even harder than it was before.

After all, you don't simply want *more* leads (or at least I hope you don't). You want better ones who are ready to buy, and this means you need to be more discerning before you start your marketing.

Now you have a clearer idea of who your audience is (or have begun the process), it's time to dig deeper into what they're experiencing and how they feel. Even when you are clear about who you serve, it's likely you're thinking more about your services than about the issues your audience is facing. When you turn your attention from seeing them as a prospect and start thinking about them as a real human person with real-life issues, it changes your marketing for good—for the good of your audience and for the good of your firm.

CHAPTER 2
ISSUES

WHEN I ACCEPT A SPEAKING ENGAGEMENT, it's usually at an event for accountants. They're the audience I know best and the one my agency serves. Every once in a while, however, my experience with marketing in an exclusive niche leads to an opportunity to speak to a broader group of business owners, and at one such event, I met someone whose problem was not what he thought it was.

The business owner who didn't know accountants like you exist

The conference and speaking sessions were over. We were all standing around with drinks in hand late on a Friday night, still talking about marketing (as you do). This person came up to me to share his appreciation and share his struggle.

"Listen, I really appreciated your talk," he said. "Honestly, I am struggling right now because cash is a real problem for me, so I'm not sure where to focus my marketing."

I asked what was making cash such a problem for him right now.

"Well, I've got some people who aren't paying," he said, "but mostly I have a massive tax bill I wasn't expecting, and I'm trying to figure out what I did wrong and how to get more business so I can pay it."

I asked him more about that. Turns out his accountant hadn't met with him or given him the heads-up that all his amazing sales that year would have an impact on what his company owed in terms of the UK VAT payment. As a result, he had gotten a notification he had no idea was coming, informing him he owed £30,000. And it was due in several days' time.

"I guess I ought to know more about taxes," he said rather shamefacedly. "I just . . . I know about woodworking and making furniture, but I don't know as much as I need to about accounts."

I was silent for a moment.

This was more than a business problem. A wrong had been done to this man, and he didn't know what to do. Now, I believe every business owner has a responsibility to understand their own accounts and finances and to be prepared for any taxes they need to pay. But the way they understand that is by working with amazing accountants—people like you. They need someone who will answer questions, and they don't have to be ashamed because they have a guide to help them. It's why you are so valuable and worth every penny you charge (and for many of you, a lot more pennies than you currently charge). But this person's accountant hadn't prepared him and wasn't guiding him to sort out the problem. So he figured marketing was what he needed to fix it.

"You can address your marketing later," I said, "but the core problem right now is not rethinking your audience or selling more products or updating your website. You need two things: one, immediate help with the bill you've been presented with; and two, preparation and guidance from a really good accountant so this never, ever happens in your business or your life again."

He stared at me. "But this just happens, doesn't it?" he asked.

"Sometimes tax bills come, and they're just a big surprise, and you have to deal with it. How could you possibly prevent it from happening again?"

I told him how. I told him there were accountants out there who could meet with him when he needed it, and be present in his life and his business to help him plan. Accountants who could work with him throughout the whole year, looking ahead to what was coming so the tax bill was never a surprise. Who could help him set aside money so when the tax bills came in, the cash was already there to pay them. This kind of accountant could be the first person he called when anything happened in the business—whether it was a new opportunity, challenges with sales, hiring, or profit margins—and to cap it all off, that person could be someone whose company he really enjoyed, someone he could have a beer with or meet up with even if they didn't talk accounts.

He stared at me in genuine shock. "That kind of person exists?" he said, dumbfounded.

I felt for him and for every business owner who has this kind of worry hanging over their heads. "Not only do they exist," I told him, "but I know many of them personally. I'm going to text a few of them tonight, and one of them will help you through this so you never have to go through it again."

And I did. I texted three accountants I knew who had similar clients with the level of sales he had and who might be a good personality fit. They were also people who would reply to me on a Friday night at 9 p.m., people who knew exactly how this man felt and wouldn't want him to go one more hour with that £30,000 VAT bill hanging over his head. They all replied to me within hours, and before Monday arrived, this business owner had meetings set up to start working through his issue.

Your clients have stories like this too. It's sad when people have financial problems in their business they didn't *have* to go through. Yes, sometimes people create their own havoc. But cases like this can be avoided. There was no reason this man, with his year of amazing sales, great success, and so many business opportunities, had to be worried about where to find £30,000 with only three days' notice.

A wrong which you can help make right

Steve Jobs spoke about business success involving a wrong we want to right. Marketing success is more than simply solving problems for clients: it's helping to right a wrong. The tax bill hanging over the head of this business owner wasn't a business issue; it was a *wrong* in his life.

When we talk about the issues your clients face, this is what we're talking about. It's not a list of phrases like "cash flow," "growth," or "business development." The people you're talking to don't simply need an accountant; there's an actual *wrong* in their life which needs to be made right.

Sometimes they know what the wrong is. Sometimes they think they know what it is but need help digging down to what's underneath. Sometimes they have no idea and don't even know where to start. When you call out the problem and recognise the wrong for what it is, they'll better see who you are and what you do. They'll also understand why getting in touch with you was the best thing they ever did.

Knowing about issues business owners tend to face is one thing. Considering how those issues apply to a specific group of people (your audience) and pointing them out as wrongs to be made right: that's what helps them believe you. Combine this with your brand (see chapter 4), and your marketing becomes truly yours, unlike any other accounting firm in the world. No one is exactly like you, has the values you have and lives them out in the way you do, serves the audience you work with, and helps solve issues for them in the way you do. Any marketing which doesn't address all of this, doesn't reveal who you truly are, is still too generic.

When clients come to you with what they believe is the problem, there may be a root problem underneath, and they may not be able to see it yet. One way to dig down to a root problem is to ask five questions which start with "what". Using the word "what" makes it a fact question, not something they have to defend. Our woodworking friend had the big problem of a £30,000 tax bill. The five what questions lead us to the following:

1. *What* did he think the bill was going to be? (The same as last time.)
2. *What* made him expect that? (He didn't understand how VAT works.)
3. *What else* didn't he understand? (How his sales were growing and at what pace.)
4. *What* prevented him from understanding it? (His accountant wasn't meeting with him more than once a year.)
5. *What* was the reason they only met once a year? (He presumed that's how accountants work.)

When you're marketing your services, it's not enough to simply list the services you offer. You need to get down to the root issue, the real problem they are facing. Asking a series of five "what" questions can help you find out the real wrong they are dealing with. Whether it's cash flow or tax planning, you're showing the prospect that you understand the real problem they are facing. When we get to chapter 6, which covers websites, we'll look at how your marketing needs to recognise their feelings and talk about those too.

Answer the questions they are actually asking

Content marketing doesn't mean trying to come up with nice words and phrases to put on a website and get people to meet with you. It means the content you create is giving helpful information to potential clients. As you show you understand their problems and even the problems they didn't realise were there, it strengthens their trust in you. Clearly, you've seen these problems and dealt with them before.

The same applies to creating content for your ideal team members. Remember, marketing is for hiring too. Go beyond the basics of what an applicant may want to know about the job and help them understand what their life will be like as an employee of this firm. Answer their questions in blog posts, on website pages, in video, and on social media. Instead of replying to thousands of emails and holding endless interviews, use your content to direct them to an answer. It will save you time and help you understand the kind of person the applicant is. Are they willing to look around, research, and make an effort to find and absorb this content? After all, if they join the firm, you'll want them to contribute to the content you create so they can work with clients they love too.

When you or your team members write a blog post, you're not trying to choose a topic no other accountant has ever written about before (you would definitely struggle there). You're writing the answer to a problem or issue clients have asked you about or one they would ask about if they knew what to ask. This keeps your marketing focused on them, not you. "They ask, you answer" is a concept from Marcus Sheridan's book of the same name, and it means you use your clients' (and prospects') questions as the core of all your content. The more you share, the more likely they are to make a decision about working with you. As we talked about in the last chapter, give away information, and charge for implementation.

Give away information, charge for implementation

As you create content to answer the questions your clients ask, helping them through the issues they face, it's tempting to give away as little as possible. You're tempted to write a generic post about "Five ways to improve cash flow," which sounds good but doesn't give away too many specifics. Or a PDF download with thirty-seven ways to reduce tax, which you feel great about but is more about getting a prospect's email address than helping them discover which tax reduction they need. You want to hold back and remain the expert, drawing them in by being helpful but not answering all their individual questions yet.

Good content marketing means you create content which helps them *enormously*. This content makes it so obvious you know what you are doing. Remember the Buyer Progression Model; the purpose of your content is to build trust. Giving away information means you create content to give away everything you know on a broad scale. If it's information anyone could find if they looked hard enough, waited on the phone with the HMRC or IRS long enough, read enough blogs, or watched enough videos, give it away. Tell them as much as you know, as much as it applies to most people. This saves them time and helps them be impressed by you. It also saves you and your team time.

Instead of writing out the same answer in a long-winded email for the tenth time, all you have to do is send a link to a blog, video, or another resource. Job done. Once you've sent it, it's over to them to do the reading and the considering. The moment they ask "But how does this apply to me?" you're in implementation land. Time to charge them for that.

As you create and share this content, don't merely tell them about your expertise; show it. It's easy to make statements such as "bookkeeping will save you time" or "we can help you improve your cash flow." But just as you ask your clients for numbers and data to prove what they tell you, your audience needs to see proof of the statements you're making in your marketing. Enhance your statements about the issues you solve by giving them the data.

Share real life examples. Even if you don't name the particular client, you can say "We worked with a business owner who had problem *x*, and together we did *y*, and now they've improved their numbers by z." Help the prospect feel it's possible you can help them too.

Show statistics and data. If a particular app has been really helpful for people in one industry, quote the numbers. You might say, "47 percent of dentists who used this app found it saved them an average of two to three hours a week." Help them believe it's possible they can have a similar outcome.

Provide specific details. Don't just say, "Look at your cash flow for the month." Tell them in detail, step by step, how to do that: "First you create a spreadsheet (by the way, here's a link to our template spreadsheet you can use). Then you fill in this information from your accounting app (and here are the steps or a video on how to get that information). Then you look at these numbers and compare them in this way." And so on. Giving them information means they can do it themselves if they want to, and that's okay. You only need to charge people who actually need or want your help.

Give them tools. Create resources—checklists, documents, and spreadsheets they can fill in and use. Record videos taking them step by step through the problem. Write blog posts providing every detail they might need. Link to other sites, books, or resources which will help them further. Be generous. Give away information so when they are ready, you can help them and charge for implementation.

Maybe this has you wondering, "What if they simply take all my information and never sign up to work with me? I don't want to give too much away. Best to hold some back." But let's work this through. Imagine you have written the most detailed blog post ever with the most intricate information about a particular area of tax, VAT, or credits. Think about the person who has looked for and is now reading the post. After they read it, they will have one of three responses:

1. "Whoa. That is a ton of information. It sounds like they really know what they're talking about. I'm not

sure if I'll apply that correctly to my situation. I better get in touch and find out if they can help me."
2. "Oh, perfect! This is exactly what I needed. Thanks so much, accountant. You've been generous and helpful. I've got enough to sort out my problem. I'll remember this and you."
3. Response Number 2, but after trying it for a while, they get lost, confused, or frustrated and shift back to Response Number 1 and get in touch.

No matter what they do with the information, it's a win. You win if they get in touch because they're already impressed with your detail, experience, and authority. You win if they don't get in touch yet because they needed a simple answer and got it. They think well of you, and nobody has wasted any time. And you win if they try it themselves, realise it's a lot harder than they initially imagined, and come to you ready to listen, believe in, and pay for the value they will receive. The people who become clients are more educated and more informed, trusting you can and will help them.

The content you create helps them decide. It reminds them the decision is always in their control. It also saves you and your team hours of valuable time, protecting you from having yet another hour-long prospect conversation only to realise the problem wasn't what they thought, they're not willing to pay, or they're not the best client for you to work with.

Gathering client questions to help you create the best content
To create this content, one of the best ways to gather a list of questions you can answer is to hold a "they ask, you answer" workshop with your team. Here's a brief guideline on how to run this workshop (and for more detailed guidance, visit the PF Vault for free resources, templates, and guides at wearepf.com/vault).

- Begin talking to the team about the kind of questions they get asked often. Start a list everyone has access to (i.e., a collaborative sheet, your team app). Whenever a client or prospect asks a question you know you've answered before, add it to the list. Help build habits so the team can easily do this as soon as the question is asked.
- Block out fifteen to forty-five minutes with the whole team or with a core group of the team who are client-facing.
- Find a creative space. A bright, open place which encourages creative thinking.
- Choose someone to write down all the questions. The answers can be recorded with a few bullet points.
- Remind the team how this will help them. Instead of having to send long personal emails or making calls over and over, they can simply send a blog, video, or resource link.
- Have the team list as many questions as they can think of in the allotted time and then stop.
- Run the workshop regularly (at least once a month) until the team are in the habit of sharing questions as soon as they're asked.

As you get into the habit of writing down questions or issues, your list will grow faster than the time you have to invest in answering them. This is when you start to prioritise the questions, and the highest priority will be the content which helps future prospects make their decision faster. Remember the Buyer Progression Model: a prospect may absorb content from you for quite some time—days, months, even years. It's okay if they take a long time to become a client as long as they have every piece of information they need to decide they want to work with you. But it's your job to create content which provides them this information when they need it so they sign up as soon as they're ready.

One firm created a Google Sheet list of questions to answer and ended up with a list of well over 150 questions. The owner felt overwhelmed. How in the world would he decide where to begin? We talked about his priorities, and then I asked, which of these 150 questions would help his prospective clients make their buying decision faster? What do they most need to know? When he considered this, prioritising the top questions became much easier. Nearly fifty of the questions were related to brand-new start-ups in his niche, and although he wanted to help them in the long run, this owner's priority was getting clients with established businesses in that niche. These were businesses with income and profits who would be able to pay the accounting fees. "I'll write the answers to start-up questions later," he said, "but I can see how the questions relating to the more established businesses are more urgent and will deliver results faster." Prioritise answering questions your *very best* clients ask. Not all questions from all clients need to be answered.

When you look at your list of questions, consider whether you've been asked this question before. The more often the question has been asked, whether to you or a member of your team, the more time you all save in the long run when it's answered in a blog post or a video. Every time you get this question in future, instead of typing out an answer taking you five, fifteen, or thirty minutes, you simply find the link and share it. Make this even faster by creating a shareable document listing all the content you've created, organised by topic, searchable by the entire team.

If the question is simple or specific, consider the greater question behind it. One of our clients was asked, "Which bank account do I pay my VAT bill from?" On the surface, it seemed too specific and not worth wasting time to create content on it. But we dug deeper. Who was asking this question? Why? Turns out it was a client who had recently switched company structure from a partnership to a limited company, and their question came from that situation. We talked about the greater issue of the change in company type, and one of the team members realised this happened fairly frequently. "We could write a post on the typical problems people have when switching from a partnership to a limited company," she said. "There are at least four or five of those I can think of."

You'll also want to consider what category this question falls into. In Marcus Sheridan's *They Ask, You Answer*, he refers to five categories of questions which drive the most traffic and leads. "When reviewing the top performing content from my pool company, we found five article topics were consistently outperforming the rest," says Marcus, referring to the company in which he first discovered the power of content marketing to drive new business. "These are the Big Five blog article topics that drive the most traffic, leads, and sales for those smart enough to write about them."

The big five are pricing, problems, comparison, "best of," and reviews. For accountants, the biggest of the big five is pricing.

So few accountants actually address pricing on their website and in their marketing, which means most prospects are coming to them confused. These prospects won't understand what's required of them, how often they have to pay, what's not included, how different services are calculated (like bookkeeping and payroll), and how the prices vary by type and size of business. You have options about how to present pricing on your website, but you must actually address it. You build trust by recognising this as a genuine question you're not afraid of answering.

You don't have to actually give a specific price or a quote in your content, and I appreciate you need more information to do so. But you can explain the methodology you follow, share the questions you'll ask, and show how the information they provide to you will help you generate the best and most accurate quote.

Some of the pricing-related content you can create includes

things like a blog post about how pricing works for your firm. A video walking them through a demo proposal and the elements within it. A pricing page on your website explaining your methodology, which would include some of the content above.

Give them enough information so it's clear to them whether they're ready for a proposal. It will save both of you hours of time.

It's easiest to answer problem-focused questions, but don't neglect the others. Have a balance of these five categories, and look for ways to turn your client's question into a "review" or "best of" category question. If they ask whether they're subject to a particular rate of tax, write a comparison post about the tax requirements for different types of businesses. If you're featuring a new app, review multiple apps and explain which one you believe is best for a particular type of business.

If you've got your list of questions already, use these priorities to help you decide which one gets answered first. The questions ticking all or most of the priority boxes get moved to the top of the list. If you don't have that list yet, create it today. Remember to put it in a shareable format so the whole team can contribute to it.

It's okay to answer questions you *wish* they'd ask. But more often than not, the questions they have already asked will cover both aspects. When you use their actual questions, the way they've worded the question will sound more comfortable and familiar to people like them (people you'd like to work with). This is what I call "marketing gold dust": taking the words they use, and turning this into your own marketing.

Marketing gold dust: Their words are better than yours

When you answer questions your clients ask, you'll be tempted to reword it, make it sound "professional," or put it in "accountant-ese." When you do this, the question stops sounding like your ideal audience and becomes less appealing to the type of clients you want. Let's imagine your prospective client visiting five or six accounting firm websites, all with similar content and wording. This means they don't have any way to distinguish your content from anyone else's because it all sounds the same:

We're modern. We're forward-thinking. We're experienced. We're chartered. We have offices. We provide services: advisory, forecasting, payroll, outsourced bookkeeping, and management accounts. We help with profitability, tax planning, personal goals, cash flow, and growth.

Even if you see this in your own content and want to do better, you might feel frustrated because you don't know how to fix it. You write something, and it sounds like every other accountancy firm website you've ever seen. You see other accountants or other businesses with amazing content, and you think, "Yes! That's what I want to say!" But it's theirs, not yours.

Great news. There is a kind of content available to you which you don't even have to come up with yourself: use the words your clients say.

I mean this literally; use what they say word for word. Most of the time you can use exactly what they say with no edits or even spelling corrections. Other times you can edit it slightly, borrow a phrase or a sentence, and incorporate it into the rest of your marketing. It's marketing gold dust because it's worth so much. There is no way you could say it better than they could because when you're writing content, you're not always able to see things from their perspective. You try, and you're doing better all the time. But you'll never truly feel what a client feels because you're the accountant, and you see things from your own perspective. That's okay! Use that difference to remind you to prioritise their words over yours.

You'll also find your clients will be more complimentary of you than you would be of yourself. When a client says, "You literally changed my life, and I don't think I'd be alive today without the advice you gave me," that is not the kind of thing you'd think to say because you don't want to brag. Besides, the advice and help you give is like breathing; it's just what you do. So, while you're glad you've helped them, it won't feel as dramatic to you as it does to them. Their words are going to be powerful, and you can use them.

When you write content for your marketing, you're trying to give a particular impression. Your clients, on the other hand, aren't trying to make their words sound like anything. They're not trying to win you clients or improve your marketing. They're just telling the honest, real truth, and *that* is what your prospects want to hear. They want an unvarnished opinion, and that will always be more believable than the tidied-up version (or worse, the "professional version") you are tempted to create. When you gather words your best clients say and share them, it's more attractive to prospects who have the traits you want. They will read it and think "Yes, that makes perfect sense to me" because it's being said in their language. Your language and their language are different. That's okay, and that's how it is supposed to be. But in marketing, it delays the buyer if they have to translate your perspective into one they understand.

Just as you answer questions your *very best* clients ask, use the words your very best clients say. You don't have to use words from all your clients. Even if someone says nice things about your firm, it doesn't mean you have to use those words. If they're coming from a difficult or frustrating client, someone you don't want more of, then by all means *do not* use those words or you'll get more clients like them.

To help gather this marketing gold dust, get into the habit of writing your clients' exact words down.

Building marketing habits: Write down what your clients say, word for word

To do this well, you have to document like crazy. You essentially become a reporter or a journalist. When I listen to a client share kind words on a call, at the time I truly believe I will remember what they said. I'll think they said something like "You really listened to what I said and turned it into an organised list of marketing actions." When I go back and listen to the recorded call, however, what they actually said was "It's literally like someone has plugged into my brain and downloaded all the relevant data to my life, business, and clients, then organised it into a tidy database of tasks, timelines, and summaries." My recollection was close, but it doesn't have the same power as the exact words.

When the words are spoken aloud, use any method at hand to document it right away. Use your phone, a scrap of paper, or the corner of an envelope. Dash it off instantly, while the person is still talking. Otherwise you will forget the amazing phrase they just used. That's marketing gold dust lost in the river. If you need to, stop them once they've said the amazing thing and repeat it back to make sure you get it right.

You could say something like "Actually if you don't mind, what you just said there was so encouraging and so helpful. Could you hold on a second while I get that down? You said you felt like *x*, and you got *y*. Okay, thanks!"

Your client will be thrilled their words are so valuable to you. Most of the time, they won't even remember ten seconds later exactly what they said. We often send quotes to clients, asking if it's okay to share, and they say, "I said that? Wow, that sounds really good. Are you sure?" You don't need to apologise for pausing to write down their words.

Record everything during online meetings. Getting into the habit of recording means when your client does drop the most beautiful statement, phrase, or kind word into the conversation, you've got it there, word for word. You'll need to train the team to make a note of when the words were said. Even a rough indicator is better than nothing (i.e., *6th June meeting, about a half hour in, mentioned how much more time they have with their family, and how they didn't think it was possible a year ago*). When you gather the raw data, your marketing team or agency can help you create great content from it.

If it's written content, copy and paste it into a collaborative place the same day it's shared. Copy that sentence from the Facebook comment. Screenshot the kind words. Save the email into a folder you can find later. I can guarantee you will forget what people have said, and it's incredible how many questions and kind words you receive on a daily basis which aren't being seen by anyone else but you. Have one central place where you save all this powerful material. You could use Trello, Evernote, or a folder on Google Drive, but it needs to be collaborative so your team can contribute to it as well. Train the team to document this way every day, and you'll gather even more marketing gold dust.

Training the team in this process *will* take some time. As with any change, it will not be a matter of casually mentioning it in a team meet, and the next day, everyone starts doing it and keeps doing it. You'll need to mention it, mention it again, prepare a system, share it, check in to make sure it's useful, listen to any observations or challenges they have, and be a good example. Your team will not write down kind words from clients, or document client and prospect questions, unless you and the other firm leaders are doing it too. Even once the habit is established, it can still slip during busy seasons, after a holiday, or if there haven't been many to share recently.

Make sure the team can see how their contributions are used and how it benefits them. When a team member shares a specific quote from a client, and the quote is later used in a social post or in other marketing content, and a prospect mentions how helpful it was, the team member will feel the impact of their actions. What they do matters. What they contribute helps the firm get more clients of the kind they enjoy working with.

Ask open-ended questions, then shut up and listen. This gold dust will help you build great gold statues, not of yourself but of your client. They're the hero. They're the ones who matter, so their words matter. And what you gather from them helps you build marketing content which sounds like the clients you *love* to work with. This leads to more enquiries from people who are like them. People who have similar issues and need those to be solved.

Their doubts are valid: How will you address those?

The practical issues your audience faces is one thing. But what about their feelings? Every prospect considering working with you has feelings about choosing a new accountant, and often there are negative feelings and bad experiences in the mix. These have to be incorporated into your content because they're very real. Recognise they may be worried, concerned, or confused. And create marketing content which recognises those feelings as valid. It says, "You feel like this, and that's okay." It's not okay for them to feel like that always, and you want them to be able to move past it, but your visitor needs to know it's okay for them to come to you with their concerns. To hear, "We aren't afraid of those questions, those feelings. We aren't going to pressure you, push you, or make you buy something you don't want or need. There are things about accounting which are unclear to you. You didn't do something wrong. It's not your fault. We're here to help."

When your marketing content focuses on complying with rules and data and "staying professional," it's more difficult for your buyer to connect with you personally. Keeping the personal and business elements of your life separate doesn't really work anymore. "Work–life balance" doesn't always mean finishing work at this particular time and then starting your life. It means you're building the kind of firm to deliver the kind of life you want to have, and it means enjoying the work you do and the clients you work with as part of your life. It means they recognise who you are as a person and what you care about. It helps you understand what motivates your client to get into business in the first place and hearing their origin stories. It means caring for them when they are crying, swearing, or burnt out because of the issue they're facing in their business. Emotions matter in marketing. Even if some of the actual accounting work you do is quite practical or even dry, the issues your clients face are never cut-and-dried. They're losing sleep at night. Having long conversations with their partner or family member. Sitting with their head in their hands, trying to figure out what to do.

I'll never forget the story one of our clients mentioned, oh so casually, as we were talking about their industry focus on farming. I asked if they had a farming client they'd worked with and delivered a positive result for. "Well, we did have one recently," one of the partners said offhandedly. "It was a family farm. Had been in the family going back several generations. Due to several dry spells over the past few years, the family were looking at cash issues which could mean they wouldn't be able to continue farming. We helped them get funding so they didn't lose the farm."

They didn't lose the farm.

Think about that for a minute. Imagine the farmers sitting at the freshly scrubbed kitchen table, cups of tea before them. Perhaps the parents and grandparents there too, Gramps rubbing his arthritic hands while he thinks about the situation and remembers past tough times on the farm. Imagine the fear, the concern as they all wonder if this is it. And then imagine them meeting with the accountants, hearing the good news, telling Gram and Gramps everything is okay, the farm is safe, they got the funding! Three cheers all round! All hail the accountants!

I was blown away by how matter-of-fact the accountants

were when sharing this story with me. Maybe the farmers seemed to be matter-of-fact about it too, at least during the meeting. But whatever way you express it, there are feelings involved in good news versus bad news. As an accountant, every day you are delivering good news or working through bad news as you help your clients sort out the real issues they face. These are wrongs in their life, and a wrong has a strong emotion attached to it, whether it's anger, fear, worry, frustration, or annoyance. Too often in marketing, the discussions about your "ideal client" and their issues are too tidy, too clinical. These are humans with feelings and wrongs to sort. And you're here to sort them. As an accountant, you are so much more valuable than you realise. Make sure your marketing never, ever forgets to include and mention the emotions your clients feel.

Go back to the list of your best clients from chapter 1. You've already looked at things you like about them, qualities which make doing business with them easy. Now consider what made it hard for them to consider changing accountants. (You can document your answers in your Accountant Marketer workbook.) Think about why they might not sign a proposal—either now, or ever. What value might they be missing? What kinds of experience have they had which makes it hard for them to believe what you're saying?

Doubts and fears are a powerful part of the emotions your prospective client feels when they're considering working with you. Yes, you can tap into motivational feelings: hope, excitement, opportunity, and enthusiasm. But even the most enthusiastic prospect will still be wondering, "Will this accountant really be able to help me? Are they for real?" After all, they already know they need *an* accountant. In principle, any accountant will do, and they have a general sense of what accountants can do. What they want to know is if *this* particular accountant can help them, if you're their type of person, if they can see themselves opening up to you about what's hard and what's weighing on them.

That's why they're reading your blog posts, watching your videos, following you on social, and arranging a discovery call. They're doing all of it with at least some level of trepidation. They're worried it might not work out, worried they will make a poor decision. Their doubts and fears are actually centred around trusting themselves.

When someone chooses not to work with you or disappears from the prospect process altogether, it's tempting to blame that on practical reasons like the price of your services. You tell yourself, "Oh well, our firm is expensive. That's why they didn't want to sign up." But it's never really about the money. Even if they're too small or don't actually have the cash, the question is whether they're the right fit for you as a client or you're the right fit for them as a firm. When a prospect says, "That's too expensive," what they really mean is one of these things:

- "I am not sure what I'm actually getting for what I'm spending."
- "I had another number in my head and am struggling to see the difference between what I used to pay and what I'd be paying now and what I will get."
- "I'm comparing you to another accountant providing different services."
- "I don't know enough to believe I'll get my current problem fixed if I sign up."
- "I'm not feeling enough of a connection to you and your firm for this amount of money to feel worth it."
- "I'm scared I'll make the wrong decision and waste all this money."

These are valid concerns because your client doesn't know any better yet. You know what you can do for others, but they don't know that because they don't fully know *you* yet. This is an opportunity for you to honour their feelings and show you're not afraid to have this conversation. You have the ability to alleviate this particular pain they have. Help them *feel* that.

Imagine a prospect coming to a page or a place on your website that went through every one of these reasons and others you've identified from the businesses you work with. Imagine the prospect reading these questions and then reading the answers. Imagine you've recorded videos of you or another team member explaining how you had a client come to you with that concern, what happened, what you did for them, and how they feel now. Imagine them watching these videos and reading quotes from your clients saying, "I felt this too, and now I'm happy and motivated and relieved and on track and living the life I want to." Imagine the relief. Those are the kinds of feelings they want.

Over time you'll begin to see patterns in the issues your clients face

The business owner with the £30,000 tax bill who spoke to me at the marketing conference wasn't asking me for a new accountant. All he knew was he had a huge bill and he didn't know how he was going to pay it. He was worried and disappointed in himself. The accountant who ultimately helped him with that didn't (fortunately) send him a list of services like management accounts, tax returns, and associated costs. He simply said, "That's so frustrating. We can absolutely chat about how we can help with that. Let's get a call booked in."

Not every prospect comes to you like this one did, with a personal recommendation and a direct link to your phone number. Even the ones who are recommended to you will go to your website and other marketing first to get a sense of who you are. Take that personal, human approach you use when arranging discovery calls and meetings and apply it when you are creating content. When you share content to help your buyer feel they know you before they meet you, it moves the buyer journey along faster. They aren't pressured to move faster than they want to go, but they move faster than they would have without the information they were wondering about already.

As you talk to your clients and think about the issues they face, you'll notice some issues come up more often than others. You'll begin to see patterns. There will be things you find yourself saying over and over about them and their journey, about your firm, and about the process of how you approach solving it. These patterns will lead you to your cornerstone piece of content, which we'll talk about in the next chapter.

CHAPTER 3
CORNERSTONE

THE JOURNEY OF A THOUSAND MILES, it is said, begins with one step. And the construction of a building begins with one stone. A cornerstone.

Historically, when constructing a building (usually one of brick or stone), the cornerstone would be the first stone set down. All the other stones are set in reference to this stone, and the whole structure relies on it. Remove the cornerstone and the building is in danger of falling apart. For some older buildings, the cornerstone might become a ceremonial stone or a replica outside the building, documenting the groundbreaking date and those involved in the architecture and building. There might even be a ceremony for the laying of this stone.

When building your marketing, a cornerstone piece of content sets the tone for everything your clients will learn about who you are.

The cornerstone: A visual summary to help clients understand your way of doing things

It is visual. It is easy to see and notice. And it sits at the heart of who you are, who you work with, and how you do business.

Without the cornerstone, all the excellent content you create is slightly disconnected. It gives your buyer the difficult and lengthy task of sifting, considering, and piecing it all together on their own before they decide to get in touch or to buy. Your cornerstone helps them see it faster, get in touch faster, and decide faster.

PF's cornerstone is a marketing map, and I distinctly remember the day this came together. We were exhibiting at an event for accountants and, over and over, we answered questions about who we are, what we do, and how we help accountants. With every conversation, we were starting from the beginning, explaining the power of understanding marketing and how this contributes to the success they're looking for. We explained how we do things, why the order is important, and the marketing philosophy our work is based on.

When we debriefed together as a team at the end of the exhibition, we all agreed it was hard to quickly explain what we do without something visual to point back to. And when we looked at all our conversations, accountants were asking where to go with marketing and in what order. That's when you need a map —not the detailed step-by-step "turn right here, turn left there" kind of GPS instructions but an overall big picture. This is when you look at a map of the whole area and say, "Okay, first, we'll go north for a while, and then we'll turn west. We'll follow that for a while until we go north again, and then we arrive."

A few weeks after that exhibition, I was in an office with whiteboard walls, presenting to account managers who worked for an accounting app. The same kind of questions came up again, so I sketched out this map. This is that sketch:

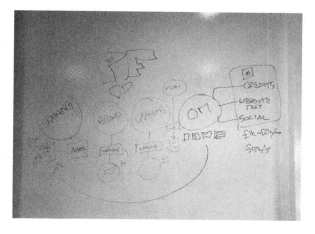

Just like that, we had our marketing map.

The next stage was to have our creative team design it as a proper branded image so we could print it, publish it, write content about it, and integrate it into all our marketing. This is the first simplified draft:

We've gone through a variety of different map images over

the years. At the time of publishing this book, this is the one we're using now:

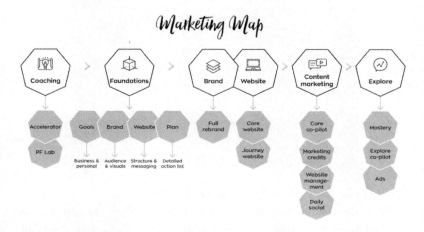

As PF changes, you'll see this map updated slightly. Every few months, we recognise something we're doing a little differently, and we adjust the map to keep it as current and as clear as possible. A visual summary like this is a cornerstone piece of content.

It's a visual graphic. It represents years of experience. It summarises a way of doing things and the journey our clients take. It expresses our philosophy and the values inherent to us and our business.

It leads to many other forms of content, including more detailed versions of the map. We have a summary video explaining where it came from and other videos covering different elements of the map. We have client stories about how they've followed the map and the results they saw in their firm. There are blog posts and articles about the map, explaining the elements in detail. In addition there are social media posts, postcards, printed material to hand out at events, and a resource guide in PDF and printed format. We have other visual assets as well. We've created an asset toolbox for these graphics, each of which summarise a principle we follow or an approach we recommend in a visual way. But the marketing map sits at the heart of who we are, who we serve, and the journey you take to great marketing.

You'll create more than one asset for your firm (i.e., visuals, manifestos, guides, and graphics), but the cornerstone sits at the heart of who your firm is and how you do things. If you were to pick one visual—and only one—to help a prospect understand what it's like doing business with you, the cornerstone would be it.

Developing a cornerstone: The three core elements

The cornerstone visual can take years to identify, and it often does. PF was in existence for six years before we finally drew and developed the visual, but we'd been doing business in line with the marketing map since the early days. We just didn't have a way to explain it so concisely yet.

In one sense, the cornerstone has its own time frame. It will not be forced. It is built on your business model, and it will take time for you to discover it, much less create a graphic which successfully shows that to others. But there are three elements which make up a cornerstone, and you can begin working on content for these. The elements may come together into a cornerstone quite seamlessly, or you can ask for help to bring it together. Let's walk through each of these elements.

Your "way": Your way summarises the processes at your firm. This is the big picture of the way you do things, differently to other accounting firms—what happens first, what happens next, and when. This doesn't mean your process is wildly different or bears no resemblance to any other accounting firm in the world. It's okay if there are similarities to other firms or businesses. The cornerstone explains *your* way: what it is, why it exists, where it came from, and how it helps the type of people you work with.

The PF marketing map includes our way by showing what

services you'll sign up for and in what order: Accelerator, the Foundations sessions, the brand and website projects, the monthly marketing.

Your values: The second element of your cornerstone is a reflection of who you are and your philosophy. This is what you stand for and what you don't. What's okay and what isn't. These values may not be revealed within your cornerstone in an obvious way, but they are inherent to it. PF's pillars and values aren't listed on our marketing map, but the reason the map goes in the order it does is because we believe in collaboration, responsibility, and positivity. Our values are woven into the very fabric of the cornerstone.

Your clients' journey: This refers to the unique path followed by your ideal client. When you've worked with a certain type of business or person more than once, you begin to see themes throughout their journey, including feelings they have and actions they take at the beginning, in the middle, and towards the end. You can say with confidence "this happens first" or "most people at this stage feel like this" or "here is where this particular thing will come up." Creating a visual of this journey helps someone see at a glance where they are and see hope for where they will be. When you look at the PF marketing map, you can identify where you are on this journey right now. Are you doing monthly marketing yourself? Is branding an area you need to sort out for your firm? Does your website need a rebuild? Your place on the journey is easily visible in this graphic.

Once you've created your cornerstone, you'll find it will save you and your team time. You'll be able to explain more quickly what you do, how you do it, and who you work with. It helps people figure out whether they want to work with you, and conversations are more focused and happen sooner than they would have otherwise. Your cornerstone becomes your first impression, your starter before the main course, your hook. It's a helpful piece of content used to draw your prospects in. And it's always free!

The best way to work towards identifying your cornerstone is to 1) keep creating content, 2) look for patterns, and 3) create individual assets. Sketch the process, journey, or path. Use your tablet, sketchpad, journal, or anything handy. Make notes about what you explain to clients over and over. While you do your work and serve clients, look for patterns. Identify the direction it is best for them to go in. Listen for clues. If you're not ready to create the full cornerstone yet, you can still create focused, specific assets.

Create multiple single-concept core assets

A core asset is different from your cornerstone. It's also a visual graphic, but it's focused on one concept only rather than showing the whole picture of why your firm exists and how everything fits together. Unless your business model fundamentally changes, you'll have one cornerstone throughout the life of your business. But as you explain and educate your clients about other specific concepts they need to understand, you'll create more core assets over time. You might even think you have a cornerstone and change your mind later. It's okay to change your mind; this is why you often create core assets before you discover your cornerstone.

A good example of a core asset is the sketch of the Hogwarts castle and grounds done by J. K. Rowling. When Stuart Craig, a production designer on the Harry Potter films, asked a question about where they might place something on the Hogwarts grounds, Rowling sent back a quick sketch to show him where she envisioned everything when writing the books. Craig noted that this drawing showed an exact, clear understanding of the whole Hogwarts world. Because the author knew how each element related to each other, she was able to draw it quickly, and the sketch became the ultimate authority, a "bible" of sorts for Craig and the design team as they crafted how the castle and grounds would appear in the films.

In this example, the Harry Potter books themselves would be the cornerstone of the films. Each book would anchor the related film. The Hogwarts map sketch was a core asset, used to help explain a particular element of the films; it was integral and connected directly back to the cornerstone.

A core asset is focused, educational, visual, and supported by additional content. We'll discuss each part in turn.

Focused: A core asset is created exclusively for one particular audience or issue. If you're running a marketing campaign, such as holding an event or promoting a particular service, the core asset unites all the marketing actions together (you'll read more about this in chapter 12). You could create an asset for creative agencies or an asset to explain a particular process within your firm. This onboarding graphic from the firm Raedan in London explains quickly what happens within the first six months of a client signing up to work with this firm:

Educational: The core asset helps your client understand an idea they would find difficult to grasp or had not thought about in this context. You're training them in a concept foundational to their life and business. You're showing your expertise by teaching a concept they can use in their business or life. You want someone to look at it and either say "Oh, I see! Tell me more" or "Hmm . . . I'm not sure I understand. Could you tell me more?" The Concentric Circles graphic we discussed in the introduction is an example of an educational asset focused on one area, the involvement of your team in marketing. As you look at it, you begin to understand there is more to learn about your role as a leader and what you will ask of your team when it comes to marketing.

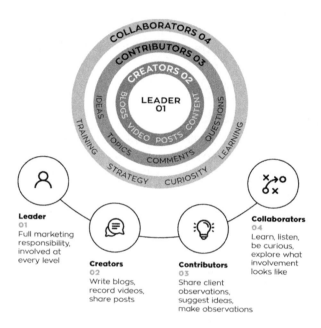

Leader
01
Full marketing responsibility, involved at every level

Creators
02
Write blogs, record videos, share posts

Contributors
03
Share client observations, suggest ideas, make observations

Collaborators
04
Learn, listen, be curious, explore what involvement looks like

Visual: The core asset is visual so the overall concept can be understood straight away. You use further content to expand on it and explain the elements in more detail. Most core assets are sketched out very quickly—often in the moment, during a meeting or presentation, or when you're trying to describe it to someone—and expanded on later. This financial maturity graphic from accounting firm MAP shows their approach to supporting creative agencies and provides a starting point for those agencies to assess the effectiveness of their finance function:

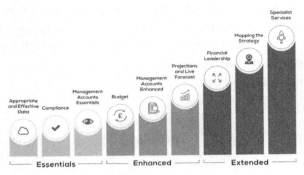

MAP Finance Maturity Curve™

Supported by additional content: The core asset is usually visual (i.e., a diagram, map, or graphic), but surrounding that core asset are blog posts, videos, live events, workshops, mentoring groups, and other content to expand on the details within the core concept. The twelve elements of content marketing which make up PF's Accelerator (and this book) are a core asset. They're core to the Accelerator, the marketing map, and to PF itself. The twelve elements of the Accelerator are summarised in one graphic, but each one represents an entire chapter of this book.

Now we've discussed core assets, let's go back to the three elements of the cornerstone: your way, your values, and the client journey. Although your cornerstone will bring all three of these together in one graphic, you may need to create them separately first. What you think is a cornerstone piece now might end up simply being a core asset later (or vice versa), and that's okay. Never feel discouraged if you haven't figured out yet what your cornerstone is. Just keep creating great content for a specific audience, keep sharing it, and the pattern *will* emerge. Next, I'll show you how you can create a core asset designed to cover each of the three cornerstone elements.

Way asset: This is a graphic focused on your processes. It helps your client feel comfortable with what they can expect when working with you. What will happen first? What happens next? Why does it matter? If you don't know how your processes work or if they seem similar to other firms' processes, dig into this further. Start creating content about how you do things, in what order, and why.

Values asset: This helps set the tone of the conversation and the expectations of the client relationship from the beginning. What qualities and behaviours are held by your type of people? What's acceptable, and what isn't? How will they do business with you, and how can they expect to be treated by you and your team?

Journey asset: This is about the business and life journey your clients go through. It illustrates your experience because you've seen businesses go through this journey before. You've worked with people who are like them, and you know the patterns. You can help them identify where they are now, where they want to be, and where they're going. It shows how you, as their accountant, are here to help them in each of these stages. It builds confidence and trust; this isn't your first rodeo.

As you read this, are you starting to get a sense of which of the three assets you might be ready to develop? Would it be based on your way, your values, or their journey? Most accountants find the process, or "way" element the easiest of all. You've worked hard to build a firm which does things in the best way possible. But if your values and their journey aren't part of it, you don't have a cornerstone yet. That's okay. You don't have to rush the cornerstone. Unlike a cornerstone used in construction, you don't have to have this element before the rest of the building can be built. This is more of a ceremonial stone, one you display to show your values and express how you've been doing things for a long time.

How to design and share your cornerstone content and message

Once you have the idea for your cornerstone (usually a sketch or concept), it's time to bring it to life and make it a part of your firm's marketing. We'll talk more about design in chapter 5, but the cornerstone must be visually appealing. People respond so much more to images than they do to paragraphs of text. In fact, the brain processes images much faster than text. Don't make your prospects and clients use extra brain energy in trying to understand the core message. Get to the point fast. This is also a good test for whether the cornerstone is ready to be designed. Do you have a sketch? Bullet points written in a document? A video explaining the process? Create your raw content and then ask for help. A good design team will help you pull these notes together and create a graphic summarising it succinctly.

Make your cornerstone easy to find. Your cornerstone will be featured on your website, and it will be prominent in all your marketing, so those who come in contact with you will be aware of it. They need to be able to quickly and easily find the cornerstone when they're researching your firm. When you've done this, you can refer back to it in conversations, sales calls, and proposals. The cornerstone leads to deeper conversations and invites the client to talk with you about how it applies to their situation. You'll back up this cornerstone with more detailed content and imagery with core assets, which will educate your clients over a longer period of time at their own pace. Remember the Buyer Progression Model. Let them absorb information at a speed that makes sense to them.

Once you have created and shared the cornerstone, talk about it every chance you get. Bring it up in conversation at events, mention it during prospect calls, discuss it in networking groups, and chat about it with your team. It needs to become part of your elevator pitch, a piece of your brand. Notice whether people grasp the concept instantly or if it takes more explaining on your part. Listen to the questions your ideal clients ask about it. Pay attention to how the rest of the team explains it. What words do you use? What order do you usually follow? Look at how and when people take action. All of this will affect the design or content. Does your cornerstone encourage action, such as asking someone to sign up for a product, service, or event? What part of the cornerstone helps them the most or moves them through the Buyer Progression Model the fastest?

Finally, let your cornerstone change along with your business. Just because you've developed a cornerstone piece of content doesn't mean it will stay exactly the same forever. Unless your entire business model changes, your cornerstone concept will usually remain roughly the same. For example, if your entire firm is built on exclusively working with one particular industry niche and you later expand that to working with more types of industries, your cornerstone would need to change or you'd need one per industry. Your cornerstone needs to stay relevant, so pay attention to the responses you get when you share it. As you notice the way people interact with your cornerstone, you'll tweak and change it to reflect those interactions. Your cornerstone is a living thing. Like you and like your accounting business, it shifts and changes slightly over time, even when its heart remains the same.

The map leads you to your firm's brand

PF's marketing map begins with learning, the very thing you're doing now as you read this book. In this space of learning, you explore and better understand who you are and who your firm is. You've looked at who you serve and the issues your audience faces. You've considered their journey as well as your values and processes.

These move you directly into the next stage of the marketing map: your brand. It's who you are, and it is reflected in every marketing piece you create. Your brand involves all the elements we've talked about in the first few chapters and goes on beyond to your firm's name, logo, colours, people, values, style, and tone of voice. Whether you know and already love your brand or are still discovering it, branding is a critical step in your journey. The clearer you are about your brand, the more accurate your marketing is. It reflects your firm exactly as it is so the prospect knows what they are getting. They know who you are and what you stand for, which means your kind of client is able to move past their doubts and fears and make their buying decision faster. It lets them see the real you so your marketing doesn't have to work quite so hard. Onward to your brand!

CHAPTER 4
BRAND

WHEN YOU START your accounting firm—indeed, when any person starts any sort of business—you're not thinking about a "brand." At most, you're thinking about your name and logo, which feel like a small task, something you throw together to get your new firm going. You're not going to spend too much time on it because you've got other priorities, like getting clients. And that's okay, at that point. You're not wrong.

At the start-up stage, you don't have a story yet. You're still in chapter one (or chapter zero). Everything is new; you'll take on any kind of client, your services haven't been fully defined, and your business model is still being developed. You don't know your cornerstone yet. Some firms know exactly who they are right from the beginning, but most don't. Even if you think you know, it might be wise to wait and let your story unfold because it could surprise you (and often does). In the early days, you're better off spending time figuring out who you are right now rather than trying to lock in your story too early.

When you're further on in your accounting firm's journey, when you're more comfortable and familiar with who you are and who you want to be, that's when it's time to dig into the brand you have and the brand you want.

.   .   .

Your brand can win clients over before they even meet you

Think about your brand like a book. This book you're read-ing, for example. When I started, I didn't even intend *The Accountant Marketer* to be a book. I was simply documenting the key points relating to the twelve elements of the Accelerator so I and members of the PF team would run it the same way no matter who was presenting. I started gathering content from years of blog posts, coaching sessions, presentations, and cour-ses. Before I knew it, I had sixty thousand words in a Google Doc, and I realised I had a book.

Then I discovered it wasn't fully ready. Yes, I had words. I had content. But I didn't have a book yet. There wasn't an intro-duction, a hook, or transitions between sections or chapters. I wasn't clear on all the chapters I needed. It didn't flow. The concept of chapter 0 didn't come until after I'd written most of the book's content. A book is more than the words themselves; it's also the images, the cover design, and the way the book is shared with the world.

As you build a firm, you're not thinking about brand. You're creating systems and processes, hiring people, and setting up a practice management system. You're focusing on getting and serving clients. Along the way, though, you will learn. You'll grow. Later, you'll find you're not the same firm you were. And that's good! That's exactly how business goes. The story changes over time, often subtly, slowly, small step by small step. But for most accounting firms, your brand won't change even once these changes have occurred.

You have the same name, colours, and logo. You haven't stopped to define the tone of voice you use and why. You haven't involved your team in the firm's marketing. Either you do it yourself when you have some spare time, or you have a marketing team who takes care of things like email newsletters and deciding whether to sponsor that local golf tournament.

You might have decided to outsource it and figure that's that sorted.

When that happens, the story your prospects are reading about is an old story. They're only understanding one aspect of your firm, or they're misunderstanding many things, and it requires actually meeting you in person for them to discover who you fully are.

Countless accountants have told me winning the client is easy once they meet them: "Once I get in front of a prospect, I can win the work. But I need to get the leads, or the right kind of leads, so I can talk to them and convert them." At face value, this feels accurate. You need your marketing to deliver the leads so you can win them over. Once it does its job, you do yours. Okay, maybe some prospects think you're a dated, traditional accounting firm, but when they come in, meet with you, or get an introductory video from you, they'll realise there's so much more.

But what about all the people who never bother to get in touch? What about those who see the old story, the dated one, and think, "No, that's not my kind of accountant. I won't bother getting in touch right now"? What about those who aren't sure and whose doubts and fears hold them back?

If you're relying on getting the prospect in for a meeting to convince them, your marketing has a problem. The process is taking longer than it needs to. It's holding you and your prospect back. Marketing is far more than simply bringing someone to you, who you then need to "win over." Your marketing's job is to tell a story about who you are so the prospect can review as much information as they can before they take any action and before you even know they exist. This is why your brand matters so much. Your brand is like a director making sure the play follows the script and tells the story the way it's meant to and in the best way possible.

When your brand is right, it directs your marketing to do its job well. This means you don't have to wait for prospects to meet with you before they understand your firm. Your prospect asks for a meeting not to learn who you are but to ask a few more questions and decide (with your help) what services they need. Your brand does the winning over for you. And because its job is to win them over, your brand is not actually for you.

Your brand is not for you

The story of your brand reflects who you are and who your firm is, but ultimately, it is *for your clients*. When it comes to your brand, the most dangerous decisions you can make are ones based on what *you* like:

- Colours, fonts, and styles that appeal to you personally
- The default name you chose when you started out, perhaps your own name or that of the founding partners
- A tone of voice which feels "professional" and reminds people of an accountant
- Stock images of calculators and people in suits laughing next to laptops in bland office buildings

Using these elements in your branding would be all very well if you wanted clients just like yourself, or people who see accountants in a stereotypical way. But you don't want to work with people who don't understand the kind of work you do. Your marketing is meant to be attractive to people who want to work with an amazing accountant (which is you). So your brand —all of it, including colours, wording, ideas, and feelings— comes together to represent you.

Branding brings both the visible and invisible together. There are aspects people can feel, see, and interact with. There are also aspects which influence but remain unseen. Your brand is who you truly are, and it is represented in the following ways:

- Visually (logo, marketing materials, website)
- Verbally (words, style, tone of voice)
- Personally (the behaviour and attitude of the people who work for the firm)
- Invisibly (impressions, ideas, the things no one talks about but knows to be true)

What the buyer sees online are the visual and verbal elements of the brand and hopefully some of the personality. The invisible aspect is communicated throughout all of these things and in any other interaction they have with your firm. The feelings people have about your brand are integrated into these branding items, and when this happens, branding decisions are made so much easier. Your logo then becomes an empty vessel you will fill and give meaning to. It becomes a part of your whole brand. This brand will change slowly, even imperceptibly. It may even change without your permission or approval.

Here's what your brand includes, and what you do with it is up to you

The very concept of a brand comes from a mark, something literally burned into the skin to let everyone know *this* belongs to *that*. Throughout history, it's been used to indicate ownership, from a cow belonging to a ranch to a slave "belonging" to a king or master. There can be negative connotations with a physical brand, but you can see where the concept of the modern-day brand came from and why it's easy to think your accounting firm brand is summed up by your name and logo. But your business brand goes far beyond that. Your brand is made up of the intangibles, the emotions—how people feel about you. It's the sum of everything you are. What you stand for. How you work. How you speak to clients. How you reply to emails and messages. How people feel when they go to your website. The emotions they experience in relation to your firm.

Brand isn't something you create from a blank checklist. You already have a brand, and it already comprises all these things. But if you're vague on any of these or if your brand doesn't reflect these elements clearly or visually, you've got work to do.

There are five elements which make up your brand. Let's look at them in order:

1. Who you are
2. Who you serve
3. Your process or way
4. Your name and logo
5. Colours, tone, imagery

As you look at these five elements, remember these are already included in your brand. Ask yourself: Is my brand representing me honestly?

Who you are: Your brand tells people what your values are

Your values are the simplest way to define who you are as a firm. You may say, "Oh, I already have our firm values identified. I've documented them, and they're on our website, so I can skip this section." Here's your opportunity to question everything. Part of building or rebuilding a brand means answering these questions:

- What do we stand for?
- What matters to me personally?
- What will we not stand for? What is not okay?
- How does this flow out to our firm?
- How do my team and I live out these values every day in every decision?

Be as specific as possible. Almost every accounting firm I speak to says they want to be known as "friendly," "professional," or "experienced/expert." Having integrity, being honest, and being reliable. Those are all good things, but the fact that I can rattle them off means I've heard them from thousands of other firms, which means they aren't unique to you. I'm not saying not to have integrity or not be friendly. What I am saying is, dig into what you mean by these words. What do you mean when you say "friendly"? Do you mean you listen, you care, you treat your clients like family, you're generous? What are you trying to get across about yourself and your firm when you say you're "professional"? Be specific about what you actually mean, or instead of values, you'll end up with a vague list of terms that describe every other accountant out there. This means your prospect has no way to understand what's different about you, so they think all accountants are the same.

There's a process you can follow to create or review your values. It's not a one-time session, but start with these so you and the whole team are clear on who you actually are and how you show that.

Values stage one: words and phrases brainstorm. Meet with the team online or in person for a forty-five-minute session. Give everyone time to think and then write down words or phrases that define your firm now and words you want to define you in the future. Remind your team there are no bad ideas! Once they've done this, share all the individual lists to create a master list. Include everything, even if you personally don't think the word or phrase is accurate. Once you have the complete list, review it and remove any of the typical words or phrases every other accountant would use:

- Modern, forward-thinking, progressive
- Supportive, helpful, reliable
- Friendly, caring
- Professional, expert, experienced
- Competent, efficient

If you're not left with very many words, go back to these "standard" words and ask the team to come up with other ways to say that word.

Look for consistencies in your list. Circle words which have been repeated over and over. Connect similar words giving the same kind of message. You might combine words like positive, optimistic, cheerful, and encouraging. Circle those words which make it easiest to understand the concept you want to get across. Of those words we looked at —positive, optimistic, cheerful, encouraging—which one expresses it best? Which one is the word you and the team would actually say? This shortlist will have five to ten words on it.

Now, set aside your shortlist for a few days. Get some brain space. Be honest with yourself about how these words are or aren't lived out by you and the team. Let the words swirl around in your mind, and don't pressure yourself to lock them in straight away. When you come back together with your team at a later date, review the shortlist. Talk about whether you're happy with these defining words and whether they fit who you truly are.

You can do the same exercise for words you feel do not represent your firm—or prefer not to have representing your firm—and then look for opposites. If you want to be sure you are not impatient, delayed, or easily frustrated, that can point you to words like patient, gracious, and deliverables. It's okay if you realise there are some things which describe you negatively and need to be fixed. Part of identifying these words is being honest about where you are now and why.

Values stage two: clients and team. Go back to the work you did in chapter 1 when you listed out your favourite clients. With your team, talk about why these clients are a favourite. Identify their specific qualities and characteristics which fit your firm's style. You can also talk about difficult clients and why they are (or were) not a favourite. What is annoying or frustrating about them? As you do this, address with your team what it means to take responsibility. This is not a time to attack or blame so-called "bad clients" as if you're the perfect company and they're the worst ever. There is always something you, the team, or both can take responsibility for. Did you take the client on despite a bad gut feeling? Did you let them get away with bad behaviour in the past? Did you fail to onboard them well? What could you have done better to help them?

There are a few clients who are horrible people no matter what you do, but that's rare. Most want to know how to be a good client but didn't know what the boundaries were, or maybe you set the boundaries but didn't honour them, so your actions told them bad behaviour was okay. Part of what you're learning in the brand process will also help you with making changes to your firm's sales systems, so you can identify ideal (or less than ideal) clients early on. This is part of your brand, too.

Values stage three: Look for patterns. Based on the words and values you identified for your clients, your team, and yourselves, look for consistent patterns and short-list them. If this is the first time you've done this exercise, it's simply a first draft. You'll continue to change and adapt these value statements until everyone agrees to live by them.

Ideally, you want every team member (including you) ready to sign a values statement saying, "Yes, I promise to honour and live by these values in my work and life." If someone isn't ready to be praised for meeting the company values or called to account for not meeting them, then either the value isn't right or the person isn't. Be honest with yourself and each other; anything else is just fake.

One firm created a list of four or five company values. The team agreed on them and began living by them. They used the team meet every week to nominate someone who lived up to the values in a specific way, and it kept their values alive and real. Over time, situations arose which caused them to think, "Well, that particular situation wasn't addressed by these values," so they'd add a few more to the list. Eventually they had ten values. These values were painted on their office walls, shared in a manifesto, expressed on their website, and lived out. After a few years, though, the owner revisited the entire process and realised the firm was getting a bit carried away. The values were becoming a list of behaviours. So they simplified it to four core values, and the expression of those core values included other words and phrases from the original ten. The true values themselves didn't change, but the visual representation as well as the written and verbal explanation did change. This provided clarity and simplicity and reflected the growth of the firm. No doubt there will be changes again in a few years' time because the firm will keep adjusting to life and the way the world works, to the clients they serve, and to the team members who deliver those services.

Make sure you and the whole team are living out these values before you start creating visuals. Having values documented in a manifesto, on a website page, or on the wall of your offices feels impressive, but a true brand is felt by your team and by your clients in every interaction and communication. When this happens, your buyer feels all this—even before they can put it into words—and when it's working well, it makes the buying process easier.

Who you serve: Your brand tells people who you will work with

Your brand is not for you; it's for the clients you want to work with, the ones who value your expertise and services, who involve you as early as possible and appreciate your advice, and who listen to that advice and follow it. If you're still not clear on who you serve, revisit chapter 1. You'll continue to define and redefine your audience multiple times throughout your business life. Once the changes become consistent or you confirm a pattern, your brand can be refreshed to match.

One of our Accelerator graduates, Katie, is an accountant in the States working primarily with therapists, counsellors, and coaches. She built her brand around psychotherapists but was not exclusive to those clients only. Part of her discovery process included questions about potential clients, including their type of business and their goals and challenges. This way, she could review those answers and be open to other types of businesses with time to decide if she wanted to focus exclusively on one particular niche. While she was deciding, she adjusted her website to reflect the words used by the clients she worked with —their issues, their concerns, their hopes and dreams. She could still create niche content for another industry, but her current brand and marketing helped her choose the right kind of person to work with. She didn't dramatically change her entire brand straight away but chose to live it out for a while first and experiment with what worked for her.

Another Accelerator graduate and the author of this book's foreword is Paul Barnes. When Paul started his new accounting firm journey, he worked with a variety of businesses in and around Manchester, where the business was headquartered. Over time, he discovered his firm, MAP, was naturally working more and more with creative agencies, specifically digital creative agencies, in the Manchester area. The more MAP worked with these agencies, the more they were referred to other agencies, and the firm became known for this focus. So he and his team adjusted their marketing to reflect this exclusive audience. Because of this focused marketing and the deep expertise the firm was building with agencies, MAP began to be noticed in areas further away, getting enquiries in London and further afield. So they adjusted again, adapting their brand message to the kind of agencies they had the experience to support and to the unique values and personalities of these agency owners.

Right now, your brand *is* revealing who you will work with. It's sending messages through your name, the content you share, and the type of website you have. It's appealing or unappealing to prospects, sometimes without your being aware of it. If you're still getting leads who aren't a fit, or clients sign up and become difficult later, your brand is still appealing to some of the wrong prospects. When this is the case, your brand needs to change.

The clearer you are about who you serve, the easier your brand (and marketing) decisions become. Instead of thinking about what you like, you're thinking about what appeals to them. It may mean using a colour you didn't initially care for but fits your ideal clients' businesses and their style. It may mean scrapping website content you were so proud of and starting over. It may mean revisiting the name you've invested so much in.

Your brand is not for you.

As you get to know your audience better, you'll also get to know better what your brand is and what it needs to be. Your job is to recognise those shifts as your firm changes and be willing to adjust your brand accordingly. The changes you make to your brand help your marketing efforts do a faster, more efficient job of appealing to the kind of people you want to work with.

Your process or "way": Your brand includes how you do things

You have a way of doing things unlike any other firm in the world. There will be similarities to other firms, and that's okay. But how your brand is expressed shows your buyer the combination of your values, your audience, *and* your way so they can see the differences when they compare you to others. Remember, they aren't comparing you only to other accountants; they're also comparing you with other types of businesses. Whenever they order something on their phone, research versions of a product, or send an enquiry to a different kind of professional service business, they are subconsciously comparing your firm to all of those businesses.

Your visual representation of your way is displayed in the cornerstone. When you reveal your process as a documented, consistent graphic, it gives your buyer confidence. You have a way of doing things which belongs to you and couldn't quite belong to any other firm. Even if someone else tried to borrow it, it wouldn't come across right because they're not you. This helps your buyer make their buying decision more accurately. To revisit your cornerstone and process, go back to the previous chapter.

Name and logo: Your brand includes your firm's name and logo

Your firm name can be anything, but if you didn't give any thought to that name or just threw it together, that, too, sends a message about who you'll work with and who you are.

When I set up PF, we chose the original name The Profitable Firm in a matter of minutes. As we grew and I got more clarity about the business I wanted to run, I realised our approach had subtly changed over the years. We reviewed the services we offered, the way we delivered them, and the approach we took to helping accountants with marketing. We thought about our name and whether it truly reflected who we had become and who we serve. After much discussion (and a great deal of hilarity surrounding suggestions like Glitter Cat and Cactus), we agreed the name itself didn't need to change.

Deciding to keep the original name did not mean we had wasted all that effort considering other name options. Putting in the effort to revisit your name doesn't mean you've already decided it will change. It's about understanding the messages suggested by that name and how they'll be expressed in every other part of your brand. It means being open and curious, considering the possibilities and how the potential names would fit with the kind of people you want to work with. It means knowing the story you want to tell and telling it. This protects you from being stuck with an old story, one which has been told for so many years it's lost its meaning.

We decided to keep the name we had, but the process led us to define who we are and who we wanted to be. We were (and wanted to continue to be) creative, positive, curious, and personable. We were also authoritative, wise, and experienced. The old visuals were cold and formal—professional in the most boring sense. Colours were dark blue, light blue, and grey: colours often used by a traditional accounting firm. They reflected who we were, not who we had become.

It was time for The Profitable Firm to express itself as the creative agency we had already become. The branding process was exciting and motivating . . . and it also took a lot longer than I had expected. There were times I felt stuck in indecision. But our final concept best expressed PF at that time. It kept the whole name and added an icon telling a story about our origins and purpose and who we serve:

Further rebranding stages have been more subtle. As we lived out this brand, sent emails, and saw our logo on screens, we noticed there were things which didn't fit. At one conference, a company mentioned PF on stage and showed a screenshot of the home page of our website. I was so proud to see our brand and site revealed on a huge screen, but I realised from where I was sitting that the logo was almost invisible at that distance. There were too many colours, and the lines were thin. The yellow words were hard to read.

Our full name was a mouthful. Our email addresses were long and bulky. Our name was being shortened naturally to PF —by us and, more importantly, our clients. PF was easier and faster to say, and it still reflected our official company name. Our brand was changing organically, almost without our permission.

Once the organic change had already happened, we reflected that in our branding, including choosing a new domain name, new email addresses, and new social media handles. We saw other companies we liked going with a "we are" approach to their branding, and it was a fit for us too. We became "We are PF" almost without even trying.

Side note: Do *not* choose your firm name based on the domain name you can get. Spend the time and effort to discover the name which is perfect for you, and then look into domains to support that name. We've helped firms find a new accounting firm name and had to reset because of trademark issues, but we've never been stopped by domain or social media handle issues. Those will always work themselves out. Don't let a domain hold you hostage to a name; stay in control by working through a proper naming process.

Now we . . . are PF. The name, together with the logo, visuals, and the other parts of our brand, reflects one of our company values: collaboration. Our clients are part of PF too. You don't hand over your marketing to us to be done while you focus on other things; you share insights, make notes, suggest ideas, and scribble out sketches on napkins or a tablet. You involve your team, you make a note of things your clients say and ask, and the members of the PF team become like a part of your team. All that is reflected in our name. We may even change names again in the future. We may adjust our branding slightly or significantly. Those changes will be a reflection of our growth as a company, as will yours.

Your logo may reveal how your marketing is really going

Your company name is directly connected to the logo, which is part of the visual element of your branding. Your logo is the book cover; all the other brand elements support it, expand on it, and tell the full story. Because of this, the state of your accounting firm logo reveals a lot about how successful your marketing really is. Below are some common problems with accounting firm logos. Read them and think honestly about which one might apply to you.

Your logo is okay, but the rest of your marketing isn't consistent. This happens when you've focused on your logo as the sum total of your brand. You've put effort into the logo, but the rest (i.e., your website, messaging, videos, social media, imagery) needs work. You pick random fonts, choose a colour which you consider to be "close enough," and sponsor an event that doesn't quite fit who you are as a firm. Your logo may initially appeal to the kind of clients you want to work with, but it hasn't been crafted based on your values and story. There's a mismatch.

Your firm has changed, but your logo hasn't. Your logo was developed a long time ago. Maybe it was thrown together by an amateur designer or someone you know. It was okay then, but the firm has naturally changed since that time and the logo has not. Perhaps the firm name hasn't changed either. You've convinced yourself it's good, it's strong, and it shows your expertise, but you haven't stopped to review it and decide whether the name or logo is right for the firm you are now. The name and logo are telling an old story, and it's confusing for your potential buyer.

You're emotionally attached to the history of your logo. One firm owner told us she still remembered clearly the day she created the original logo for her firm. She was sitting at the kitchen table in her house, and a good friend who was a designer pulled out her laptop, and they created it right then and there. It was colourful, it was exciting, and it reflected the new firm she was creating. Considering a change to that logo was hard because it brought up all the memories of those early days and the helpful friend. Even though the name of her firm was still right, the logo itself was complex with over eight different colours represented. The firm had grown. They needed simplicity. Moving to a simpler logo with two core colours made everything easier, including website page design, swag and merchandise, and signage.

Your logo is poorly designed. This happens when you think of the logo as something which stands alone rather than being an integrated part of the whole. The logo wasn't designed to work in many varied situations. The colours are hard to display or see. Perhaps the logo doesn't scale down well or is an awkward shape. It's cumbersome or includes a long, detailed tagline that confuses your buyer. This can be the result of working with a designer who simply creates an image, an icon. True branding involves looking at the logo as a very small part of the entire brand picture, which includes your goals, purpose, and values. You need far more than a meeting or two to tell them what you want and the colours you like, then leave them to "design something nice." You need a logo to be part of the fuller brand.

You've only thought about whether *you* like your logo. The biggest mistake you can make when having a logo designed is considering only what you like. Or the preferences of your team members or family members. These people already know and like you, so they're not seeing the logo as part of the bigger picture. When a logo has been designed for you, it only reflects you. It hasn't been crafted to appeal to your buyer first and foremost, so it takes them longer to decide to work with you, if at all.

Your logo is actually quite good, but you don't know why.

Some firms have a beautiful name and logo, and it actually fits who they are as a firm. But this doesn't mean you've done the hard work of digging into it, asking why, questioning everything, and being open to changes which reflect who you are. It's time to be open to adjustments which may be barely noticed by your audience but move your marketing into a more grown-up place. It's time to consider your story and how you tell it. Change the About Us page on your website so it actually does tell a story rather than simply listing facts and dates and showing pictures of the partners, directors, and team.

One firm in Ireland shared with us in a brand session how their name reflected a story about the owner's grandmother. She was ambitious and strong, ran her own business in a time when not many women were doing that, and was a daily inspiration to the current owner. He had a photograph of her shop framed and hanging in the firm's offices. We spent time talking about her, her values, and how these fit with the owner's values, as well as the importance of bringing this into his brand story by telling it, showing it, and letting people in.

Even having the most amazing logo isn't the end of the story. There's work required for you, your team, and the firm to promote the brand itself. The logo is part of the foundation, how you promote and share your business, but you, your team, and the firm have an active role in branding. A logo doesn't bring you clients on its own. It is not the magic bullet. You are the magic bullet.

When you have the right brand elements (including a logo), your confidence will rise in who you are as a firm. You'll feel braver about doing marketing that you wouldn't have considered before, things you wouldn't have had the strength to do because your platform was weak. You'll use that logo to help you build a solid brand identity, one strong enough to hold a serious level of marketing.

•   •   •

Colours, tone, imagery: Your brand gets into the detail too

When you have the major decisions made—who you are, who you serve, your values and way, your name—the detail comes after to support those big statements. Detail includes colours, tone, and imagery.

Colours

Confirm the specific colours you will use, usually one or two core colours. You may also have supporting or complementary colours. These are included in a branding identity document. If you don't have one, you must get one created. The process of creating one could show you what's missing or what doesn't match and help you understand it's time to step back and review what makes up your brand and why.

There are two important things to remember about choosing brand colour

One: Do the deep work first. Never pick colours before you've confirmed who you are, who you serve, what your values are, your way of doing things, and how you want to be known. Colours complement, remind, show feelings, and stir up emotions. "We picked purple because we like purple, and we didn't want to be like other boring accountants," an Accelerator graduate once told me. "When we went through the branding session, I suddenly realised we hadn't thought about what our audience might like. They're construction businesses. So we went back to look at what we'd written down about who they are and what they care about. And we looked at their brands and colours for consistency. We realised orange, red, and yellow were much more of a fit for them than purple."

Two: Confirm the concept before deciding on colours. Because colour distracts, you could look at an amazing logo that's perfect for your ideal audience, yet dismiss it because it's blue. Or you might say, "Let's try it in orange!" and then decide that doesn't work at all and go back to the drawing board. Branding projects include days and weeks of research, strategy sessions, discussions, ideas, conversations, and notes. We sketch out hundreds of concepts. But choosing from more than one concept is distracting; you'll be tempted to say "Ooooh, I like that one" based on a random feeling rather than digging into what it represents. Remember, a logo doesn't stand alone to wow you all by itself. That's like deciding whether you could live in a house based on the coolness (or lack thereof) of the front door. Once we have the best concept, only *then* do we look at colours to enhance the concept and add meaning to it. Your brand is an empty vessel you fill with stories, conversations, people, and life. Don't put the burden on your logo or its colours to do all the hard work on its own. Let all these pieces work together.

Tone of voice

This means agreeing how your firm will "talk." If your firm was a person, what would it sound like? Do you have a fairly formal tone and use "professional" wording? Are you friendly and relaxed? Tone of voice includes wording and intention, helping people feel what it's like to work with your firm. It's helpful to consider specific words too. Are there words you will or won't use? Do you swear, ever, in anything written for your firm? How does this flow through when you have a larger team and each person has their own personality and style? Values tell you *what* you say. Tone of voice tells you *how* you say it.

Paul, the owner of the firm with the four core values I mentioned earlier, told me there were values he had personally that weren't among his firm's four core values. "I have a view on whether we call our clients 'mate,' and I have a view on what to wear in the office, but we're not going to fire team members if their view is different," he said. "We want people to bring their personality into the office and to be able to express themselves. So we have these softer values which aren't at the core. We don't hire and fire by them."

There are core values, there are personal preferences, and there is space for humanity. As long as something doesn't dilute your message or go against your core values, everyone in the firm will have a different way of living out those values. The whole firm is still consistent as a brand even when the individuals within it are different.

When you decide on your tone and document it, all your content is consistent. It helps your prospects feel comfortable and safe because there is continuity everywhere. Your tone comes out in website content, blog posts, social media posts, emails, and PDF guides. It's reflected in the presentations you give, your careers page, and how you conduct interviews. It's the same in your prospect calls, proposal documents, and videos. Anything which represents your firm is revealing your tone of voice. The question is whether that tone is intentional and consistent or if you simply hope for the best.

Imagery and graphics

Choosing imagery is not a matter of going to a stock photography site and picking photographs you like the look of or feel like you ought to choose because you're an accountant. If you do a Google search for the word "accountant" and look at the images, the vast majority of those you see include an array of calculators, desks with laptops, serious-looking individuals (usually male) in suits, and piles of paper. This is not what you want. To truly show your brand, you need images to fit the story your brand is telling. You can still use stock photography sites at times, but you're not grabbing a photo at random. You're selecting images to support your content's message. The whole point of an image is to explain what's behind the message more quickly. A picture, as it turns out, is still worth a thousand words.

There's no need to be too literal with choosing imagery. You may be an accountant writing about tax, but does that mean you have to have a stock photo of wooden cubes spelling out the word TAX? Think about the message you want to get across and the emotions people have coming to this topic. If you're writing an article about a tax allowance or credit, how might this affect their business or life or what they can afford to do? You can even choose a stock image and change the background or highlight colours to fit your firm. One firm's brand colours are black and white with a complementary colour of a bright orange. When we found a beautiful background image for the home page of their website, everything fit except for the colour of the coffee cup. We changed that to orange, and suddenly it was their image, not a boring stock one.

Being clear about your values, name, logo, colours, tone, and imagery helps you build the right brand for your firm. But what if you're not there yet? What do you do when you're unsure about your name, you know your logo isn't right, or you know a branding process won't give you quick results? What do you do during the brand process when you're painfully aware your website, logo, and branding are bringing you the wrong sort of clients?

Good news! You don't have to wait until your new brand is ready to get the kind of business you want.

You can still get business with an ugly logo

The sales process is a little harder and takes longer when the visuals and representations of your brand aren't a fit yet. But you can still make progress while you're reconsidering your brand. People can still decide to work with you even if your accountancy firm name is boring, your website layout is similar to other (bland) accounting firm sites, or you aren't consistent on social media. It can happen, and it does happen. It simply takes longer.

Your buyer cycle might be two days, two months, or two years, depending on the person or type of business. It's never right to rush someone into buying before they are ready, but you do want them to buy the very second they are ready, with no delays which your firm or your branding has caused. Brand confusion can result in your potential buyer saying things like the following:

- "I'll get in touch later."

- "I'd like some more testimonials first."
- "I'll think about it."
- "I'm really busy right now."

This is what people say when they're not sure, when there's not enough driving them to take action. It's not a "no," but it's certainly not a "hell yes."

What are these delays costing you? Is the buying cycle taking two months instead of two days? Or twenty months instead of two? Is the buyer coming to a discovery meeting with hesitations, uncertainties, or confusion rather than enthusiasm, interest, and a few questions to be answered? While you're waiting for your brand to become the visual representation of who you truly are, start creating content that will fit perfectly with your beautiful new brand when it's ready.

The message is what matters.

When the message is right, when you're speaking to the exact type of people you want to work with, they'll connect with you even if your logo, colours, and dated website aren't as good as they could be. Use the "show, don't tell" mantra. Instead of saying "We are brave," say brave things like "There's no accounting problem too big for us to tackle." Remove all the typical accountant-speak words such as "modern," "forward-thinking," "professional," and "innovative." Use words and phrases they'll hear when they talk to you. Think about the questions you always get asked in the proposal process and answer them aloud as if the person is sitting right in front of you. Then take those words and use them on your website and in all your marketing.

Photographs and video don't need to wait for your new brand before they can be changed. You can use your phone to share photos of your team members, offices, and even pets. Keep it human and real. Video is the fastest way to establish rapport and build a sense of trust. The more personal and real your videos are, the easier it is for the buyer to know and like you.

Don't make them wait for the in-person or online meeting to figure it out, and don't wait for the new brand before you start recording your videos. Remember: not perfect, but done. The message is what matters, not the perfect professionalism of a cinematic video experience. Answer their questions. Interview clients and team members. Tell stories. You can always replace the video later with an updated one.

All this will contribute to your new brand, so once you have finished your amazing rebrand, renaming, website rebuild, or all three, you've got the content, videos, imagery, and values to support it. A good brand helps your buyer make a decision as fast as they want to make it.

When considering a rebrand

Finally, a critical point on getting a new brand developed for your firm: *You may not love it at first.* The idea that you will see a new brand concept, fall instantly in love with it, and start plastering it everywhere is a myth. You may not even like it at first, and that's okay.

Look at some of the most popular and well-known brands in the world. At their most basic level, what are they really? A swoosh, a box, a circle, an apple? As you're learning, a brand is not comprised simply of a nice-looking logo or a new website template to make your home page cleaner. Your brand will be crafted to fit your business, and it will be an empty vessel for you to fill. You'll fill it with your personality, your people, your values, your clients, and the words you use. Everything that makes you, you.

So the question is not "Do you like it?" but "Does this concept match who we agreed you are? Does it appeal to the kind of audience you want to serve?" When you turn your attention from what you prefer to what matters most to your audience and what they are impressed by, this changes how you look at your new brand concept.

You may be surprised at what you come to love. When we started the brand process with a firm who were considering changing their name, they told us they were open to any kind of change except the use of the colour red. We encouraged them not to worry about colour at this point and went through the brand process, exploring who their audience was and what they cared about. As we did so, we agreed on messages reflecting what was wild, adventurous, confident, and a little crazy. There was still an element of authority and expertise, but the firm name itself came from the image of who they most wanted to be and how they wanted to be seen. These were not boring accountants; they were mavericks of the accounting profession.

Together, we realised red was the best colour to help show those messages to their ideal client. The red we agreed on in the end was more of a cherry red or, as our head of branding explained it, "not a blood red or a danger red, but something friendly and cheerful whilst also getting across the message of authority and confidence." Those messages fit their new name and the style and approach they were taking. It wasn't the colour they initially thought they wanted, but it fit their audience, and once we had a final concept, they loved it.

Put your ideal audience clearly in your mind: the type of client you absolutely love and want more of. Think about how they feel, their experience of accountants in the past, and the situation they're in when they begin looking for a new accountant. Evaluate your brand concept based on all of this and take your time. You made early decisions on your brand and logo almost instantly, without much thought. Now you know who you are and who you serve. Give yourself space to really consider whether the brand concept reveals that well.

As you're considering this, take care when asking friends and family for input. One of the quickest ways to railroad an amazing brand design is for you to go through the whole branding process, learn about what branding truly is, get excited, see the intention and story and meaning behind it . . .

and then show the new concept to a close family member who says, "Ehhh, I don't like it." You feel confused. Lost. Betrayed. You thought this was going to change the perception people have of your firm, and now someone who knows you better than anyone else in the world is telling you it won't work! Back to the drawing board, you think.

Actually, it's an opportunity for you to remember who this brand is for. This brand is not for you, and it's not for your part-ner, sister, or best mate (unless they're exactly the type of person you want to work with). Are they a business owner with the sales, employees, or type of products you're aiming for? Are they in the niche you've defined? Are they happy to pay the monthly fees you quote? If none of those are true, take care when asking their opinion or taking their suggestions.

I remember being asked by a complete stranger to evaluate logo options. I was with the team in a co-working space filled with other creatives. As we walked down the corridor, someone stepped out of a room and said, "Hi. Would you do us a favour? We're reviewing our new logo options, and we'd like an outside perspective." My mind swirled with everything I know about branding and how a random stranger picking one logo out of three wasn't going to help them at all, but I stepped in anyway. There were three logos displayed on boards, each wildly different and in different colours. Honestly, I didn't like any of them. But that wasn't the point. I began to ask questions. What was their business? Who was it for? What kind of person were they trying to appeal to?

They answered all my questions, and I never ended up telling them which one I liked best because it didn't matter. I wasn't their audience. I suggested they were the ones who knew their audience best, so it was better they chose the logo which best reflected that sort of person and would help them trust this business and be more likely to buy from them. I indicated I didn't believe any of those logos would achieve that, and I could feel their disappointment. They were hoping for a quick answer from a random stranger, as if everyone in the world was their audience.

When it comes to family and friends, those closest to you love you because they know you already. They know your heart, your expertise, your talents, and your skills. They've seen you in good circumstances and bad. They already believe you're amazing. But your audience doesn't know any of that yet. They don't know you. They are struggling to trust you at first. They may have had bad experiences, and even if they get a personal referral to work with you, they might still be fearful or unsure. This is how your brand helps you. It gets across a solid message, subtly and subconsciously. It combines your name, logo, colours, style, tone of voice, imagery, and content together to give hints of who you are to someone who's never met you. Your family already know you, but your audience doesn't yet. Build a brand which does the work for you.

True branding makes your marketing easier

Once you have your true brand in place, a brand which reflects the real you and which appeals to your ideal audience, the next part of marketing—design—is so much easier.

You're becoming an Accountant Marketer, but you're likely not a graphic designer, and that's okay. This is why you need a clearly defined brand. This way, everything coming from your firm will match, fit, and tell the same story. Whether you create or edit an image on your phone, or a team member writes a blog post, or you have your website designer create a new page, you are all following the same script. There's nothing vague or undefined; the guidelines are clear. You and your marketing team still have the flexibility of creativity within those brand guidelines, but the overall impression your buyer receives is one of consistency. This consistency builds trust.

CHAPTER 5
DESIGN

WHEN CHILDREN ARE STARTING school at the age of five, 98 percent of them think creatively.

By the time they are eighteen, this number has gone down to 2 percent.

Two percent.

Sadly, this makes sense. They, you, we all quite literally get the creativity taught out of us in school. There are rules, after all. You don't colour outside the lines. It's not time to play unicorns; it's time for maths. Be responsible, small children. Fit into boxes. Do what everyone else is doing when they are doing it.

As an accountant, this is locked in further when you go into accountancy. At university or once you started work, the message was clear: "Accounting isn't creative, and accountants aren't creative. There's no place for that. If you want something creative, you hire someone to do it."

When it comes to design, you may have looked at a logo or a selection of images and said, "I'm an accountant, not a designer. You're the designers. You tell me what looks good." After all, you trained and qualified as an accountant, you learned the accounting rules, and you built your accounting firm. You didn't train as a designer, and it does make sense you'd feel less familiarity with what you consider "artistic." If asked to choose an image for a blog post, how would you choose? What looks good? Which font works best with that banner image? Does this website page "work"?

It's tempting to pass off any understanding of design because it's not your area of expertise. But there are two reasons why you must know something about design as an accountant.

First, you're more creative than you realise (return to chapter 0 to remind yourself why). Second, understanding even a little bit about how design works helps you direct your marketing. You may not be the one sketching the artwork, taking the photograph, or designing the website page, but when you understand the principles of good design, the marketing your firm puts out will be the best reflection of who you are. And that's what good marketing is: a true and accurate reflection of you.

Design is not about making something "look pretty". Anyone with some level of artistic skill can make something look a little better, at least on the surface. What you learn about design doesn't necessarily make you a designer, but it will impact the quality and truthfulness of your marketing.

The Golden Trio: Strategy, content, design

True design incorporates three things: the purpose (strategy), the message (your content), and the visuals (design). Design doesn't stand alone; it works together with content and strategy to help your buyer quickly understand what's being said.

From your buyer's perspective, the visuals register first. They get an instant impression of some kind. It could be subconscious; they don't realise it, but they're already making up their minds about the kind of person and accounting firm you are. How friendly are you? How human, how welcoming, how experienced? Whatever they're looking for, they are evaluating from the moment they connect with you, your team, or any other part of your brand whether this relationship will be a fit. After they've made that connection, the design draws their eye to the words you want them to read.

From a design perspective, the marketer begins the other way around. Think about the words and content first so the designers can build around it. Think about the purpose of what you are creating (this image, this social post) and how it fits into the whole picture (a website page, the enquiry process). These three areas have to go hand in hand:

1. Strategy: the purpose (why you're creating and sharing it)
2. Content: the message (what you're trying to get across)
3. Design: the visuals (how it's presented)

These are the Golden Trio.

Each one affects the other. It's not enough for a website to look good; the messaging has to be right. And the only way to get the message right is to spend time thinking about who your audience is. What they care about and why. After you strategically think about the content (messages), the subsequent design will reflect all of that thinking.

Good design affects how (and whether) people engage with your content

We'll look at the Golden Trio in order, but first, let's remember why we're doing this. It's so your buyer can engage with you and your marketing in the most efficient way possible.

We know we're not supposed to judge books by their covers . . . but we do.

It's why so much effort and skill are put into book cover illustrations. When a book's cover is designed well, giving you a sense of the style and tone of what's inside (perhaps without even consciously realising it), you're far more likely to pick it up or click the buy button. The same applies to what you share about your firm. You can write the most amazing content based on your clients' issues and problems in blog posts, guides, and emails. You might have social posts, case studies, and stories. But the presence or absence of good design affects how your prospects engage with your content. And good design which fits your brand helps your buyer make their decision faster.

In chapter 4, we saw how your logo and brand can cause someone to hesitate or hurry up. We showed how you can still get business even if you have an ugly or outdated website or bad imagery; it simply takes longer. Your buyer is used to high-quality design. They're not comparing you with other accountants; they're comparing you to every other company they see and do business with. These companies have good quality imagery, design, and branding.

At a minimum, your firm needs core branding and design requirements so a designer knows what the boundaries are. If you're doing DIY design at first (which is okay), you'll need to know the brand and boundaries yourself. When everything created for your firm is designed to be consistent with your brand, it helps your buyer feel confident. Your buyer makes their buying decision faster because you are

- **More easily found**. When a buyer sees something of yours, they'll know it quickly and subconsciously. This is why it's helpful on social media when all your firm's usernames and profile images are similar to each other. The visitor recognises your firm regardless of which social platform they're on.
- **More trustworthy**. Good design says you've invested time, effort, and money. Early start-ups and those who aren't ready or able to invest at this level will cobble things together or have someone do it cheaply rather than well. We've all been there. But a higher-quality,

more consistent design means trust is built much more quickly.

- **More quickly understood**. Ideally, the buying process is so clear they don't have to use extra brain energy to figure out what you're trying to say. Good design reveals the core message clearly and directs them to the one call to action you want them to take. It's their choice whether they take that action, but any delay is on their part as they consider who you are. If the delay is on your part because the design is confusing or not on brand, it could take them too much time to figure out what you're really saying and they may take no action at all.

Good design is simple. You don't need paragraphs of text with swooping graphics for a well-designed website page; clean lines, white space, and a few words is enough. As we talked about in the last chapter, a logo doesn't need to include every element of the concept behind the name. A simple shape, icon, or even one word is enough. Unless you're designing a comprehensive PDF guide, don't crowd the design with lots of words. Get to the point fast. It's much harder to come up with five words which get the message across instantly than it is to write five hundred words saying it in a roundabout way. It's easier to ramble on in a one-hour video than get your key points across in a one-minute video. Simplicity is harder than verbosity.

In order to get to this place of simplicity, know what you're having designed and why.

Strategy: Why you're creating and sharing it

You don't design a website by picking a nice-looking Word-Press template, picking some images, and then filling in the text boxes with words. Well, I realise some people do. Sadly, this is still how some websites are "designed." The accountant picks a nice template from a list, and the designer adds some branding and style. You may even be asked to write all the website content yourself, after the design work is already done. Or they may give you content from a generic template, something written for . . . anyone. Any accountant, any audience. The problem is, "anyone" means no one. Remember when we looked at your audience in chapter 1? Good marketing divides. Its intention is to seek out and find those who are the absolute best clients for you and to send everyone else away.

If your marketing isn't dividing, or is for "anyone," it's not going to work well. Unfortunately, that means the website template you thought looked nice, the words you wrote based on what other accountants have on their websites, and the images you selected from a stock photo library may not be coming together to create the amazing website you want.

Perhaps you've shared it, and other accountants and connections have told you it's good. When you compare it to your previous site or other accountancy firm sites, you feel proud or even relieved to have a shiny new site which isn't as dated or ugly as your last one. Over time, though, you realise something is still missing. Although your site has had a slight lift, the core message is the same. You still have long, boring services pages which sound the same as every other firm's services pages. You still use all the standard words accountants tend to use. Your imagery feels like stock imagery, your call to action is a contact form or a free consultation, and the end result is roughly the same. You realise your site hasn't been strategically thought out. It hasn't been built around your unique client journey. It doesn't reflect your true human style, your brand.

You've hired someone to build you a website, and they have. But you're the one who has provided two thirds of the design: the strategy and the content. You, the accountant, have been asked to become a world-class designer, strategist, and copywriter.

Instead, you and your designers need to collaboratively work together on the integration of the Golden Trio. Instead of simply picking some "nice" images and a pleasant-looking website template, you and your designers need to take time to think about the integration of content, design, and strategy. You need to consider your brand (i.e., who you are, who you serve, your values, your way) and the purpose of the item you're having designed (i.e., a website page, a PDF guide, a book). What is it for? Who is it for? What one message do you want to get across? Then think about the words involved in that message. *All* of that comes together into how the item is designed.

Imagine you're building a page on your website, perhaps a Services page. Before you choose a template and start filling in words about management accounts and payroll, stop to think. Why do you need a Services page? Is it because every other accountant or professional service business has one? It's a reason, but it may not be a solid one for you. Everything you create needs to be something your audience wants and needs.

Question everything. Do you actually need the page at all? Put yourself in the mind of the person coming to your website and to this page. Think of the creative agency owner, the person starting up their new business, or the restaurant owner. How do they feel? What information might they be looking for? What questions will they have? The more you think about it, the more you may realise the following:

- They already know they need an accountant. They've got a problem which has drawn them to see what you're like and whether you could help them.
- What's listed is in accounting language, and it may not make sense to them yet.
- Most of the services you offer are similar or, indeed, exactly the same as every other accountant website they've visited, so it's all blurring together.

Even if they did read every detail about what you've written on management accounts, bookkeeping, and tax consulting, they still need to understand how your process works, what kind of experience you have, and whether they trust you to work with them on it.

After years of building websites for and with accountants, we've noticed the questions you get asked by prospects aren't "So do you do management accounts?" or "What is payroll?" Instead, they say (or feel) things like these:

- "I'm not sure what I need, but I have this problem." (i.e., "I'm running out of cash and I'm worried")
- "I don't need all the strategy and consulting. I just need . . . this." (i.e., "I just want to get my bookkeeping sorted without stressing about it at the end of the year")
- "I want to be able to retire / get offices / expand my restaurant / hire more employees."
- "My business is expanding, and my local accountant isn't able to handle the work anymore."
- "I'm confused about what services I need and how much they cost. I don't know what to expect or budget for, and my mate down the pub said he only pays *this* much per year."
- "I don't get how accounting quotes work, how the numbers are calculated, and what my choices actually are."

You know people with these feelings and concerns. You've talked to them. You've heard them share these things. Imagine them coming to your Services page having never heard of you before. A person like that is not going to look at a long list of accounting services they don't understand, a page which looks, literally, exactly like every other accounting firm's Services page they've seen, and say, "Oh wow. I have *got* to get in touch with these people."

Instead of creating a services page because everyone else has one and focusing first (or only) on the design of the page, think about the strategy. How might you answer your prospects' questions better and bring in your brand so they feel they really know you? Now you're thinking creatively. You're being curious and considering how to solve the prospect's problem. This kind of thinking provides you with other options:

- **A "How We Work" page**. Explain what happens first, what happens next, and what they do to start (i.e., fill in a questionnaire, book a discovery call, download a guide, watch a video).
- **A client journey page**. Show you understand the journey they're on as a person or business owner. Help them identify where they are today and where they may be going. Put your cornerstone graphic here.
- **A pricing page**. Give as much information as possible to help them see the approach or methodology you use in pricing. This could include an explanation of the software you use, the calculations and where they come from, or a demo video walking them through how proposals are created.
- **An FAQs page**. Address everything they may be wondering, including how to start, how the proposal process works, what happens first, what happens next, what's required of them, and what you do and when.
- **An "About" page**. Help them understand you. Something far more than "Our firm was created in 1492 and has fourteen partners and twenty-six team members, and here are their names and pictures, people wearing suits and smiling fairly stiffly." Instead, show some humanity. Share your values and explain why they matter. Tell the story of how the firm was created and what your name means.

Your strategic thought process may lead you to an entirely different kind of page, requiring a different design and layout. It may even lead you to a whole new website structure. We'll get to this in the next chapter, but your website needs to begin with your client's journey. It's not about your need to tell people about the services you offer. Your brand is not for you. Your website is not for you. And anything you design is not for you either.

Whether you're considering a website page, a PDF guide, a mural on the wall, or a coffee mug, once you've planned the strategy by considering the purpose of what's being designed, and confirming whether it needs to exist at all, *then* you move on to the message. What is it you are actually saying?

Content: What are you actually trying to say?

When I am presenting or speaking for a very short period of time (say, five or fifteen minutes), it takes far more preparation than when I'm presenting for an hour. When I have a longer period of time to speak, I can take the time to search for the right word or go on a tangent. I have time to adapt what I'm saying to the comments and questions of those listening. When I have only a few minutes, my words need to get to the point and fast. There's no time to waste.

The same applies for the core message of anything being designed. Even if it's a forty-page PDF guide, there's still a theme message, a reason you are creating this piece of content. The right message affects the design. And as we saw above, getting the message right can change everything about the design. As you prepare content for design, think about what you're *actually* trying to say:

- How would you say it to a child? A five- or seven-year-old?

- How would you say it if you didn't care what it sounded like?
- How have you described it to a new client?

Presume the prospect is not familiar with all the words and terms you use every day. This is especially true when it comes to names of services. Do they know what management accounts really provide? Does tax planning mean the same to everyone? Talk about what the service does. What it enables them to do. The results they get.

When we work on the content for an accountancy firm's website, the home page takes the longest. There's more back-and-forth between everyone involved—the content team, the design team, the client marketing managers. The home page is where you grab attention and make the statement.

You do not use the incredible real estate of your website's home page to say something bland like "Welcome to XYZ Accountants." You don't need to *say* a welcome; you need to show it. You don't need to repeat your firm name when it's already evident in your logo and domain name. Because your website is not for you, the content for the home page message is about the people you're talking to. Instead of something bland, like "We are accountants to help you with all your finance needs," be specific. Talk to your audience. Tell them you are accountants who know tech. That you provide businesses in this particular kind of industry with the professional finance team they need but aren't ready to recruit for.

The design: How do you show it?

When PF was first set up, we used outsourcers and free-lancers to do design work. We talked with the clients, got to know them and their audience and messaging, and then hired someone to design what we needed. After a year or two, we were spending so much on outsourcers it was more cost-effective to hire full-time designers, website developers, and content writers. We wanted to bring it all in-house and have a team working together on all client work.

When we did this with designers, the calibre of design level went up significantly. This was not because the freelance designers we had weren't good (many of them were excellent) but because we were at last combining content, strategy, and design together in every conversation, every communication. For each client, the whole team knows what the person and the firm is like, who they serve, and what their style is. We can talk about client projects as a team so the content writer learns from the brand conversations. The marketing manager learns from the social media posts. And the designers learn from all of it.

So when one of our designers has a website page, a PDF guide, a social media image, or a mug to design, they know the whole story. They can review recordings, notes, and conversations with the client about who their audience is and why. Our designers have access to notes about the client's values, the way they speak, interactions within their team, and the quotes or testimonials from people they work with. The designer sees far more than the words on a design brief; they feel who the people in this firm are and are able to show it. The draft design is created, reviewed, and discussed with the whole team. Further edits and drafts are made upon reflection and discussed with the client. More edits are made, and the design is placed where it needs to be. Often, it is reviewed again to make sure it's doing what it was born to do.

That's how good design works. It thinks about who this item is for, why it was created, and what it is on earth (or on a website, email, or social post) to do. It considers the message and the words and how those are visually supported. And it brings them all together in a glorious unity, the Golden Trio. This is the gift of design.

If your design is merely a nice picture, or something you think is impressive, it isn't necessarily good design. The more you know about how these three elements work together, the more effective your design will be, even if it looks a little different than you initially imagined or how other accountancy firm websites or designs work.

Having a good designer makes all the difference. Not everyone is ready to hire a full-time marketing manager or team. That's why PF exists: it's all the beauty of an in-house marketing team . . . without having one yet. Even if you're not ready (or not sure if you're ready) to work together with an agency like PF, you can still prepare. You can build a relationship with an agency or a designer so, when you *do* need good design, they already know you and are ready to go.

Get ready to have good design created for your firm

If you wait until you have a big opportunity, you'll be rushed, and so will your marketing agency. You'll need good-quality design fast. You'll be pressured into making decisions without strategic thought, which means you're not paying attention to the message. A good designer will always take time with you to understand your brand, style, tone, imagery, and everything else we discussed in the chapter on branding. You can help them.

Start by exploring and questioning your brand. Even if you feel absolutely certain your brand fits who you are right now and what your audience needs and wants, it's still wise to regularly revisit it to make sure it reflects what has changed in your firm within the past few years. What worked a few years ago (or longer) could begin to look dated, especially as design trends also continue to change. I recommend reviewing your brand, including your name and logo, every three years. If, at the end of this brand review, you and your branding agency are confident this is 100 percent the brand you still are today and it's perfect for your audience, good. Carry on in that confidence. If there are changes to make to your logo, imagery, or tone of voice, you have the opportunity to make them. Most of the time, in three years your business has changed, and it's right to reflect that, even subtly.

Invest in one core piece of properly designed content for your firm now. You don't have to redesign every single marketing material you have. Unless you've recently done a full rebrand, this might not even be the best use of time and money. But getting a core content piece designed really well is a great start and well worth seriously investing in. This could be any of the following:

- **Your cornerstone content:** An image, a graphic, a visual of your way.
- **A website page:** Most likely your home page, which is a summary of your whole website. We'll talk about this in the next chapter.
- **Media templates:** Core template images based on your brand and style which you can edit easily yourself. This could include templates for social media posts, documents, or PDFs. All of these can be set up with your branding and style so you can upload them to an app and add wording or imagery. You could also change headings and content for long-form content you edit regularly.
- **Brand book:** Have the core of your brand summarised in a brand book.

Your brand book includes the following:

- *Logo guidelines*: How and where your logo is used (or not used). This also includes your logo colours, fonts to be used as headings for body copy, exclusion zones (spacing around your logo), and restrictions (dos and don'ts when using your logo).

- *Fonts and typography*: The font used for the words in your logo usually stays exclusive to the logo (as opposed to being used in your other marketing in website headers or designed work). A good design agency will suggest other fonts to be used in the rest of your marketing.
- *Colours*: The specific colours relating to your brand, listed in hex code, RGB, CMYK, and Pantone format. Most brands will have primary and complementary colours. For example, your core colours could be formal or classy black and white with a complementary colour of bright orange to be used for buttons on the website or places where a call to action needs to stand out.
- *Photographs, imagery, and design*: How do you define your firm's style in terms of imagery, photographs, and designed work (i.e., icons, illustrations, sketches, cartoons)? There's design expertise in choosing the right images or designing the right illustrations for your brand, but you can include examples of the type of imagery which is or isn't a fit in your brand book.
- *Tone of voice:* Values tell you what to say. Tone of voice tells you how to say it. If your values aren't identified or documented, you won't know what your tone of voice is yet. Tone of voice can also include phrases, philosophies, tag lines, and sayings you use all the time and sound like you. As you read this book, you're absorbing sayings we use at PF which are part of our brand. When you speak to someone from PF, you'll hear us say things like "not perfect but done," and "good marketing divides." A full list of these phrases can be found at the back of this book! These are part of our tone of voice, our culture, and why we exist.
- *Culture deck or manifesto:* This gets into the more nuanced elements of your brand. Your culture deck or

manifesto could include feelings and emotions you want to inspire, values you stand by and where they came from, or a history of the firm and why it exists. It could include a personal history of the owner or founders.

Your brand book could be one document summarising these, or you could split it up into sections: a logo guidelines document, a tone of voice summary, and a culture deck. Eventually, you'll have it properly designed to beautifully summarise your entire firm's brand, but to start, document these in your Accountant Marketer workbook so you have a place to begin when you're ready to get your brand book designed.

Small ways to improve your design now
Finally, there are things you can do yourself, even on your phone, to improve the design you're using for your firm's marketing now.

- **Know your brand's specific colours.** When you know exactly what the colour codes are, you automatically have more consistency when you create an image on your phone, add text to a video, or highlight something in a Google Doc. There are other formats such as Pantone and CMYK for printing, but we'll focus on the digital formats as those are the ones you're most likely to use yourself. Ask your designer or get help from the PF team to confirm the exact colours you use in hex code and RGB formats:
- *Hex code:* This is a six-digit number you enter into an app or share with a designer so the colour is absolutely accurate. It starts with a hashtag symbol. PF's yellow colour, for example, has the hex code #FFC60A.

- *RGB format:* This is the percentage of colours which make up your specific colour, ranging from 0 (black) to 255 (white). The RGB code for PF yellow is 255/199/0.

When you use apps or online tools, they'll ask for one or both of these, and when you are consistent, the colours you use better reflect your true brand.

- **Create a collaborative folder of imagery everyone can use.** You can start with stock images that fit your brand. Remember to let your brand guide the imagery. You're not choosing photos you like; you're choosing those which best reflect the people you want to work with. Stay away from the photos which look "stocky." You know the ones: a perfect blend of diverse people with fake smiles standing awkwardly around a laptop, laughing and pointing at the screen. One of our clients worked with us to build his brand based on an audience of business owners who work globally and travel often. His values include adventure, independence, and boldness. His colours are red-brown, orange, and cream, which reflect the places he's travelled and the feelings he wants his audience to have. As he looks at images, he might choose hiking boots, mountain scenery, a camping tent, or a tin coffee mug. When you find photos to fit your brand, save them as they are, and later you can ask for help to have these stock photos customised with your exact brand colours so they feel more like you.
- **Build a photo library of real photographs from you and the team.** Stock photographs (even edited ones) are still generic. The more real photographs you have, the more honest your marketing becomes. Here are some ways to add to your collaborative image folder:

- *Take photographs on your phone of things which are on brand* (either in colour or style). You always have a high-quality camera in your pocket. When I was a wedding photographer, I used to carry around a massive bag of very expensive equipment, but I can honestly say some of the photographs I've taken on my iPhone are as good (if not better) than ones I took using that heavy-duty equipment. The best camera is the one available to you at any time.
- *Ask the team to take pictures.* The more *real* photographs you all take—of real life, real things, and real people—the better your on-brand library will be. As they're out and about, working in the office, or with a client, your team can take photographs of what it's really like to do business with you and add these to your firm's own stock library.
- *Hire a local photographer to take photographs of you, the team, your offices, and the surrounding area.* You could use an amateur, someone building their portfolio, or a friend if they do high-quality work. Even if your photographer is just getting started, always pay them; their time is valuable. When you've confirmed your new or refreshed brand, you can hire a professional photographer and give them your brand book and all the brand guidelines. They'll love it and appreciate knowing how to showcase your brand through imagery!

Bear in mind taking photographs of real people (and children even more so) needs care and requires asking and receiving written permission. I suggest including a permission clause in your employment terms and conditions document for all team members so you can take and use photographs of your team. This document can address the usage of these photographs after employment has ended, and I recommend checking with your

HR professional to do this document right. Until you have this signed document, focus on detail shots, landscapes, and things rather than people.

- **Create a simple DIY asset.** Think of something you're always saying or showing to clients and prospects. Something you keep repeating which would be handy in a more clearly summarised form. This could be a diagram, a process, or a list of questions. Create your own asset (hark back to the Cornerstone chapter) by using some of the methods we discussed in chapter 3:
  - Sketch it out on paper or a tablet
  - Create a mind map or diagram
  - Write down the core points in a document or spreadsheet
  - Build a simple form or page on your website

You don't have to have it "properly designed" yet, and actually it's better not to if you haven't actually used it with clients. Play with it in draft format, with no major design costs at stake until you have proved the concept. Once you get to the point where you're saying and showing the same things every time and the asset answers questions or stirs up good conversation about how it applies to prospects and their business, then you can hire a designer to make it on-brand and impressive. Then you can include it into your brand book, your website, your culture deck, or paint it on your office walls.

- **Download and use the PF design brief.** You can access this brief from the PF Vault. This document helps you ask good questions about anything you're designing, even if it's as simple as an image with a quote you're creating on your phone using a free app.

Accounting isn't creative: but you can be

It's true accounting itself is not creative. It's governed by rules and laws. When we talk about an accountant being creative with those, we're moving into a negative and even illegal territory. That's not the kind of creativity we're talking about. We're talking about the creativity built into each of us as human beings. When it comes to your marketing, what you tell yourself and what you practice will flow into what you do. If you tell yourself, "I'm not creative," you reinforce the belief, and you'll be less likely to try. "It's not going to work," you say, because you're expecting things to "work" according to certain rules and laws. What are the marketing rules? What are the design laws? And yet creativity doesn't work like that.

You certainly don't have to be a designer. No one is asking you to learn Adobe apps or pull out the paints or start sketching on a tablet, although you're certainly welcome to, and I love to see it. But why not play with that a little? Why not tap into that latent creativity you imagined for years didn't exist but has been hibernating since you were five?

I've seen accountants learn to use a free design app on their phone and, using solid brand guidelines, quickly create images that look good and fit their firm's brand. I've seen accountants learn to write and discover they enjoy it. After all, marketing is not meant to be a burden on you or an obligation, something you "have to" do. It's meant to relieve your burdens, and it can actually be quite interesting, perhaps even quite fun. That's creativity too.

Now that you know design doesn't stand alone but works in tandem with purpose (strategy) and message (content), you're ready to look at the place much of your marketing comes together: your website.

Your website is a place where all you've learned so far—including your audience and their issues, your brand, who you are, your cornerstone and process—comes together into one central hub. All this is summarised in one place belonging to you, and only you, where you're in control of guiding prospects through the journey you want them to take, the journey they need to take to work best with you. You are the guide directing them along that journey. And your website will support those efforts in a way which will draw in the very best kind of clients for you and will send everyone else away.

This is where your marketing begins to really work for you. It begins to relieve the burden of having to explain yourself. It's all there, summarised and explained in the right order for the right people. They have everything they need to take action, and that means they are more likely to do it.

CHAPTER 6
WEBSITE

BUILDING a website is a natural part of starting a business. It also naturally reflects changes to your business and brand. The original PF website we created in 2012, when the company began, bears little resemblance to the one we have today, although it continues to share the message of helping accountants with marketing. People change. Businesses change. Your focus changes.

Right now, you may feel like your website is good enough. But the more you understand how your website's job is to speak to prospects on your behalf, the more likely you are to want to improve your website.

Martin's story: Do you change your brand and website first, or just improve your content?

One accounting firm owner, Martin, works with creatives and creative business owners. He came to us for help creating consistent content for his firm. We went through four foundational sessions in which we reviewed Martin's goals for the firm, their audience and brand, and the messaging they wanted to get across. He told us when people came to their website, he wanted them to feel like they had "come home." After reviewing the firm's brand and website, we suggested it was time to change both of these so they fully reflected their creative audience and this concept of coming home. Martin disagreed. He felt those were good enough and wanted to focus his monthly marketing on strategy and design projects based on the current brand.

It's hard to prioritise big foundational projects like a new brand and a new website. They're time-consuming. They're costly. And it's difficult to see the direct impact of their results since they often work in the background, delivering visible and invisible messages to clients and prospects over a long period of time. Whilst we still believed a new brand and website would help Martin achieve his goals, we also recognised content was a priority too. So we started working on that.

Three months later, Martin messaged us to say he'd had a realisation. He was more clear about the kind of clients he wanted to work with and who the firm needed to speak to. And yet, as he reviewed his website and content, he realised the messaging was resonating with early-stage entrepreneurs instead of those in the growing stages, whom they were best placed to serve.

This meant the picture these creatives were getting about the firm wasn't the right one. So it was, after all, time to revisit the firm's brand and build a website which would get this message across straight away. Together we updated the brand, its visuals, and the website, which showed off that brand, including the messages the firm's ideal clients needed to hear. The updated messages sounded more like him, his team, and the people they work with. There were phrases like "Creatives have the power to change hearts and minds" and "You want to build a meaningful business, and you want to smash a few perceptions along the way. Prove success isn't all white men in suits and hustling till you're burned out. We're with ya." Once the content changed to reflect the true audience, there were more qualified leads coming in.

You will not find those phrases on a traditional accounting firm website (with those men in suits), and even if you're a firm who also works with creatives, your own brand, style, and messaging would be different from other firms'.

Your website represents you and guides the buyer in their journey

Like your brand, your website reflects not only who you are today but also the business journey you're on. As your accounting business changes, your website changes too—or it needs to.

If your website hasn't changed in three years, it either needs refreshing or you need to ask some hard questions about why your business has remained static for that length of time. This might mean a slight refresh with a few new pages and some custom imagery. It could mean an entire rebuild from the ground up, looking at who you serve and the journey you want them to go on as they start working with you and custom building the entire thing to reflect that journey.

Your website is a visual summary of who you are, who you serve, and how you solve their problems. And when you have a problem with your website, it's either because you have some things to work out in those areas or your website isn't accurately representing you to the people who visit.

Your website is the only marketing platform which 100 percent belongs only to you. When you use other platforms (i.e., social media, video sites, apps), the content is yours, but the platform isn't, and you may be at the mercy of algorithms or changes in platforms which can be changed at any time. Your website is your hub: the central point of marketing owned by you and entirely within your control.

Like your brand, your website is not for you; it's for the people you want to work with. And you're the guide, drawing them through the process in the way you want them to. This is why, when you record a video, you embed it into your own site. When you write an article, you publish it as a blog on your site. When you get something designed, it goes on a page on your site.

The message matters most

Before we go into the elements that make up a really good website—one which draws in *only* the kind of clients you want and causes them to take the action you want them to take—remember this: you can get results from a terrible-looking website when the message is right. It's the same principle we mentioned in relation to your brand and logo. You can still get business from an ugly logo; it will just take a little longer. And you'll miss some of the best potential clients.

The message is what matters. It matters more than anything else. You can have a site cobbled together on an old WordPress template or built on a platform which no longer has any support. You could have built your site yourself. Maybe your images have been very obviously downloaded from a stock photo site. But when the message is absolutely spot on—when you are talking to an audience so specific they instantly say, "Oh, that's me!"— they will be more likely to take action.

It will still take them longer to make their decision if your website isn't well designed or easy to use. That delay could be a few seconds or minutes. It could also be weeks or months. Even if they've been referred by someone who said you're amazing, your prospect will still hesitate slightly if something doesn't work well on the site or they don't easily find what they need. This doesn't mean you put off the website rebuild. It means until that new site is ready, you focus on the message. Help visitors feel you're talking specifically to them. Help them understand how you work and what happens when. Show success stories of people who had the problems your prospects have now. The message matters. Their feelings matter too.

We buy based on emotion. Think about the last thing you bought which you'd been thinking about for a while. New office equipment, gardening services, or a bean-to-cup coffee machine. It's never purely emotional; there are other factors such as need, urgency, finances, and your current personal situation, but emotions are a significant factor which, if ignored, prevents your buyer from engaging with you as quickly as they want to. When someone is considering changing accountants (often the majority of people who come to you), they'll have an issue bothering them:

- "I can't get a hold of my current accountant."
- "We only talk once a year."
- "I don't know how much tax I'll have to pay" or "I got a surprise bill last year."
- "I'm profitable according to the accounts, but I don't seem to have cash to buy what I want to buy."

When you look at these statements, you better believe they are full of emotions. Not only the emotions themselves, but the impact on your client. These issues reflect frustration, fear, worry, and lack of sleep. Behind these statements are arguments with a partner or a family member. Discouragement about the future. Inability to make decisions.

Think about the last great prospect you had a meeting with. What emotion words did they use? Did they say, "I need compliance reporting and management accounts"? Or, rather, did they say, "I'm not sure whether to sell my business or grow and scale it"? What did you spend most of your time talking with them about? And once they signed up to become a client, what kinds of things did they say once you started to help solve these problems? Most likely their words reflected relief. Thankfulness. Appreciation. Hope.

This is what matters to your prospect, to your new client—what's motivated them to look for help, how they feel about it, and how you might help them with it. They still need to know about the way you do things at your firm and what your people are like. And yes, they need to know how much it costs. But their buying decision is impacted by how your marketing, especially your website, addresses how they feel and the value they'll receive. The hope you stir up, through the stories and examples of people who used to be in the exact same situation but aren't there anymore. They are convinced by the practical help you give them with resources, content, and videos, all the training and learning they experience before they even meet you. That's what your website can do. On the other hand, that might be what it's missing, which means they don't have all the information they need to make their buying decision as fast as they want to.

They need to build trust first, and it takes time. They also want to know who you and the team are. People do business with people. It's still true and probably always will be true, especially when it comes to professional services. Even for larger firms, prospects still want to know which humans they'll be working with, and they want to be reassured they'll be dealt with as a human. For smaller firms, they want to know who you actually are—not the royal "we"—since they'll be working primarily with you. The more humanity you share, the faster they can make their decision to buy.

For accountants who are on your own: say "I" and "me" as opposed to "we" and "us" on your website. It builds trust faster because you're honest. If you genuinely have other team members who will be talking to your clients and prospects, then you can change it. Always be who you are rather than trying to have the imagined professionalism of an "accounting firm with global reach, local touch" which doesn't exist.

Because your buyer needs trust in this potential relationship, the words and flow of your website matter immensely. You may think of a website as something you need to have, a sort of "base" from which you post a few news items and provide your contact details. You might not feel like you need to invest too much in it, because, after all, many of your prospects are referred to you anyway. The others will just get in touch using the contact form, and you've got it covered from there.

You just need a nice-looking template, you think. You'll put some information on it and include a home page, an about page, and a services page, a contact page, and a few others, and you're good to go. As long as it looks clean and modern with lots of white space and maybe some good photographs and a half decent logo, that's all you need. Your website (you think) is all about you and your people and services.

It's not.

Your website exists for your future client—the person you want to work with, the buyer of your services. They're the hero, the reason you're saying anything at all.

Contrary to popular belief, a prospect does not simply get referred to you, get in touch, and decide to work with you. There is a great deal more to it than that, much of which is unseen. People who sign up with an accounting firm follow a typical path. Remember the Buyer Progression Model; a prospect doesn't start at the "nothing" stage and jump instantly to a long-term retainer. They listen, watch, read, pay attention, and notice. Eventually, they start connecting in small ways and consuming your content. At some point, they'll sign up for something small which feels safe and isn't a big commitment. When they're ready, they'll sign up for a big project, a monthly retainer, or both. Depending on your audience, this could take anywhere from a few days to a few months or even years. Your prospects want to have everything they need to make their small decisions in order and at their own speed. Let them do it.

Your first goal is not to sell something. It's to start a conversation.

Because of how your buyer buys, moving through the progression model, the first goal of your website may not be to instantly sell them something. Of course, your ultimate goal is to sell your services, appealing to the right kind of people so they sign up and become a client. But your very first goal, what you want them to do first, will be a specific action to start the conversation. This is why your action button needs to be more specific than "Learn more" or "Explore." Instead of telling them what services you offer and a few facts about who you are, use your website to give them what they want to know when they want to know it. Give them the opportunity to start building the relationship by taking a small achievable action.

The call to action (CTA) on most accounting firm websites is some version of "call us today," "get in touch," or "arrange a free consultation." This implies the person visiting your website is ready to have a sales call today. They've done their research and simply want to know which services apply to them and how much it will cost. Actually, most of your website visitors are not ready for that yet. Make the connection so they can start the conversation.

Your website visitor generally comes to you at the awareness stage or free things stage. As they move from the awareness stage, give them an easy or simple way to connect with you. This could be your cornerstone piece of content. You could share a video, ideally a specific one connected with a particular free thing or a small paid product rather than a vague welcome video. You might give them a helpful resource such as a guide to download or a series of training videos. You might even offer them a product like a course or a membership.

As they begin to build trust and consider the potential relationship, they want to know (and feel) these things, usually in this order:

You understand their problem. The more your website can

do to instantly answer this, the better. The more specific you are —about them, their problem, and how it's impacting them—the faster they take action. Think about the research you do when you land on any kind of website. If at first glance it draws you in, reassures you, points out what you already know or what you thought no one understood, you're far more likely to stay.

At this point, they will explore, and consume, and consider. They'll read articles, watch videos, flick through pages on your website, download guides, and sign up for things. Look for testimonials and stories and follow you on social media. Over 70 percent of their buying decision is made before they get in touch with you—and certainly before the meeting they have with you. Give them as much information as possible so at your eventual meeting, you get to the good stuff faster.

There's a process you follow to sort out that problem. This is your opportunity to build trust and show your experience. It's not enough for your website to tell them the problem they already know they have. What your prospect wants is an actual process, a way, a path. This is why building your cornerstone piece of content is so powerful. It shows the visitor quickly and visually you've been here before. You're there to guide them and lead them, and you have a tried and tested way of doing that. You'll still work with them individually as a human, but your process makes sure nothing gets missed. Without a process, your buyer has to rely on the referral they received, their general impression of your firm, a few testimonials, and a vague hope you know what you're doing. When your process is not only defined but also visually represented by an on-brand asset they find easy to understand, their impression of your firm (and the price they can expect to pay) will go up.

You seem like their kind of person or company. They're looking for your humanity. Are you the people they want to work with? Do you understand them? Are you on their side? Do you talk in a similar way, like the same things, or have the same values? Even the website for a larger firm with many team members can still give an impression of the firm's style and personality. Values aren't words on a page; they're an integral part of who you are, and this needs to be evident in everything prospects see and read.

It is possible you can help them. The questions and concerns they have need to be answered. At this point, they need to feel hopeful these questions will be answered. They may ask questions directly in an email, form, or on a call. They may ask them in their own mind or to others. They may not even know what their questions are yet. But only when they feel like there's a possibility of help will they begin to ask those questions.

It's clear what they need to do first. Many accounting firm websites have so many calls to action it can result in fewer leads, not more. Call us today! Download this paper! Also this paper and this guide and this report! Request a free, no-obligation consultation! Fill in this form! Read our blog! Watch this video! Follow us on all the socials! Your poor visitor may have been vaguely interested but doesn't know what to do first, so they either half-heartedly choose one of the many options or choose nothing. When you share too many options, you're not showing leadership and authority; you're letting the potential client lead by starting where they want to start.

"Wait a minute," you're thinking. "Didn't we say to let the prospect decide? Sign up when and where they want and move at their own pace?" Yes, they decide but only within the boundaries of how you work. If you don't want people phoning you up out of the blue with no information about who they are, what kind of business they have, and what they're expecting from an accountant, then do not make your phone number the biggest or most noticeable CTA.

Make whatever you want them to do *first* the most noticeable CTA. Repeat it on every page. This is your primary CTA. You can have secondary CTAs, but those will take longer to find and require some digging. Make it so that if prospects decide they want to explore working with you, it is crystal clear what their first step is.

When you know the buyer's questions, you can craft your accounting firm website to follow the pattern. Every accounting firm is different and has a unique brand, though there is still a typical buyer journey for the person who needs accounting services. In the earliest days of PF, well-meaning people suggested we create templates based on the standard journey the buyer followed. It would be more efficient, they said. You only work with accountants, they insisted, so you know what an accounting firm website needs. Why not simplify it? This kind of advice bothered me because I was (and still am) passionate about the unique qualities of each accounting firm. I wanted to make sure every website uniquely reflected each firm. I didn't want templates, generic content, or anything which could act as a "cookie cutter," because there is no firm in the world exactly like yours, and it's unfair to the visitor to pretend they're all the same.

However, as we built website after website for accounting firms, we did notice that buyers of accounting firm services follow a fairly predictable pattern. They have the same questions. The same confusions, the same concerns, and many of the same problems. I still believe every accounting firm is uniquely different, so your website must be fully yours, "on brand" as only your website could ever be. But because we know how your buyer buys, we know there are five elements which always need to be on your website.

Five elements your website must include

1. Who you serve (Chapter 1: Audience)
2. What their issues are (Chapter 2: Issues)
3. How you solve these—your process/way (Chapter 3: Cornerstone)

4. Who you are (Chapter 4: Brand)
5. What they do *first*—their action

The first four items we've covered in previous chapters. It's worth revisiting these now to remind yourself how they apply to your website.

Who you serve

When it comes to your audience, you want to be so specific they're shocked. You want them to say:

- "I didn't know it was possible to find an accountant who works with exactly the type of business I have—and understands it."
- "Wait. Is this an accounting firm? Their website is so *cool!*"
- "Oh, what a relief. Yes, this sounds like exactly what I need."

As we've discussed, you'll be tempted to make your website appeal to everybody—to be all things to all people. You're afraid of marketing that will send people away. You wonder, "What if the most perfect client ever comes to this website and then never gets in touch?" And yet the very best accounting firm website *does* send people away. That's its job. Good marketing divides. A good website divides.

A good website is appealing, interesting, and welcoming to the kind of clients who will be the very best clients for you, and it is unappealing, frustrating, and dismissive to the sort of clients who aren't best for your firm. Your website—with its specific messaging, on-brand design, journey, and calls to action—isn't about appealing to everyone who visits. It's appealing to people who have the type or size of business you are best placed to work with, people who have values to fit yours and are willing to work within your process. When your website is built and written to appeal to the most perfect client you could ever have, you'll never send away a wonderful client.

What their issues are

You've begun to address the issues your best clients face. On your website, bring those to the forefront. Remember how you've already asked yourself what makes doing business with them *easy* and what makes doing business with them *hard*. Why might this amazing potential client choose *not* to do business with you? What might prevent them?

Their doubts and fears are absolutely valid, and your website needs to help them feel comfortable, reassured, and helped even before they sign up. Address their questions about your services, pricing, and the approach you will take in the proposal process. Talk about what happens first, what happens next, and what the client experience is like.

At every stage of the sales process, your prospect can reach a point where they are confused or they find what you're sharing doesn't match their expectations. They may think your firm is too big or too small. They might believe they need to work with an accountant who is geographically close to them. Maybe they expect to leap into the accounts before the bookkeeping is cleared up. Maybe they don't know what they need or want.

All these fears and concerns you can answer throughout your entire website, and you must answer them. Some prospects will read every page, every blog post, watch every video, and connect with you on all the social platforms. Others will glance over it and book a meeting with you. Either way, the content must be there so they can see it at the right time.

Remember, the fresh content you create based on clients' questions helps you to be found. But if you're wondering "How do I get more business using SEO?" or "How can my website be number one on Google?" you're asking the wrong questions. There are many, many questions to ask, and they're not about you. They're about the people you want to work with. Who is it you want to reach? How long does their buyer journey take, and what do you want them to do and in what order? What issue or problem is talked about most? With this mindset, when it comes to SEO, the question then moves from "How can SEO help me?" to "What are you SEOing?" If you are using SEO for standard keywords, the ones you figure people are searching (i.e., "accountants," "accounting firm," "bookkeeping," "payroll," "cash flow"), you may not have stopped to think about your audience. Think about the questions they ask, the fears and doubts they have. Those are the words they're typing in, and not necessarily your firm's name or location.

How you solve these issues (your process, your way)

Your cornerstone helps people understand how *you* do things. Despite other accountants offering similar services, sometimes even in similar ways, you still have an approach to delivering these services which is yours. If you've created a visual for your cornerstone, share this on a website page along with supporting content such as a video explaining how it works, blog posts giving more detail, stories from clients (or even videos from clients), or a sign-up form to receive emails or updates.

- *Share process and onboarding graphics.* A visual diagram of their journey or your process will help them see what happens first and what happens next. This is not your first time doing this kind of work, and it's clear. This could include pre-onboarding or qualifying (i.e., a list of resources they can read, download, or absorb before they sign up). It will definitely include sharing a visual of your onboarding process, which will be either a description of the first three to six months of the client relationship or the same information broken into sections, such as a detailed version for the first month of the new client relationship, showing everything both you and the client will do during that time.

- *Show stories and proof of how you've done this before.*
Include specific proof of those you've worked with
before. This could include case studies, video stories
from clients, testimonials, and quotes. These could be
embedded or screenshotted from social platforms or
another public place to give further social proof you
didn't make this up.
- *Skip the Services page and create a How We Work page.*
Having a Services page feels . . . typical. Expected. You
figure every site needs a home page, an About page, a
Blog page, a Contact Us page, and a Services page. Of
course. But actually, you may not even need a Services
page. As we talked about in the last chapter, most
potential buyers already know what accountants do or
have a rough idea. They don't want to read long,
detailed descriptions of professional-speak about
management accounts; they want to know if you can
help them with their problem. If there are services you
offer they don't know about, it's unlikely they'll sit on
your website for hours reading pages about budgeting
and payroll, especially if every page or paragraph
sounds the same as other accounting firms' or doesn't
give much detail. They'll glance over it and then get in
touch—not based on your services, but based on your
style, your approach, your people, and how easy it is
to find the CTA.

Better than multiple generic service pages are website pages
addressing a specific issue your clients face and a
service/product to solve that issue. Instead of having a page
listing bullet points about credit control services, your page
declares, "You deserve to get paid for your hard work." Below
that, the content shares why this is true, how you address it,
people you've helped with this issue and the results they got,

and one specific CTA for those who are interested. We'll talk about this more in chapter 12 when we discuss campaigns.

Your "How We Work" page shows you recognise prospects need an accountant and they want a really good one. But they might not yet realise what a good accountant actually is. They might think a "good accountant" is one who does their accounts once a year, gives them a tax bill that isn't "too high" (however they define that), and doesn't cost more than what their friends or fellow business owners pay. They don't realise a good accountant is a confidante, a friend, an expert, someone you can ring about *any* issue with the business from hiring, profit margins, or funding and who will either help you or direct you to someone who can. They don't know what's possible. Because of this, it's essential you redefine what a "good accountant" looks like, and a list of services won't do that.

In your How We Work page, explain what happens first, what happens next, and why. Explain how your pricing works, or have a separate page for that resource. Explain what prospects need to do to get started or to enquire. That's what they want to know. They also want to know who you are—as a firm and as individual humans.

Who you are

Your brand is the summary of who you are. On your website, this is represented in four ways:

- *Visually*: Your logo is there, but is it only sitting in the top left-hand corner? Ideally, your website's design brings in elements of your logo, brand, style, icon, font, and even personality on every page.
- *Verbally*: A good test to determine whether the words and the tone of voice sound like you is to ask yourself this: If you removed the words from their context and sent them to a client, would they know it was you without being told?

- *Personally*: Your website isn't only about a company in a broad sense. It's about people—those who serve your clients, the owners and founders, and clients you work with. How the website reflects the people gives your visitor an impression, an understanding of who you truly are.
- *Invisibly*: These are the impressions, ideas, emotions, and feelings you want people to have when they connect with your website and your marketing. Your website is there to make the invisible visible.

Now you've given them all this information, it's their turn to act.

What they do *first*

You can have many calls to action throughout your site, and it's likely you'll have more than one. We talked earlier about primary and secondary calls to action. There will be different actions your buyer can take depending on the stage they are in, how much research they've done, how ready they are to buy, and what page of your site they land on.

There is one clear call to action that must be everywhere. This is your primary call to action, the one readily available when they are ready to buy or take an action leading to a proposal. Put this button at the top right of your website. Keep it in a banner which remains static as they move down the page or throughout the website. This means when your buyer *is* ready to take action, they don't have to scroll endlessly to find it. It's there, it's always there, and it's ready when they are. You may also put it at the bottom or end of almost every website page, but this is something to discuss with your website developers and designers when working through your buyer's journey and the path you want them to take.

Your home page is like a mini website. It includes the five core messages: who you serve, their issues and problems, how you solve them, who you are, and what you want them to do.

The home page gives your visitor a quick overview of everything they'll be exploring in more detail as they move through the site and helps them feel the freedom to go to the section or page which relates best to how they feel right at that moment. Your primary CTA is the first step they take when they are ready to talk with you about what services they need. It's visible no matter what page they're on, encouraging them to take action. That action could be to

- book a discovery call;
- fill in a form;
- download a resource guide;
- sign up for an event; or
- watch a video (which ends with a specific CTA).

If you don't know what your primary CTA is, use the Buyer Progression Model to work it out. What do they need to be aware of? What free thing will help them understand what's possible and build trust? What small paid thing is next on the journey? Choose the action which offers the fastest route to working with you with the lowest barriers to entry.

In the early days of PF, our primary call to action was our free things. By providing free resources, we were building relationships and directing accountants to learn more about how marketing works for them. After over a decade of working with accountants, most people coming to our site are already learning these things and finding them on their own. Because we're a collaborative agency working one-to-one with every accountant we serve, our primary CTA is now a discovery form. For those who want a little help but aren't ready to outsource yet, our secondary CTA is the Accelerator coaching group. It combines the learning and the doing, and it's a small paid thing compared to the other monthly or long-term services.

You may need to try several different calls to action before you discover the one which moves the buyer along their journey in the most efficient way for both of you. Stay in control of your website and the journey it shows your visitors. Don't be distracted by what other accountants do or other websites. Direct your visitor to the action you know they need to take, and make it easy for them to do it quickly. Those who don't want to start there will find your other calls to action and move at their own pace. When your website is constructed this way, you'll find your buyer taking the action you most want them to take at the time they are most ready to take it.

You're being asked for a five-second presentation

When I'm given a full hour for a presentation, I prepare some key points, but I won't memorise the entire talk. Depending on the size of the audience, I may make it interactive, take questions, and talk about how these principles apply to their specific situations. When you have a longer time available, you can plan a variety of content and then, on the actual day, pick and choose what is most relevant to those you're speaking to.

But if you're given only five or fifteen minutes to speak, you need to know exactly what you're going to say. You need to get to the point fast, choose your words carefully, and not ramble. You don't have the luxury of jumping around from this slide to that one. You might not even have slides at all. You choose an opening sentence and memorise it. You write a closing sentence and memorise that too. You might even memorise the entire speech. I've given one-hour presentations, fifteen-minute presentations, and three-minute presentations. For ease of preparation, I'll take the one-hour presentation any day of the week. It's easier. It's faster. I can adapt it on the fly. It feels comfortable, and it's okay if I don't know exactly what I'm saying until I say it. But for clarity of message, there's nothing in the world like a short presentation.

Remember the speaking engagement I mentioned in chapter 2? It was a fifteen-minute talk to over a hundred people. Because

I knew how quickly the time would go and I had so much to say, I wrote out the entire talk and memorised every word. I recited it on my morning walks in the woods. I practised it whilst driving in the car or sitting on the train. I kept it on my phone and read it aloud when I had a few spare minutes or was waiting for someone. I used the timer on my phone to track how long it was taking me.

I put in massive effort because I needed to make an impact fast. I didn't have time to ramble. There was too much to say and not enough time to say it all. I had to be concise. There were points I would have loved to make, but they weren't as important as others. There were points I had to make quickly at the beginning and others which needed to wait until the end.

When it comes to website content, it's like you've been asked to make a five-second presentation.

That's about how much time you have, and that's being generous. Sometimes it's more like one second. Website content isn't merely words. If you ramble, use "professional speak," or sound like another accountant, you'll lose your audience. They may not take the primary action or any action, and they may leave entirely. You lose potential clients by being vague, boring, or too focused on yourself.

By now, you know designing a website isn't about picking a layout that looks nice and fitting some words and images into it. For your website to work, it needs to instantly impact prospects with the message you want them to hear. It requires the Golden Trio of strategy, content, and design, which we talked about in the previous chapter. If you're creating a new website page, you'll start in the strategy phase by identifying why you're creating this page and how it will fit with the rest of the site and all your marketing. Consider who you're talking to, the order in which you want them to take in your content, and the action you want them to take. Then for your content, craft words to fit the audience and journey, and finally use design to make those words and actions more visible. Use this approach throughout the whole website process. What seemed like the best idea on the first few drafts might be revisited by the time you get closer to launch, and that's okay. As long as you remember who you are talking to (they're the hero) and what you want them to do and why, you can keep adjusting the words, design, and calls to action accordingly.

We worked with a firm in London called Thrive who weren't getting the right kind of leads. They needed a new home page to explain who they were, who they served, and what action the prospects would take. Strategy considered why this page existed and how it would change the whole website. Through brand conversations, we got to know this firm and who they serve, and the content included words like:

- We are accountants who know tech.
- We're the professional finance team you need but can't yet recruit.
- You believe business is a force for good and impacts people you may never meet.
- Generalist accounting firms aren't specialist enough for start-up and scale-up tech businesses.

In the design process, these words were included in the page in a particular order to get the visitor's attention quickly and to move them to take action.

When you see the words laid out so they're easy to read and moving people towards an action alongside the imagery, you see them differently. Sometimes we write what we believe are the most amazing words, and when they're laid out on a website page design, we realise it isn't appealing at all. Or it takes too long to get to the point. It's okay to keep changing website content until it's the right fit, and your marketing numbers (such as website visits, length of visit, and actions taken) will tell you if you are appealing to the right type of person and they're taking the action you want them to take. We'll talk about this more in the final chapter.

When your website is working as it's meant to, it is accurately reflecting you and your client's journey in the most truthful and efficient way possible so the clients who will be best for your firm will take action faster, and other prospects will qualify themselves out. It's not about more leads; it's about better ones. Your website becomes a place where they start the conversation, start the relationship, and continue the client experience.

Your website will keep changing, just as your firm does. You'll revisit your brand, your cornerstone pieces of content, and the way your clients tend to behave. You'll create content you share in blog form, resource form, video form, and many other formats. And as you do this, you have the opportunity to build a list of people who want to hear from you. These are people who want to be the first to know what's new, what's different, and what's available. This is your permission-built email list. Let's talk about email.

CHAPTER 7
EMAIL

EVER HEARD the washing machine advert story? Back in the days of physical newspapers, someone might open a newspaper every single morning. Glance it over, flick a few pages, read a few articles. Then one morning, their washing machine breaks. They're feeling frustrated and not sure who they'll go to, to get it fixed. They pick up the paper as usual, flick through it, and hey presto! A washing machine advert! "Well look at that," they say to themselves. "You know what? Maybe buying a new washing machine is actually the way to go. It's probably cheaper in the end. How helpful that this advert was here on the very day I needed it! I didn't see it yesterday."

The fact is, the washing machine advert was there yesterday. And the day before, and the day before that, and the week, month, and maybe even the year before. They didn't see it because they didn't need it. They didn't have washing machines on their mind. This particular day they did, and their eye saw what was already there.

Email is a part of creating awareness of your firm

Now we have many more places for businesses to be seen

besides one advert or one email. Whatever you do regularly—flicking through socials, watching videos, watching the news, seeing billboards flash past as you go to work, listening to podcasts—there are products and businesses you're vaguely aware of or not aware of at all. Then one day you do need them, and suddenly you're grateful for that notification.

Email is a part of creating that awareness for your firm. And unless people unsubscribe from every single form of communication you use, your messages can still be a presence in their life.

Email is not dead; it's still alive and likely will be for some time. But it's less about quantity (i.e., number of people, number of opens) and more about quality (i.e., how they respond, what they do after reading). The key in using email is to recognise people always have a choice.

They can choose to be connected to you by email, social media, text, or some other platform. They may only be aware of you through word of mouth, and they haven't signed up for anything or followed you anywhere else. All these formats are available to them, and none stand alone. Emails on their own do not hold full responsibility for the message you deliver about your firm. Even people who have been recommended to you will still check out your website, follow you on social, or sign up for emails. There are many methods of sharing your presence, and email is only one of them.

I've made it a personal mission in my life to make email something which (if it has to exist) doesn't interrupt my life, doesn't run my business, and doesn't become my to-do list. I still sign up for emails, but it's either to get a special offer or to access content unavailable any other way. Sometimes I get hundreds or thousands of emails over a long period of time from a person or company and read only a few or even none. But I stay on the mailing list because I like the reminder appearing in my inbox, telling me this company still exists. Is still around. Is still helpful and helping. Every once in a while, as with the washing machine advert, I get an email on a day I need or want what they're offering, and it works out perfectly.

Everyone gets emails and reads them, but we do that with people and companies we actually want to hear from. As accountants, you don't need to get hung up on subject lines, open rates, or click-throughs as much as whether you are making it possible for people to hear from you in the way they want to. At the speed they want to. On the platforms they want to.

When you send emails, you can test different subject lines or preview texts. You can do split testing, which means sending the same email with one slight change to see which performs better. For example, Email A has one subject line, and Email B has a different one, but the content is the same. You can split test the A/B emails and see which one is opened or engaged with more. But your entire email marketing strategy doesn't rely on these specific numbers for one specific email. Subject lines don't matter as much as who the email is from. Once they know who it's from, they're far more likely to read what you say. You're building trust over time. Yes, they're reading some of your emails; they're also watching your videos, following you on social, downloading your guides, and looking at the assets you provide. Let them decide how and when they'll do that.

We'll talk about setting up email lists and permission-based marketing so you have a list of people you can send emails to. But first, what do you actually say?

What to say in your emails

The most important advice I can give you when sending emails from your firm is to make sure to show your personality. Whether you write emails yourself, your team does it, or it's outsourced to an agency who works in collaboration with you, these emails need to reflect your brand. This doesn't simply mean putting your logo at the top of all your emails. Remember that branding is who you are as a firm and what you stand for. It's your style. Your tone of voice. The words you use.

I assure you, the more "professional" you try to be, the more boring it will be and the more difficult for your buyer to actually understand it. Even if your style is more formal or serious, you can still help them feel they're receiving an email from *you* or from a person on your team rather than an email from the company as a whole. Your firm is made up of people who serve people. Your reader needs to feel that.

Ask yourself, "What am I *actually* trying to say?" Ask it aloud and answer it aloud, like you were saying it to a client or a team member. When I'm running an Accelerator coaching group session online and ask those in the group to type an answer, the words they put in the chat box are always more genuine and more easily understandable than the jargon we often see used in emails and on websites.

Speaking of jargon, get rid of it. Remove the phrases you'd find hard to explain to a ten-year-old. Using phrases like "game plan," "avenues for success," "analytical insights," and "competitive advantage" could cause your reader's eyes to glaze over. Yours may be glazing over right now. What are you actually saying? What does it really mean? How does it really change your prospect's life? Question everything. Does your audience use that term, or are you simply trying to sound important and experienced? Do your clients actually call it "compliance," or do they say "accounts" or "bookkeeping"?

To write an email which isn't jargon-y, isn't boring, and says what is real, start by writing down exactly what you wish you could say. Write it without corrections, without worrying about how someone could respond, and without worrying about offending anyone. Put in some swears. Make mistakes, ramble, and repeat yourself. Leave it for a few minutes, an hour, or even a day or two, and come back to look at it.

Researcher and storyteller Brené Brown calls this the SFD ("shitty first draft," a nod to Anne Lamott's term from *Bird by*

Bird). Or you can call it the "stormy first draft" if that fits better with your brand. Everything gets dumped in, helter-skelter, without perfection. This is the freedom of creativity, and it's usually a lot closer to the final version than you might think. The more real it is, the more people will engage with it. The first draft is always perfect because its only job is to exist. Leave your imperfect first draft to sit and then revisit it. Make a few tweaks but not too many. Keep the personality in there. Within a few minutes, you'll realise what needs to go, what needs to stay, and you'll have your email. I do this with blog posts too.

Reduce the use of product or service names. I mention the term Accelerator throughout this book to refer to the core coaching group we run several times a year because it's the natural next step for you after reading this book. But I need to be careful how often I use it and the context in which it's used because, if you don't know or remember what Accelerator is, your eyes will skim right over it as you try to figure out what it is based on the other things I say, which takes more brain energy. In emails, talk more about what your service does rather than what it's called.

I love the example a copywriter used of receiving an email proclaiming a "premier service." The email went on and on about how it was premier, why you needed the premier service, and how you could sign up to the premier service today. The copywriter skimmed it, didn't care, and deleted it. Then, being a curious copywriter, she went back to figure out what was wrong with that particular email. She realised it was the overuse of the word "premier." If your service has a vague name—something like "premier" or those classic gold, silver, and bronze packages—people don't know what it means. They're trying to figure out what you're actually saying, what it actually does, and how it helps them. They don't care if you call it "Gold" or "Premier" or "Dragon." Being too clever with product or service names is worse than using a boring name. I remember in the early days of PF having an entire brainstorming session around our products.

At one point we considered naming them after animals, like Tortoise, Hare, Jaguar, and Dragon. Fortunately, we realised how confusing that would be. Call your service what it is so prospects can understand it quickly.

As you prepare to write your emails, the questions you ask yourself are the same as those you ask about writing a blog post, recording a video, or creating a website page. Why are you emailing at all? Who are you emailing? What one thing do you want them to do? Let's look at each of these questions.

Why are you emailing? Ultimately, you would like people to buy something. To become a client. To work with your firm. But asking this question reminds you this particular email may not be about you getting more clients. When selling services, you're building on previous conversations and setting the stage for future ones. You're addressing a need they have, an issue they're facing, something weighing on them. So when you ask why you're sending this email, you're asking it in relation to the recipient. Remind yourself who this email is actually for. Your brand is not for you, your website is not for you, and the emails you send are definitely not for you.

Think about the problem you're trying to solve. What's in it for your client or prospect? How does this help them? Consider how they might feel upon receiving it, and you can even try to imagine where they might be or what they're doing at the time. Above all, you need to know why this email matters to them. This will help you write an email they actually want to read.

Who are you emailing? What you write will change depending on whether it's a client, a prospect, the owner, or a certain type of business. You'll consider how they feel, what they're going through, and what they need (or think they need). The more you consider who you are sending this email to, the more likely they'll read and care about it. Start by writing your email for only one person. A particular person who has the problem you're addressing. Think of that person, and keep them firmly in mind. You could even address your first draft to them: *Hi Paul, you were asking the other day about how you can know which of your products is most profitable. We've created a worksheet to help you determine this, and here's a video about it . . .*

Once you have your draft, change what is specific to that one client, and you've got a personable email focused on the problems this human is actually facing. This goes beyond the one client and becomes an email capable of reaching anyone who feels the same way they do. This is also why you write emails to the type of clients you want more of.

What do you want them to do? In an email, your CTA needs to be very specific. If you say "get in touch if you have any questions" or include an "explore now" button, that's vague and doesn't inspire action. It's similar to the approach we talked about with your website calls to action. For an email CTA, figure out the *one thing* you want them to do after reading this email. If they did nothing else, what would they do? To figure this out, think about what exactly you want them to do and when. Will they fill in a form, download a guide, book a call, register for an event, or request a proposal? Make it possible for them to take that action instantly upon receiving the email.

If you ultimately want them to sign up as a monthly client, think about the small steps they'll need to do first to move them towards that. You might think your CTA needs to be "Sign up today as a monthly client," but if you haven't done the preparation work, it's unlikely people will do that. Think about the Buyer Progression Model. Consider the order in which you want them to do things, and send your emails with the related calls to action accordingly. Below is an example of what this could look like (the CTAs are in italics):

- **Email 1:** Thanks for downloading this guide. Here's one of the points from it and a video to watch. *Watch video now.*

- **Email 2:** You may be feeling like x now you've got all this information. You can talk to us about it to figure out what's best for you. *Book a free discovery call.*
- **Email 3:** Want to talk with others who feel like you do? We have a client community you can join to connect with others like yourself. *Join community today.*
- **Email 4:** This topic has been mentioned in our community a few times, so we're running a workshop to help you work through it. *Register for the workshop.*

Each email needs to tell the reader exactly what you want them to do at that time. When you have a plan instead of a one-shot email you're pinning all your hopes on, not every email needs to have a specific CTA to buy. You could send helpful information and leave it at that. Try different calls to action and see what responses you get.

You could also choose one call to action and repeat that in every single email. Repeat the CTA within the body of the email and in any buttons you include. Keep repeating it so they're not distracted by too many different options, and eventually, they'll either take the action or unsubscribe. If someone unsubscribes, don't worry about it. You have no idea all the reasons they don't want to get your emails. Maybe your firm's messages are not for them. Maybe they get too many emails and want to stay connected another way. Maybe there's something going on in their life, and it all feels too overwhelming. Once you send your emails, the choice to keep getting them is entirely up to the recipient.

Once you've written out an email and edited it, send it. Send it as is, warts and all. Emails can take a few minutes or an hour to write, so if you're not careful, they'll become something you obsess over as you work to get every phrase right, the call to action perfect, the message exactly what they need to hear. If you feel a little nervous about sending an email because it's "not perfect yet," it's probably a lot closer to what it needs to be, which is the most human and the most honest.

Permission, permission, permission

Now you've got something to say, how do you get them to sign up for it? Your goal is a list of people who want to hear from you. Better to have fifty people who really are interested in what you have to say than fifty thousand who don't care, block you, and don't read your emails. Seth Godin says when you practice permission marketing, as the clutter gets worse, your efforts become more profitable. These days, we all get so many emails that we protect our inbox fiercely and rightly so. When your email subscribers have all the information they need, they can sign up for what they want and unsubscribe when they want. The choice is theirs. Not everyone wants to receive emails. Those who sign up may not stay on your list forever. Those on your list may not always see your emails. Knowing this, we'll now discuss what you can do to make it easy for people to sign up to your emails when they're ready.

Choose one email platform and use it as your sole place for everyone who wants to receive emails from you. This can be particularly challenging for accountants because you usually have project management software and other software apps to manage the accounting and tax work you're doing. Not all of them play nicely together or make it easy for someone to pick and choose what emails they receive from you. Some countries have specific rules about what constitutes spam emails, including a "legitimate interest" element—meaning if the person is a client or has purchased from you at some point, you may have good reason to email them about other things they would be legitimately expected to have an interest in. Solve the problem by using one email system where all new subscribers are added by them opting in rather than you signing them up yourself. This could be a link you send to ask them to confirm their interest in receiving emails from you. Or, an app integration which records the email addresses of everyone who has signed up to hear from you and puts them somewhere you can access them easily.

Make it really easy for people to sign up and really easy for them to unsubscribe. Making an email sign-up easy doesn't mean making it spammy or presuming they want every email you'll ever send. Ask for permission to send certain kinds of emails, and show what these are so they know what to expect. If they sign up for one type of email, don't send them all the other emails as well, overwhelming them with content they didn't expect, didn't ask for, and don't want. It will only result in them unsubscribing from everything rather than happily receiving the one email they did actually want.

Use double opt in so they need to confirm their email address. Most email systems include this as a standard part of their service. Don't look at it as a frustration; look at it as a fail-safe and a help. Those who didn't really want to sign up won't confirm. Those who entered the wrong email address will have to figure that out, and you won't be sending emails for years to an address which doesn't exist! Even if for some reason they receive emails from you they don't want, they're still in control and can choose not to receive these emails and know you will honour that decision. Reassure them when it comes to cancelling or unsubscribing. Depending on your audience and how they might feel about signing up, you could add a message on your website or in the first email to be clear they can unsubscribe at any time. Most people know this already, but if your audience needs to hear it, be transparent and ease any fears or doubts they might have.

Create free content they access after providing their email address. Asking for an email address to give away free content brings us into the slightly confusing world of gatekeeping content. This is the practice of asking someone to share information about themselves and their business before they are permitted to access the content. You literally place a digital gate around the information you're giving them. It's like a trade. You are providing something helpful, and they are showing they value it. An email address is very valuable to its owner and worth protecting. Because of this, you are not asking for nothing by gatekeeping your content; you're asking for access to this person. What you give them must be valuable enough to them so they feel comfortable providing you that level of access.

The rule with gatekeeping is this: the more you share, the more you can ask for. If your content is extensive or extremely detailed, you can ask for an email address as well as other information about them or their business. If it's light content, which means the information could be found anywhere or you want them to access it with no delay, provide the content without putting a gate around it at all. If you are sharing a four-page PDF with a few tips about cash or a leaflet about your firm, you don't even need to ask for an email address. If, however, you have invested your expertise in building a forty-five-page PDF with extensive practical content you've custom-written yourself with your own unique assets and approach, you can ask for more information.

Depending on the value of the content, you could ask for their name, email, company, type of business, number of employees, sales, or other details relevant to the content you're providing. If the PDF is about payroll, you could ask multiple questions about the size of their team, payment processes, and deadlines. Having this information helps you create emails relevant to the person receiving them, right down to the smallest detail.

Tell and show them what they'll get when they sign up. To help them decide whether they will share this information with you, tell and show them what they're getting. You can do this by sharing one or all of the following, usually on a website page with a form to complete that unlocks the content:

- *Images of what the content looks like.* Think of Amazon's "look inside!" feature when you're considering buying a book.
- *Quotes or short clips from the content they will access.* This is a similar concept to my making available one chapter of this book to help people decide if they want to read the whole thing.
- *Samples of similar content.* If it's an email newsletter, add links to the full body of content from the previous week's or month's newsletter so they can read it and decide if this is what they want.

Use your creativity to show as much as you can and to give as much information as they need to decide. Asking for an email address can feel like a big ask. Make sure they feel in control.

Write different emails to different audiences. This is why segmenting your list and creating categories is so important. We'll talk more about that in a moment. It's far better to send a custom-crafted email which is perfect for this particular person or business—and have five of these emails received, opened, read, and appreciated—than to blast out a more generic email to fifty thousand people, most of whom ignore it.

Write a text-only email. We get it into our heads that a "business email" is only worth sending when it has a properly branded header, is structured with sections, and contains a call to action. Actually, some of the best emails you can send are text-only with a message from you personally. It could have one simple CTA that is not a button but a link. It could even (gasp!) not have a call to action at all. Some of the emails I appreciate the most have no fancy headers or images at all. They simply share things I care about. I save them. I read them later. I stay on the list. It feels less like they're trying to get my business and more like they're sharing something they care about or want me to know or learn.

Your text-only email doesn't have to be long. You could send a three-sentence email which is more applicable and helpful to those on your list than a super-long version with lots of buttons and links to click.

Write an email from you personally. When I started PF, I wrote "Karen's Marketing Tips" for over seven years, sending them out by email every Friday without fail. I'd write helpful how-to articles, educational training articles, and practical marketing help exclusively for accountants. I put the content on the PF website as blog posts and invited people to sign up on the email list so they could get them in an email as well. Turning email content into a blog post (or vice versa) helps make sure everyone can benefit from what you share, whether they're on the email list or not. It also helps your website to be found when someone is searching online for words appearing in your email or your blog post.

As the team grew, I began to involve all the PF team members with the marketing articles, and they began writing too. This expanded the value of the content we share. Our graphic designers write about choosing stock imagery and how to edit videos, our content team writes about tone of voice and how long a blog post needs to be, and our Client Marketing Managers write about strategically choosing an audience or involving values in your hiring process. This made the articles more relevant, more well rounded, and more helpful. It also meant they weren't coming from me personally anymore. So I started writing my own "Karen's Notes," which I send out (most) Saturday mornings.

"Karen's Notes" come personally from me, and while the PF marketing articles are focused on practical help, "Karen's Notes" are about mindset. I talk about things like leadership, culture, creativity, and rest. I share what I'm writing in my current book or thinking about for my next project. Although they're still written for business owners, anyone can sign up for them (and some family and friends do!). The list of people who receive this email is shorter, but my primary goal isn't more numbers. I write to keep connection with those who have signed up. Sometimes I simply write them for my own sake. I often get personal replies (sometimes many long paragraphs) from people who have been receiving them for months or years, and we connect and talk about real things. As a result, we know each other better. Sometimes they become clients; sometimes they become friends. It's another way to connect.

Create website pages for specific issues. When you have a website page relating to a particular issue or problem (i.e., what's deductible for tax, how to start a business, which type of business you need to set up) or a niche audience (i.e., dentists, creatives, writers, farmers), the CTA might include the opportunity to sign up for emails about this particular problem or niche area. Your page could include helpful tips, videos, free resources, people in your firm who help with this issue, and an email sign-up. This is why segmenting your email list is so important; the more information you have about what they care about, the more relevant your email will be and the more likely they'll not only sign up but stay signed up.

Use speaking, presentations, and events to get email sign-ups. Anytime you are speaking at an event or delivering some kind of presentation, create a specific website page relating to that event. Before the event, you can include a pre-event video ("here's what I'm going to cover"), and afterwards, either upload the entirety of your talk (if it's recorded and you have permission) or a summary of it ("here's what we talked about and why it matters"). Include helpful resources specifically relating to this topic or ones you mentioned in the talk, such as checklists, downloads, PDF guides, your book, or community memberships. These can be something you gatekeep, or they can simply be there, easy to access. You can also include a link to sign up for emails on this topic—again, this is why we segment!

Make the website page URL easy to remember. It's far easier to mention wearepf.com/book than it is to explain wearepf.com/accountant-marketer. However, if you type either one of those in, you'll get to a page about this book! Most of the time people will access a website page from a link you or someone else shares, but especially for an event it's handy to have a phrase that's easy to remember in case they're looking for it.

Use a waiting list. One of the most powerful uses for an email list is the waiting list. This can be useful when:

- You have too many leads and need time to breathe so you can serve your existing clients well.
- You have a new product or service, and you aren't ready to sign people up yet but want to know who's interested.
- You are writing a book, want to build momentum, and are giving extra or free stuff to those who have been following your journey.
- An event is coming up, and sales or tickets aren't open yet.

Harness the power of the waiting list by creating one and staying in touch with those who have expressed an interest. It might feel backwards to you; after all, you're thinking, "Surely if someone is interested, they want to buy *right now!*" But the truth is a waiting list builds momentum better than an always-available product ever could. We'll talk about this more in chapter 8 on following up.

Segment, segment, segment your email list. To make sure what you're sending is actually helpful, segment your email list so those signing up receive the content most relevant to who they are and where they are in life or business. If you send out one email to thirty thousand people, chances are it will only specifically apply to a few hundred or maybe a few thousand of them. It won't apply to every single person or be relevant to their situation that day. Not everyone has a broken washing machine today.

Once you've segmented your list, you are better able to write emails relevant to that particular audience and only them. You craft the emails they will get (or not get) depending on those segments. This makes it far more likely they'll read and appreciate your emails, which means they'll want to keep getting what you send them. If you're sending an email blast to everyone, but it only applies to parents, or to owners of companies with more than one million in sales, everyone else for whom it doesn't apply could think they're on the wrong list and unsubscribe.

You can segment your email list within your email software or customer relationship management (CRM) system in one or more of these ways:

- **Niche/industry:** creative agency owner, manufacturing business, construction business, ecommerce
- **Type of person:** business owner or tax-only client
- **Type of service:** those who get management accounts, payroll, tax, or all of the above
- **Services not signed up for:** You could mark those who do *not* get a particular service so you know to include them in an email relating to how helpful that would be. This also prevents someone who gets this service from being informed about something they already have.
- **Type of business growth:** fast, scaling, slow, start-up

Segmenting allows you to take one email you've written and adapt it for the specific type of people you're sending it to. This isn't merely a "find and replace" exercise in which you change "business owner" to "dentist" and call it good. You need the content of each email to be relevant to that particular person. But often, once you've written the core email, a few small tweaks are enough to send similar content to a variety of people and help them feel it was written just for them.

Getting people to sign up to receive emails from you and segmenting that list so they get the right emails is one thing. Now let's look at the system you'll use to send them.

Get the core elements of a CRM system working before you actually invest in the system

One of the reasons you don't send emails consistently from your firm may be the lack of what you consider a "proper CRM system". You're either using a simple or free email system, which is not integrated with all the information you have on your clients and contacts, or you don't have an email system at all. So you hold off on email because you want to get the system right first.

With any business problem you face, it's tempting to look for a solution in technology. When it comes to video, you think, "I'll buy all the equipment first"—instead of recording video with the phone camera you have. You want to start blogging, so you decide to sign up for a new app and create a full year's content strategy calendar instead of writing a blog post to answer the question you got yesterday. You know you need to be on social media, so you research automated-posting apps so you can share content from all the platforms instead of choosing one social platform and figuring it out by using it daily.

The same mindset can hold you back when it comes to email. You wait to create and send emails because you want to get a full, proper CRM system which integrates with your project management and accounting software. In any of these instances, there are two reasons you're looking to tech before you take action:

1. **You've leaped in before without a plan, and it didn't go well.** You skipped the research and planning step, signed up for a random app, and fired in with no thought whatsoever. You were tired of waiting and

wanted to get it done. But the app you signed up for didn't work, or wasn't for you, and you feel like you wasted a lot of time and money. You don't want to do that again. Next time you're going to plan properly, do your research, and spend your money and time wisely. This will take a lot of time, and you've got a lot on, so . . . you'll do it later. Later becomes later still, and instead of planning well, you simply put it off.

2. **You have fears and concerns about what you're taking action on, and planning is actually a way to avoid starting.** A good example of this is video. You have perfectly good videography equipment in your pocket or handbag—the phone you use every day. But even if you had the right equipment, you'd still feel worried, nervous, or confused. You feel imposter syndrome or play the comparison game. You tell yourself you're going to wait and buy the right video equipment, and then you'll feel a huge sense of relief when you've ordered it. Because now you have done everything you possibly could, and you can wait for the equipment to come and solve your problems. Only it doesn't. It arrives and sits there in the box, and you set it to the side to deal with "when you have time." Later.

Both of these reasons reflect a genuine desire to do marketing well. They also reflect a desire for perfection. For people-pleasing. For getting it right with no mistakes. That's not how creativity works. To lean into your creativity and be a true Accountant Marketer, you're going to try things. You will discover later some of those things were definitely not right for you or your firm. Yes, it will feel like a waste of time. Yes, it would have been nice if you had known that system you spent a lot of money and time setting up doesn't integrate with your core accounting software. Yes, you wish it would magically be sorted for you and you didn't have to learn, try, send emails to the wrong people, or make a mistake.

Time to lean into the unknown.

When I set up PF, we started straight in using a system called Infusionsoft (which was nicknamed Confusionsoft for good reason). It had all the capabilities, all the bells and whistles. It could tag people, segment them, create a sales cycle, flag opportunities, send automatic emails, delay emails, set up reminders, link to your and your team's calendars, read your mind, write book chapters, and grind coffee beans to deliver fresh coffee to you upon waking.

Okay, maybe not those last few ones. But that's what we wish for when choosing a CRM system or any kind of tech which is going to solve the problem we've identified. When we realise it's not going to magically do that with no input from us whatsoever; when we realise it requires collaboration and effort and planning and setup and trying things and breaking things; when we discover we could use another system and have all the same challenges or successes . . . it defeats us a bit. And we put it off. For longer and longer.

Like marketing itself (which requires collaboration and input), you aren't going to be able to delegate your emails to a CRM system. You aren't going to solve your "what do I say to people and how often" question by signing up for more tech. You need to first solve the problem in the most minimalistic way possible. This may mean creating a form directly on your website, or with a free form tool, so people can request to hear from you. It may mean signing up for a free email system. It's not a CRM, and it's not meant to be. But you can create a sign-up form, embed it in your website or share the link, and start building a list of people who want to hear from you including preferences and segments. And then you write emails to send to them. That's really all you need to start. It doesn't significantly matter which system you choose. Pick something that works in these areas:

- You easily understand how to use it.
- You can segment by the categories you determined above.
- It integrates with your website (or it can, if you use a plug-in or app).
- You can and will actually send emails using it.

If you already have that, great! You can move on to segmenting the list further, integrating your email system with all your other systems, and building that list by sharing the kind of content people want to receive by email. You can also create templates and automate some of your emails so they go out consistently based on what someone has signed up for.

Automation: the machine with the human on top

The idea of automating your emails can feel similar to the promise of the magic CRM system or email software: "If I set this up, everything will happen without me, and I can focus on other things while emails go out and money magically comes in." But automation is another kind of tech that, on its own, doesn't solve the marketing problem. It supports marketing and helps you be more efficient and reach more people, but automation doesn't do the marketing. You never want to entirely remove the human element from your email marketing because you're in the business of serving and helping people. Your emails are going out to real humans with real-life problems weighing on them, keeping them awake, and preventing them from achieving goals.

Yes, emails can go out automatically, but you want people to engage with you and your team personally. Email replies, direct messages, and conversations during client meetings will flow from the awareness you're building with clients and prospects, including the emails you send. No matter how perfect your email is for some people, there will be others who read it and aren't sure. Who have more questions. Who have doubts and are wondering if they're going to waste their money or if you're the right fit for them. You and your team need to be present and available to answer those questions when they come up.

Automation is really helpful in saving you time with questions which are asked over and over. These are problems and concerns you've heard many times before and know the answer to before the person even finishes asking. The principles behind these questions apply to many different clients at once. To determine what emails you can automate, ask yourself, what do we do or say over and over, so many times we've lost count? Consider these questions, and for each one, write down the answer. Create a template you can use either manually or automatically so you don't have to write the same things again and again. Here are some brainstorming exercises designed to help you create these kinds of templates:

- **New enquiry:** Write down the questions prospects always ask. Make a note of information you know they'll need and the information you'll ask them for and why.
- **Proposal process:** Consider what they might be fearful of or what might delay them signing the proposal. Create emails addressing these directly (i.e., *You might be worried about this, or wondering this. Here's a video we created to answer your concerns*).
- **Sign-up:** Think about how they feel and the first thing they'll want to know. You could send one onboarding email with the answers to their first few questions and tell them what's coming up (i.e., *In the next few days, you're going to get emails from us about setting up payment authorisation, a video from your client manager, and some forms to fill in. Look out for these soon!*).
- **Deadlines:** Be clear about what they are responsible for and what you are. Explain what happens if they don't do their part or miss deadlines. Share the

consequences or penalties they need to be aware of
and how they can avoid those.

- **Onboarding:** Provide the whole picture. What
happens first, what happens next, and how long it
takes. You could include a graphic, a PDF guide, or a
website page explaining all this so they always know
where they are in the process.

Prepare a series of emails giving them all this information in
order. The first email could explain the big picture of what's
coming over the next month or so, and subsequent emails could
be drip-fed over a period of time. Send an email a day at first,
then every few days, then every week, then every few weeks,
then monthly. Once the full onboarding or sign-up process is
complete, they'll be on your email list to receive the other emails
you send out—segmented for their particular needs, of course.

**Integrated marketing: Don't measure success by individual
emails**

It is tempting to determine ROI by one specific action you
take. One of our Accelerator members shared her experience
about what felt like "instant success" from posting a video on
LinkedIn. She posted a video about management accounts, and
within a few days, she had seven messages from people
contacting her with questions or asking to meet. Within the
week, she had booked calls with at least three of them.

Another Accelerator member, Sharon, said, "Spoke to a
potential client today who contacted us SPECIFICALLY because
of our blogs!! He quoted some of our comparison blogs and said
that's the service he needs. He is not speaking to anyone else. He
is our target niche. This makes me so happy!" She later shared
this prospect signed up for over £30,000 worth of work within
the space of a year.

It is tempting to think of these successes as if they stand

alone. You think, "Okay, I got seven people messaging me because of one video, so if I post one video a day I'll get seven messages per video, which leads to three calls, which leads to one client signing up." Or, as in Sharon's case, you might think writing one blog post will result in £30K worth of new business, so if you write ten blog posts, you can expect a £300K return.

Both of these accountants know that's not how it works. The one video, the one blog post, isn't the only thing this prospect saw or connected with. I know these two accountants, and they have been consistent with their content marketing over a period of months and years. They've posted written content and images consistently, even daily, on multiple social platforms. They've recorded and shared a video at least weekly, if not more often, on at least one platform. They've written regular blog posts (at least weekly) based on the questions their clients were asking. Shared those blog posts on their website and on socials. Updated their website with new content, adding pages, writing new blog posts, creating and sharing resources, changing messaging, and adjusting calls to action. Consistently sent emails to their list of clients and prospects.

They also made sure to review their brand: not only their name, logo, and colours but also their style, tone of voice, and values. They refined and kept refining their audience, documenting exactly who they serve, moving beyond industries to consider characteristics, values, and mindset.

You may be tempted to feel elation or despair when you look at the results from sending one email. Your click-through rate was low. You wrote another, and many people opened it, but no one took action. You sent another and got four people replying but no sales. Your doubts and fears multiply. Is this even worth it? Why are you bothering? These emails aren't working! Conversely, you could be thrilled at the success of sharing a new PDF guide and getting fifty new subscribers. This is it! This is the answer! More PDF guides!

That thinking is the one-platform approach to marketing ROI:

- Sending one email and expecting instant results.
- Posting a few times on one social media platform and wondering why no one is liking or commenting.
- Recording videos every day for a week and despairing because you have no new followers yet.

But your marketing is a web, connected (with some fragility) and every thread affects the others. It combines email, video, website, blog posts, and socials. It flows from your brand and reminds people you're still there. You're looking for results over time, not an instant reaction. From time to time, you'll have an email, blog post, or a video which seems to "get results" on its own. For example, you post one video and get five, fifty, or five hundred people signing up. You did it! You found the magic bullet! And then things go quiet, people's attention shifts, or the world itself changes, and you need to adjust again.

Marketing is relational, not transactional. Emails are about engagement, not click-throughs. As a service provider building a relationship, you want people to reply, to connect, to ask questions. Even if you automate some of your emails, you'll still need to be personally present because you're a people business. Even if you have products for them to buy or resources for them to download, you still need to be talking with them about how it impacts their life. Focus on engagement with individual humans, and create emails which encourage more of that. Your return comes when that relationship is built in such a way the right people trust you, want to work with you, and start when they're ready. They may need to follow you for days, weeks, or years. They may want to receive emails; they may not. Either way, make email available to the right people so they can sign up whenever they want to.

Everyone still uses email and will for some time. But again, as with all marketing elements, don't rely on email alone in your marketing efforts. Some people won't want any emails from you. They won't sign up, or they'll unsubscribe as soon as they get a few emails. They still want to be connected to you and your firm, but they want to connect in another way through their preferred social media platform or direct messages. Maybe they are content to be aware of you from afar, without the personal connection of email yet (or at all).

As we'll discover in the next chapter, email is only one small part of the communication methods you use to be a continued presence in their life. Website pages, video, downloadable guides, community groups, and other platforms and tools work in tandem to keep you top of mind. They enable you to follow up pleasantly, patiently, and persistently.

Unless prospects unsubscribe from every single form of communication possible, you can continue to be a presence in their life. Make it easy for them to choose and contact you when they are ready.

CHAPTER 8
FOLLOW-UP

SELLING FEELS HARD. It feels awkward and uncomfortable. You're aware how good you are at what you do, but you don't want to have to persuade people who aren't ready to buy. You yourself don't like to be pushed when you're being sold to, so you don't want to do that to others.

That's a good quality. You care, you know yourself, and you're not pushy. Unfortunately, when it comes to following up with prospects, this quality can turn into something which prevents you from signing up the very people you want to work with and who want to work with you. "Well, I never heard back from that prospect," you tell yourself. "I guess they don't want to work with us." You go through mental gymnastics to understand why they never got back in touch, what you said to throw them off, what wasn't a fit about your firm, and why they went somewhere else.

Don't give up simply because you haven't heard back yet

On the other hand, you might presume you know why and go on the defensive. You say, "Oh well, they found us too expensive. And that's fine—we know our value, and clearly, they don't. I don't want to work with people who don't understand our value." Or they just wanted a tax return, and that's not the sort of work you do. Or they were a bigger company, and you work from home on your own, so it makes sense they went somewhere else.

Think about a recent prospect. They got in touch, asked for a meeting, and maybe even met with you, shared about their business and learned how you did things. They got a proposal and then . . . nothing. You sent a cheerful email and gave them a quick call. No reply. You left it a week or so, then tried again. Nothing. By this point, it's been two weeks. You don't want to be a bother, pressuring them and being salesy, so you leave it with them, thinking, "If they're really interested, they'll get back in touch." But they don't. And you forget they ever were interested, and you never find out what was going on or what happened to prevent them from working with you. So you guess.

Maybe they got really busy. Things are overwhelming them right now. Or maybe they decided their current accountant wasn't so bad after all. They got in touch with you because they were annoyed, but they managed to work things out, and it was too much hassle to change accountants.

Maybe it's pricing. They found you too expensive. They got your proposal, and it was three times what another accountant quoted, so they went with another firm. Or they didn't want all the services you provided. They just wanted basic accounts, and the advisory and management accounts with quarterly meetings was too much for them.

When you think about why someone might not get in touch, the "maybes" are endless. You could continue this exercise ad infinitum and never actually know the real reason. The truth is a vast majority of the prospects who get in touch and then seem to disappear off the face of the earth are actually still interested in working with you. They are. It's also possible some of these objections you considered—or a combination of them—are also true.

Maybe they did find you too expensive, and they're still interested in working with you if they can understand where the pricing comes from and how it benefits them. Maybe they're busy because someone in their family went into hospital, and they had to put everything on hold. Maybe they went back to their existing accountant but have since been reminded the relationship isn't great, and they really liked the meeting they had with you.

Until you know, the reason could literally be anything, and it's a waste of your time to spend hours trying to figure it out, defend yourself, or pretend you don't care. Use that time instead to actually care and to build a follow-up system which will keep you in touch until they *are* ready. Or at least until they give you an answer.

Good follow-up keeps you connected while the buyer decides

We've gotten so obsessed with not being "salesy" we've forgotten the whole point of sales. As my friend James Ashford says in his book *Selling to Serve*, "Selling is your ethical obligation. If you avoid selling somebody something that they really need, whose interests are you really putting first?"

The point isn't to focus on us—how we feel and whether we are being seen as salesy or pushy. *Are* you being salesy? *Are* you being pushy? Are you doing this simply to make money? Do you care more about the sales and profit numbers your business makes than about the human beings you serve?

For most accountants, that is 100 percent not the case. With so many of those I know personally (and I know a good few!), you are some of the most honourable, kind, and caring people on the planet. You know the pain a business owner can go through when their finances aren't right because you are a business owner yourself. You also have the accounting expertise to know how the numbers can make or break a business. Your training and experience have been applied to your own business's numbers as well as those of your clients. You feel for the person dithering at the edge of signing your proposal because you know what's coming. And you have the power and know-how to prevent a train of loss, pain, or even bankruptcy from barrelling towards this person at full speed. You know what track they need to be on, and you're ready and willing to help them.

Your follow-up process needs to be created for them, for those confused and lost business owners who are standing on the tracks, wondering which way to turn. Yes, send a few emails and make a phone call to follow up. But don't give up there. Don't *let* them keep standing in the middle of that track. Create everything possible they can read, watch, listen to, and get their hands on so they know what you know. Or as much of it as they can handle. As my friend Paul Barnes says, "If you had their business, knowing what you know, what would you recommend they do?"

This is what follow-up is all about. It's not about "getting the sale," feeling proud and relieved, celebrating another new client, and moving on to another one. It's not about pretending you don't care and saying if they really wanted to work with you, they'd stay in touch. It's about sharing everything you wish you'd knew if you were in their place so they can make the most informed and educated decision the moment they're ready. To do this, you create content every step of the way. And it starts before they even request a proposal.

A good follow-up system will follow the Buyer Progression Model. Create content for every step of their buying journey, and present them with what they need to know. It's always their choice when they take action, and they must feel they're the ones making that choice. Let people sign up as fast as they want to sign up. If the person who really did want to sign up in one day ends up taking months or years because they didn't know how you did things, or they didn't realise the difference and the value, that's on you. It's your responsibility to provide them with the answers, the process, the pricing, the proof of value, the stories, the numbers, the humanity, the connection. When you create content which answers questions at every stage of the buying journey, you don't lose prospects anymore.

There are a multitude of studies showing over 80 percent of sales happen after at least five points of contact. Here are some additional statistics that make this even more important:

- 44 percent of companies give up after the first point of contact.
- 22 percent give up after two points of contact.
- 14 percent give up after three points of contact.
- 12 percent give up after four points of contact.

This means 92 percent of people working to make a sale give up after making contact no more than four times. And yet the vast majority of the people they're talking to need at least one more follow-up before they say yes.

When you are persistent, stay in touch, and keep following up in a variety of ways, you're beating out the other 92 percent of firms who have said, "Oh well, they said no. They must not be interested. We must be too expensive. I don't want to bother them. If they're interested, they'll come back." When you think about how many contact points we have now—from social media messages to website forms, online meetings and emails, text messages and notifications, it makes sense to keep following up beyond only one or two points of contact.

It also makes sense to have a variety of content for prospects to read and engage with. Everyone has different preferences for how they take in the content you share. Some people want the detail and will read every word of your blog posts, PDF guides, and books. Some are more visual and will appreciate a graphic so they understand the concept quickly. Some prefer video and will literally watch videos from you all day long until they get the answers they need. Some prefer audio and want to listen to a podcast or an audiobook. Many prefer a combination or a variety depending on the topic, how fast they need the information, and what kind of product or service they're interested in. Whatever your buyer's preference is, give them enough they can choose from so the information they need is available and they can respond to it when they're ready.

Creating this helpful content for prospects also helps you decide who you want to work with rather than accepting every enquiry which comes your way. This is called prequalifying content, and it's some of the most important content you'll ever create. Before we talk about prequalifying, though, let's talk about pricing.

The pricing question

We've talked about the doubts and fears your prospects have when they're considering signing up because they don't understand the fees accountants charge, or the way you specifically approach pricing and proposals. For their sake and yours, it is your responsibility to give them *some* idea of the level of investment they could be looking at. You don't have to lay out your exact prices; in fact, doing so might encourage them to make their decision on money alone, but you must address the pricing question.

Show you're willing to have the pricing conversation. When you're looking for help from a professional service provider (especially one whose pricing you're new to), you're thinking, "I just want to know if we're talking hundreds or thousands or hundreds of thousands." And once we know the initial price— the setup fee, the clean-up work—we want to know what's next. How much will we be paying over the next year, or two years, or ten years? What's coming? Why might it change and what would it be based on? When your prospect comes to you, this is how they feel and what they want to know too.

Some firms we've worked with decided to share a range with

wording along the lines of "our pricing for bookkeeping ranges between x and y." Some share ranges depending on a sample type of business and its needs, saying, "A limited business with two owners and twenty-five employees and sales of this much might pay between x and y." Some give a starting or minimum fee, saying, "Our services start at x." Whatever you choose, don't make your prospect feel like you're hiding the numbers on purpose. Help them see any apparent delay is a protection for them to help prevent a wrong quote which would get them overexcited or over-discouraged. After all, their previous experiences may lead them to expect you to hide things or make up numbers to try to get as much money from them as possible, and they need to understand you're not like that.

Saying "everything is bespoke" or "we always provide custom quotes" doesn't mean anything to the prospective buyer. Your bespoke packages could start at £2K per month while your prospect is still a start-up. On the other hand, your custom quote could be a few hundred a month when they're expecting thousands. The more questions you answer before you even meet with them, the faster they can make their decision. Your buyer will make 70 percent of their buying decision before they ever get in touch; give them everything they need to understand what it's like to work with you. They want to be invited into the pricing conversation instead of being emailed a number they don't understand, don't know if you plucked out of the air based on what you know about their company or, worst of all, based on the budget they shared.

When you create content answering the questions you already know you're going to get in the proposal process, it saves you a vast amount of time in the follow-up process. It helps them compare apples with apples. It protects them from presuming your firm is like the last accountant they worked with or believing two different services are priced in the same way. They may be comparing you to one of the following:

- *A different kind of service.* Maybe they've only had bookkeeping services and have never worked with an accounting firm with a team and bookkeepers who provided help with payroll and tax planning. Show them what's involved in this new way of working with an accountant and this type of service.
- *The same kind of service from a different person or company.* "My mother-in-law does some bookkeeping and only charges this," they might say. Or, "My mate down the pub said his accountant sorted out the whole tax problem for this much." Explain the costs and penalties they'll face when they follow this kind of advice. Paint them a picture of what it will cost them years down the road.
- *A different service they got from you.* Perhaps they're a legacy client, have worked with you for years, and had a low price because you never revisited it. Maybe their company wasn't growing much before, but now it is growing and has more transactions, and they want and need more from you, and the budget has increased. What they paid for the past service is setting the tone for the number they're expecting to get for the new one, even though they're very different services. Explain how the number of transactions and the size of the business impact the pricing and how it's calculated. Show them everything you've invested in for your firm, what they get for these fees, and why that fits with a new price.

Prequalifying content also helps them understand the cost of *not* doing this now. Every moment they delay working with a really good accountant, the right one for them, will multiply their cost over time. Every decision they have to make in the next few months could be made on the wrong numbers or a financial statement they don't understand. They could be saying

"My gut tells me this is a great opportunity" or "We have to start hiring now because I'm so busy." They could be buying equipment or a new van for the business based only on their bank balance, which they checked on their phone. And the position they're in a year later could be far worse without you—or far better with your help—and saying no to this proposal could cost them. You know it, but they may not realise it yet.

We can always find money or save it up for what we value, need, or want. But our expectations will affect what we spend and when. It is the same with our prospective buyers.

If you want your whole kitchen renovated, you know there will be a lot of money going out for it, and you plan accordingly. But if you think you're buying a new oven or some flooring and, once you start the process, realise you need a whole new kitchen . . . that requires a serious mental adjustment, and it could take months or years to be ready. Maybe you buy a cooker you install yourself, or try to install the flooring using tutorial videos on YouTube, and along the way realise it's not solving the core problem and it's time to rip the whole thing out and start over. Prospects can do the same kind of thing. They could read and absorb the information on your website, meet with you, say they understand it and are excited . . . and then, when they receive the proposal, they aren't ready and tell you they're finding it too expensive. What if it's not about the money at all? What is the real problem?

It's possible they don't know yet what their real problem is. You may know what the real problem is and they don't see it yet —or you may have no clue either. After all, people think they know what an accountant does. They think, "I need taxes done," "My business is outgrowing my current accountant," or whatever else is motivating them to get in touch. But they don't always really understand who you are and what you do. And that's okay. But it's not okay if you don't help them understand.

. . .

Create content every step of the way

When creating your follow-up content, there are four stages of the buyer's journey to consider. Let's begin with the prospect who is just beginning to consider working with you.

Stage 1: Prequalifying Content

Think of a client you had to let go or who left and the financial, emotional, and mental cost that was to you. Think of the hours you spent emailing them, calling them, and talking with the team about the situation. Think of how exhausting it was and how relieved you were when it was all over. By creating prequalifying content, you're saving yourself from all of this, and you're saving that potential client from it too. You're saving them pain and heartache. You are releasing them to work with the firm or person they most need, if it isn't you. Be okay with that. Be strong in what you know about yourself and your firm and the way you do business.

You do not have to please everyone, and you know that's ultimately impossible anyway. You do need to be true to who you are and accept only those clients you absolutely love working with, the clients who will enjoy and appreciate the relationship and make your business better by being present within it. Good marketing divides. Part of the content you are creating in the prequalifying process exists to send away those who are not ready, who are not a fit, and who don't live out your values. Most of the time, they will become a very difficult client later on and cost you and your firm more than money.

It's your job to educate them about the following:

1. How accounting works and what they need
2. How *your* firm specifically works
3. What they might *want* in addition to what they need

Just because someone queries a price doesn't mean they've said no. We are far too prone to panic or jump to conclusions when a prospect says, "Wow, that's really expensive." When you do that, you aren't listening to what they're really saying or asking; you're leaping forward to a conversation you've made up in your head. All they're saying is, in their mind, knowing what they know at this moment, it feels like a lot of money. More, perhaps, than they were originally intending to spend. It's the whole kitchen instead of flooring or a new oven. When someone says, "That's really expensive," one of the best things you can say in reply is "Yes, it is." Leave a long pause for them to think. Don't fill the silence with your speaking when it needs to be filled with their thinking.

Once they've had a moment to think, it's likely they'll say something or ask a question which reveals to you more about what they are expecting this service to do for them and their business, what pain or trouble they need relieved, and what outcome they're hoping for. You could share some of the experiences and success stories of people like them. Seeing someone who was in their same position getting results helps them realise they could get those results too and that would be worth spending money on.

This is why you need to create prequalifying content based on the qualities and values of the person rather than simply the size or type of business. You're taking on a person or a handful of people, not a company. Remember, it's not a "company" who sends you a rude email; a person does. A company doesn't fudge with the tax rules; a person does. If you focus entirely on the company, forgetting the human person or people you'll be dealing with, there could be problems later which make for a very difficult client relationship. One of the most common problems for accountants signing new clients is discovering later this client you thought was going to be so amazing, so exciting, and so profitable . . . isn't. They complain, they are slow to pay or don't pay at all, and they don't listen to your advice. The team member working with them gets a sinking feeling when a call comes or an email drops in from *that client*.

When this happens, it's a warning light which lets you know

you need to address your prequalifying process. To prepare content which will help both you and your prospect decide if this relationship is right. Creating prequalifying content reduces conversations and meetings. Prepare enough information for them to absorb ahead of time so if they do have a meeting with you, they're already familiar with you, your services, and your way. They're comfortable with you or your team because of the videos and articles you've been sharing. They know you have the same values because they read about them on your website and see those values lived out by you and your people in small interactions online and offline. When this happens, the point of the meeting is not to tell them who you are, what your services are, and how you do business but to identify which of the services they particularly need, when, and the amount they'll pay.

Some content you create for potential clients has to do with facts: the size of their business, the number of transactions, and the amount they'll pay. Some content will have to do with your process: what's required from them, what you'll do, and the consequences if they don't do their part or you don't do yours. Be willing to go deeper. Every sale is an emotional sale, whether it appears to be one or not. Give them everything they need to have their fears or wonderings relieved. Let them be able to rest in the process.

This doesn't mean everything will work out perfectly and they'll never have another moment's doubt. They may struggle or get frustrated, or you may forget to send them something on time. That's okay. That's how life and business go. When you've prepared them ahead of time, you can refer back to it and say something like "Remember how we said the first few weeks would feel really exciting, but then we might discover there's more to fix than we first thought? Remember how we talked about the challenge it is to bring your entire team on board with this? Remember, remember . . . ?" And you can work it through, step back to the process and the way, reset, and go again.

Back in chapter 1, we talked about the qualities of the clients you want and the values fit. If it's been a little while since you've done the exercise, go through it again. List out their qualities, look for patterns, and see who you love to work with. Who you're best placed to help. Who is most profitable to you. Your ideal client could be characterised by something as simple as the industry they work in, or it could be a mindset. Maybe the kind of person you like to work with is ambitious. They're focused on family. They're small. They're fast growing. Be as specific as possible and look for that values fit with your firm and your philosophy.

When you've done that, move on to the flags. You're familiar with the concept of red flags and green flags. Are you seeing bad things or good things about this prospect? There are actually four categories of flags: red, pink, green, and gold. This more detailed flag system helps you determine who to follow up with. You only want to follow up with people who indicate they're going to be a great client. If there are uncertainties, this enables you to catch those earlier.

Red flags: qualities you *for sure* do not want. Red flags are obviously a problem. To determine what they are and where they come from, start a list of things you know will cause serious problems with the client relationship.

Be very specific. "They don't value our advice" is a problem, but it takes ages to see it. You don't know if someone values your advice when they don't even know you yet. You won't know if they push back on fees if you haven't sent a proposal yet. And if you create a form asking "Will you value our advice?" they'll probably say yes because they think they will. So think about what makes a little bell go off in your mind. What feels wrong in your gut. Put names and titles to these because "it just doesn't feel right" works okay if it's only you working on your own, but it's not scalable and it won't help your team make decisions without you.

If you want people who value your work and are willing to

pay for it, a red flag could be multiple pushbacks on small charges, insisting on a discount, or sending long emails back and forth for weeks trying to reduce fees. Those are definite details and can be measured.

Look back at the last five or ten clients you sacked or who left and you were relieved. Make a list of things they did which were really frustrating. Again, be as specific as possible, whether it's the fact that they sent fifty-two WhatsApp messages in one day or refused to set up a payment authorisation. Yes, these things are frustrating; they're also opportunities to help you discover where the problems came from so you can improve your prequalifying system. Look at each item and add notes about what the problem or result was. Write out a "this is not okay because" statement. Follow this structure:

- The client [did this].
- It was frustrating to us because [we felt like this].
- It meant [this result happened].
- This is not okay for us because [how it prevents you from helping clients].
- This is not okay for them because [how it makes their life more difficult].
- Their actions set the tone for [other things to happen].

Say you use a payment authorisation like GoCardless, and you require the client to sign this before you start any work. The client said they'd do it but kept putting it off. You didn't want to lose the client, so you started the work. Then a few weeks later, the client eventually said no, they didn't want to; they preferred to just make bank payments whenever they were ready. Here's what went wrong:

- **The client** did not set up GoCardless (even after multiple reminders).

- **It was frustrating to us because** we thought they were such a great client, and we know they have the money or are keen to start work, and it felt disrespectful.
- **It meant** we took longer to get started, and it took hours of time from me and the team.
- **This is not okay for us because** it's inefficient and casts doubt on whether they will fail to do other things we ask for.
- **This is not okay for them because** their work doesn't get done on time, and they could have to pay penalties.
- **Their actions set the tone for** them to ignore other things we ask, for them to be in control of the relationship, and for us to take on more clients who are like them.

There are ways you can help people who initially balk at following your processes, but wherever possible, you want to figure out if you're even a good fit in the prequalifying stage. You don't want to get to this point. You want to be so clear, so up front with your expectations and how you work, that nothing is a surprise to either of you. If they query something, you point them to your lovely How We Work page, your partnership success agreement, or your terms and conditions—and all is well, and you both carry on. That's how it's meant to work. That's how it can work. Or they leave with minimum hassle and none of the exhaustion, stress, and cost you would have had if the relationship carried on for months.

When you explain the consequences of behaviours, focus on how it affects *them*. It's tempting to focus your prequalifying process entirely on you. You may decide you don't want clients who won't set up a payment authorisation because you want to be sure the money comes in first. That's nice for you and a wise plan for a profitable business, but from their perspective, this isn't why they'll set up the authorisation. They'll do it because it means they never have to worry about whether their bill is paid, their work will never be delayed, and they don't want surprise penalties or fees.

Red flags are more obvious. Pink flags can be harder to spot. **Pink flags: behaviour which is not worth instant rejection, but could go either way.** Pink flags are for behaviours which aren't obviously bad but could be either red or green depending on the other behaviours which go along with it. If you have one pink flag and ten green flags, the relationship will probably be okay. If you have six pink flags, they're starting to make one big red flag.

If a prospect asks questions on every line item in the proposal, you explain, and they agree everything makes sense, all is well. It was a pink flag, but as you explained, it became evident these were sincere questions. But if the questions and emails never end, there's a lot of defensiveness, and then they ask for a discount . . . you're in red flag territory.

I asked several accountants what their pink flags are and many replied almost instantly with some version of "when they say how bad their previous accountant was." This is a pink flag because, every once in a while, someone really did have a bad accountant and this is backed up by evidence. The accounts were submitted late or you can see penalties and fees they paid that you know they didn't have to. When that happens, what was a pink flag disappears. But when a person explains at length how horrible their previous accountant was (or current accountant is), what you may really be seeing is a tendency to moan. To complain. To be defensive and not take responsibility. And then you're in red flag territory.

And that's okay.

Do not get angry, or bitter, or defensive at these red and pink flags; they are a *gift*. When you encounter a flag with a new prospect, stop and listen. Don't leap to put the blame on them; take responsibility for what you can do or learn. Ask yourself about the specific behaviour shown and why it is not okay.

Think about how and where they showed that quality. What did they say and when? How often did they do it over a period of time, and how long was the period? If you compare this person's behaviours to your core values list, consider how they measure up. And be ready to make changes to be more clear about your core values and behaviours. Consider anything you haven't explained which would have helped your prospect understand much faster how you work and why. Explain this visually and in multiple formats (i.e., diagram, web page, video, blog). Look for any formats you are missing.

Red flags help you create instant weed-out questions. When you see them, look for ways you can adapt your prequalifying and proposal process, making space to ask qualifying questions right at the beginning. It saves time. Use the "show, don't tell" rule: create questions which *show* you red or pink flag behaviour, rather than requiring the client to *tell* you. Ask the question so you get an honest answer: "How's your relationship with your current accountant?" or "What did you like about your previous accountant?" can reveal a lot. One person might say, "They were really friendly and responsive, but they weren't able to train our bookkeeper, and that's a big need for us." Another might say, "They were a disaster, nothing was ever right, and they cost too much." You may have a red flag.

Use these red and pink flags to look at your follow-up system again. Do you have a specific, clear process for following up on every enquiry? Who took this enquiry, and what did they do with it? Did they follow the process step by step, or did they skip any? Is there anything in your automation or system which could have been missed by you or one of the team, preventing you from seeing or acting on these red flags?

You can also consider whether there's another accountant or firm where you can send people who aren't a fit for you. For example, if the prospect is a start-up and you don't work with start-ups, is there another accountancy firm who loves to help start-ups? These kinds of referrals are for type of business or situation, not values. Don't send pain in the ass (PITA) clients to anyone else; it's not kind, and you wouldn't want it done to you.

Every prospect who turns out to be the kind of client you don't want is a gift. They've helped you. They've taught you something. You may have taught them something as well, but it's okay if they choose not to learn from this experience. That's their responsibility, and it stays with them.

Your prequalifying content gives them all the information they need, asks questions to help you and the team see patterns, and tells you what kind of person this is. The "show, don't tell" rule applies here too. How they act in the prospecting phase is how they'll act as a client, only more so. Depending on your audience, your first point of contact could be a short questionnaire to weed out the most obvious red flags, and once that's completed, you could send a more comprehensive questionnaire later in the process. Some firms have a short form with four to five questions leading to the discovery call being set up (assuming they didn't qualify themselves out straight away) and then another, longer questionnaire for the person to fill in before the call.

If they don't fill in the longer questionnaire in time despite multiple reminders, you've already got a pink flag, and it's up to you how you deal with it. You could say, "We haven't gotten this questionnaire from you yet, and we need it to make sure we give you the best advice and proposal in our call, so let's rearrange for next week to give you more time. If you get it done by x time, we can still go ahead." You've set the boundaries, made it clear how it benefits them, and held firm. If they push back, it's an indicator they'll likely push back on other things.

Green and gold flags: good behaviour indicating a positive client relationship. Green and gold flags are easier because they're so refreshing. A green flag is an obvious good thing, a behaviour you want to see more of in your client relationships. This could be someone who asks questions and nods attentively when you answer them or who has already watched most of your videos and remembers what's in them. A gold flag is so good you want to sign them right away; this is the behaviour of someone who thanks you profusely, recommends you to three other businesses just like them, or sends a video to help you understand their business better. When determining green and gold flags, the same principles as any other kind of flag apply. Be specific. Don't merely say "I love this person!" or "They have the most amazing company!" Ask yourself what they've specifically said or done which indicates a positive relationship and good potential. What values have they lived up to? What character traits do they have which are a positive sign for the relationship?

You're not looking for one flag, a gut feeling, or the fact your friend or brother recommended them. You are looking for client patterns. You want a client whose patterns fit your values as far as you can tell with the information you have. Once you've asked questions and shared content to help both of you feel it's a real possibility they're a fit, you move on to the proposal process and its follow-up.

Stage 2: Content for the Proposal Process

The proposal stage of your follow-up content may feel the most familiar to you. Someone expresses enough of an interest to get an actual quote crafted for them and their business, based on their needs. You've sent emails and messages and possibly a few videos. You've had a meeting, or several meetings. You are getting to know each other. So it feels doubly confusing or discouraging when, after all that . . . radio silence. Ghosting.

This is why you need a solid follow-up process going beyond a few personal follow-up emails or a phone call (although those are worth doing). Your process protects you from being overly discouraged, and it protects them from letting slide what they are actually interested in. It encourages them to ask every question they have, share every concern or fear or doubt, and be heard. Your process allows them to take their time and, if they do sign up, do this as fast as *they* want to.

One small thing I encourage my team and clients to do when it comes to follow-up is to listen to that little voice. You know the one: it pops into your head and says "I wonder whatever happened to that person. They were so keen!" or "I never heard back from them. I wonder if they went with someone else." When that voice speaks, *listen to it and act immediately.*

Drop them a quick text, email, video, or message to say "Hey, I was thinking of you and wondering how you got on!" If you're walking or running or talking to someone, stop for one second and send the message. Then go back to what you were doing. Don't overthink it; say what you want to say without worrying too much about how it comes across. You legitimately thought of them and wondered, so you may as well tell them that. You could ask "Did you go with someone else in the end?" or "Did you decide if you wanted to work with us?" The worst they can say is "Yes, I did go elsewhere," and you can ask more questions to find out what it was they found so appealing about someone else. This will either make your marketing better because you've found a gap in your marketing and questions you haven't answered in the prospect process; or it will confirm the type of person you don't want to work with because you realise they are not your perfect client.

I mention that now because, no matter how great your follow-up process is, you are never going to automate that little voice. It pops up because your mind is telling you something. The voice recognises it's been a long time, they said they were going to think about it, and you really liked them and weren't sure why they said nothing. Best of all, at least eight out of ten times the person will reply with "Oh my word. I was *literally* just thinking of you as well!" They might even add something like "I meant to get in touch but this happened or that happened." And they're really grateful you connected with them.

As an accountant, you are showing them you are going to be

there for them during some of the toughest times of their lives. When they're exhausted or worried or swamped with work—or excited and motivated by an abundance of opportunities—they want an accountant who is going to have their back. Be ahead of the game. Tell them what they need to be doing or listen to what the newest opportunity is so they can implement and benefit from it. As their accountant, you're going to look out for them when it comes to penalties, tax laws, or higher tax rates. They don't have to worry about their finances; they simply focus on doing the work they do really well, and you're there to make sure they don't experience the hassle they've faced before.

The way you stay connected in the proposal process helps show them what kind of an accountant you're going to be in the relationship once they do sign up. It shows you haven't forgotten, you still care, you remember.

You can automate so many things—emails, reminders, deadlines, checklists. But your follow-up process, your onboarding process, and all your other systems always need to be a machine with a human on top. Let the machine do its work. It's your job as the human to top that up with the message, the reminder, the personal connection, the gift, and the listening ear. No automated message will ever do that.

Some level of automation will help support your human touch. Here's how to automate your follow-up to the proposal:

Write a series of follow-up emails. These emails can be based on the questions you expect them to ask, the objections or wonderings everyone else has had. Cut those off at the pass. You know when to share them too because you've had enough experience to know the kinds of things holding them back if they haven't gotten in touch after a week. Or if it's been two months since they replied, these other things are preventing them from going ahead. The further out you get from the proposal without receiving an answer, the fewer emails and the less direct you become. It can go like this:

- **Day of Proposal:** Follow-up info (something helpful such as a video)
- **Day 1:** A typical question or concern with answer
- **Day 3:** Reminder of what happens next and in what order
- **Day 7:** Did you want to go ahead, or are you still deciding?
- **Day 14:** A helpful resource relating to something you discussed in the meeting
- **Day 21:** Option to receive further emails, newsletters, event invites
- **Day 30:** We're presuming it's a no for now, but if you still want to chat let us know.
- **Day 60:** Another helpful resource

After this point, they remain on your main email list and receive updates along with everyone else. This way you're still in touch, but you're not giving the dreaded salesy vibes. If you're honest, sometimes what you fear is rejection itself. You're afraid they'll say no, and you don't like getting a no, so you don't follow up at all. "Best to leave it with them and let them come when they're ready," you think. What you are really doing is absolving yourself of any responsibility and leaving the ball in their court. But you don't want the ball in their court. Your job is not to do anything you can to avoid responsibility: it's to deal with it, fully, because that's who you are. You're the accountant. Take it on.

Record a personal video and send it with the proposal. If you're not doing this already, you need to implement it for *every single proposal you send*. There is no good reason to avoid this, and it will always help them make the most informed decision possible. Sending a video reminds them of what they need to know. As soon as the meeting is over, they've forgotten at least half of what you shared. They're thinking about themselves and their business, they're focused on the price and trying to figure out where that comes from, or they're wondering what their business partner is going to say when they talk about it later. What they do remember has been converted to how they understand it in their mind. Repeating the key points in a personal proposal video helps them not to turn those things into something they're not. You don't want them thinking "I'm pretty sure they said the price would double in six months" when what you actually said was "A lot of companies we work with do so well that in six months their accounting fees go up because their transactions and sales and profits have gone up."

A video gives you the opportunity to include personal details. You can mention how fun it was to meet their child, or dog, or partner who walked past the screen in your meeting and said hello. You could mention the love for whisky, or barbeque or tacos or tea, which you have in common. It will matter to them. It certainly matters to me when I'm on the receiving end of it. It shows you care about them personally. Yes, you can send a general video to every prospect covering things like "here's your proposal and a few points to think about." Nothing wrong with that, and if it's helpful, go for it. But sending a video which is clearly personal (i.e., "Hi, Dave— great to chat today and hope you enjoy the bike ride later" versus a generic "Here's your proposal") makes it more likely they will watch it. People do business with people, and your personal video is a reminder you care about them, not just a signed proposal, or more money, or another client on the books. They're a human.

A video also lives on beyond your meeting. People need time and space to put together what they're considering. Some people make decisions instantly, but that's rare, and sometimes it's simply rashness, not bravery or boldness. Even when we do make what feels like an instant decision, it's usually the result of days, weeks, or months of gathering information, mulling things over, and considering what matters. Giving them a video means they have something to go back to if they are still deciding or reconsidering or need to share it with a business partner. We'll go into more detail about the power of video in chapter 10.

Create a specific thank-you page. Having a general "thanks for getting in touch" page on your website is good; creating specific thank-you pages for different purposes is better. Create a "thanks for requesting your proposal" thank-you page and include the kinds of things they need at that point—such as a video about what's next, a visual diagram of what happens and in what order, or a link to your FAQs.

Include only the information which is the most helpful and will answer the questions most people have to move the buying process along faster. You may be moving the buyer process to a yes, and they sign the proposal (Yay! They figured out you are the accountant for them!). Or you may be moving it to a no, and they don't sign it (Yay! They figured out you're not the best fit, and you can move on to others who are!).

If they sign the proposal, move them to the onboarding content. For everyone else, stay in touch and keep marketing until they say no.

Stage 3: Content for Onboarding

Creating a great onboarding process is not merely about saving time and being efficient. Those are lovely benefits for you, but onboarding is not about you. The goal of your onboarding process is to deliver on the promises you made during the sales process. To make sure the incredible experience they signed up for actually happens. It's also to continue connecting beyond the sign-up date. Despite what you're tempted to believe, signing a new client doesn't mean you never follow up again. Their agreeing to become a client does not mean every doubt has been washed away, every fear covered, every question answered. You're bringing them into the fold, and you've got more to do during onboarding to help this relationship be a success. Your buyer is signing up with you as their new accountant because, at the moment of the sale, they feel confident you are the one who can solve their problems and help them grow. You're going to support them in opportunities and improve profitability. Keep delivering on these promises throughout the onboarding process.

Onboarding can be quite detailed, but it doesn't have to be complex. At its heart, onboarding is extremely simple. It addresses what you promised to do during the sale, what will happen as soon as they sign, what will happen over the first six months, and how you will improve on the success of your client's business over the lifetime of your relationship.

How you do this could be similar to the way other firms do it, but your personality and culture will cause it to stand out. Your onboarding could explain the half-day strategy session you hold to kick off the relationship or the communication methods you and the team use (i.e., WhatsApp, Slack, or something else) for quick questions. Create a document, guide, or website page explaining this in detail, and use visuals to illustrate what happens when. You could even colour code sections of it to show what they will do and what you will do. Make it easy to access and easy to find. Create automated emails to send them this content at the right time.

It's really helpful to point out what will happen first, even in the first few days or weeks of the relationship. Your onboarding content could include a financial details questionnaire, a welcome call with their client manager, and a connection with your client community.

The first month is usually the most critical time period of the new relationship because your client is equally the most excited and most concerned they will ever be. The slightest positive thing may thrill them, and the slightest negative thing may really discourage them. Make sure they know a few things might go wrong and that's okay; it's not so much about what happens as how you respond to it. An invoice didn't get automatically generated? The welcome pack never arrived? The welcome call never happened? Whatever it was, communicate with them at every point. Thank them for pointing it out, apologise, explain what went wrong on your end, and show how you are fixing it for the future.

Your onboarding process then continues on to explain, at a minimum, what will happen in the first six months of the client relationship. It takes time to get all the new client's information, set them up on a new system, integrate relevant apps, and begin to get to know them as a person. They will be slightly overwhelmed in the early days, so you don't want to give them too much too fast.

When I check in at a hotel, I'm often tired from traveling and simply want to get to my room (the most important thing to me). If the person checking me in goes into detail about breakfast and dinner, where these are in relation to my room, the hotel's spa services, and the extras I can add on, I'm going to nod and say thank you, but I'll take in hardly any of it. The same concept applies to onboarding: tell them as much as they need to know in the first month. Then, in the second month, tell them what they need to know then. And in the third, and so on.

This could include setting up the new accounting system, training their finance team on how to use it and their role in it, integrating new apps, and educating the leaders on what their numbers mean. Telling them about the half-day setup workshop for their new accounting system could be exactly what they need. On the other hand, going into detail about all the client training videos, monthly meets, your webinars, client events, and check-in calls could be too much. Give them what they need only when they need it.

Beyond the six- to twelve-month time period, you're moving away from onboarding and into a client experience process. At every step of the onboarding process, you're including the content you create in blog posts, website pages, videos, courses, guides, and resources. Start by creating one piece of content which will be the most helpful for almost all new clients, and add a new one with every new client you sign up. Before you know it, you'll have a whole library of content answering most of the questions any new client would have. This circles back to prequalifying content, educating them and ideally getting them to sign up faster.

Create a visual graphic summarising your onboarding process

Before you pull everything together, it helps to have a graphic designed which clearly represents what you will do and when. This visual can be shared once someone signs the proposal, but it can also come in handy before the prospect has made their decision. Your team can use this visual in the sales process, both during a proposal call and immediately after the proposal is signed. When you begin delivering on it, your new client feels justified and confident in their choice of you as their accountant, and they're encouraged to stay with you. Use this graphic in some of your onboarding marketing, which we'll look at next.

Pull it all together: the elements of your onboarding process

Your final step in creating all this onboarding content is to combine it into a process. Create website pages, questionnaires, emails, and designed elements which show this visually to your new client. These include:

- **Who we are/About us website page:** Reminder of the values you and they will live up to.
- **Our process page:** Summary of what happens first and what happens next. This could be used while you are talking to prospects, as well as throughout the entire client relationship.
- **Onboarding page:** This page is specific only to your onboarding process. Include a visual graphic of the

full onboarding process and a video. Tell them what they need to do first.

- **Questionnaire(s):** Put these on individual pages or have a summary page linking to all the questionnaires they'll need.
- **Email reminders:** Set up emails to remind your very busy new client of the website pages, questionnaires, videos, and training sessions you've created for them. Some CRM systems allow you to set it up so the email reminder will not go out until the client has completed the previous step so they're only getting the right information at the right time.
- **Welcome pack:** This is a tangible product or gift you send out. It could include swag, food, fun and helpful tech, a T-shirt or other clothing, a card, a book— anything you know they will find useful.
- **Video, video, video:** At every stage in this process, include a video. A welcome video from the firm owner(s) or the client's new manager. A video from the whole team explaining what you stand for and why. How-to videos on the questionnaires or a summary of your process. These don't have to be longer than a few minutes, and in the early days, shorter might be better. Most people prefer video, and it helps them get to know you quickly.

One firm owner, Andy, records a personal video for every single new client the firm takes on. He told us he recorded a lot of custom videos, keeping in touch or sharing useful information. He didn't want to make one generic video for everyone because the individual video showed his firm were invested in helping their business, bringing them value before the person even became a client, before they even received a proposal.

Before the initial meeting, Andy would record a personal video sharing knowledge he believed would be helpful. He would ask them to watch it before the meeting and sent reminders leading up to the conversation. The type of people Andy and his team love to work with always watch the video and comment on it in their discovery call. Over time he discovered if a prospect didn't take the time to watch the video, that was an indicator they wouldn't be the right fit.

Once the prospect became a client, Andy would record a personal welcome video. It only took a few minutes, he enjoyed providing the personal touch, and it had a big impact on each new client who invariably loved the personal attention and care. I asked him whether he'd eventually have the team do the welcome videos, and he replied, "I might do that, but for now, I really enjoy doing the welcome videos. It's a personal touch from me as the owner, and they really appreciate it. It only takes a few minutes, and it has a big impact."

Wherever you're able to begin, start there. It might be an app page for a particular industry. Perhaps an events page for online and offline events, making it easy for them to sign up. You could create a resources page relating to their business or industry, film training videos, or create a client-only page or log-in area. Rather than trying to create everything all at once, start small and start safe. Create one piece of content which will be the most useful for new clients and help train them to become the very best kind of client. Then add another with every new client you sign up. Use your creativity and apply it specifically to your clients and their needs. You can always add more.

Stage 4: Content for Existing Clients (the client experience)

The average time a business owner stays with one accountant can be as long as fifteen to seventeen years. Make sure they know it's your intention to be their accountant for life (presuming this is the case) and why. Show your commitment. If onboarding is about delivering on the promises you made in the sale, then it's easier for them to believe this will extend into the life of the relationship. It's not about onboarding someone and leaving things to tick over and hope they go well. That approach could backfire in the same way as having no onboarding process at all (in which you make the sale, hand the client over to one of the account managers, then go back to selling).

As onboarding moves into client experience, create content to show how your firm delivers on your brand values over the lifetime of the client relationship. This presumes you have brand values, clearly identified and shared from your initial marketing through to your onboarding and client experience. Take those values and explain how you use them to keep the relationship. For example, if your values are fun, family, tech, and innovation, you could explain what you do in this way:

- Fun: We will have regular events for clients simply for the purpose of having a great time. We're not solely about numbers and business meetings.
- Family: We'd love to get to know who is important to you. Twice a year we have an event and we encourage you to come and bring your family members.
- Tech: We deliver an online or live event once a month to share the newest app which will help you run your business better.
- Innovation: We send our team to creative events so they can learn new ways of doing things in your industry.

Automating Follow-Up

Automation saves you time once you've created all the content we've talked about above. Pick out the things which happen the most often and the questions which come up more than others. Then set up your CRM system to deliver those responses, saving you and your team time. Preparing automated follow-up helps keep you connected to the leads even when you are busy, swamped, or have issues with clients or your services to deal with. To automate your follow-up, follow this process:

Document and answer the core questions. Choose the top questions you always get asked, and put them on an FAQs page on your website. If the answer is longer than a paragraph or so, use a blog post or a video (or both) to answer it in detail, and link this to the question on the FAQ page.

Set up emails on a schedule. Write content for the emails we talked about above and set up templates in your email system. Within the email itself, link to the content you've created on website pages, blogs, videos, guides, and other places so it's easily accessible at the right time.

Play with the process and change it. Pay attention to how the system is working (or not working) and keep changing it. If you have an email scheduled for Month 3, and most people seem to be asking for it in Month 2, schedule it to be sent earlier for future clients. If you're sending a long video for them to watch in Week 1 and no one seems to have time to watch it, send it a little later or break it into several short videos. There are no hard and fast rules; you're building what works for your firm and your clients based on how they behave.

Think back to those prospects you never heard back from. Every once in a while, one of them does get back in touch. And what do they say?

- "I'm really sorry I never got back to you. My mum was in hospital, and I had to put everything on hold."
- "When I called you, it felt like good timing, and then I lost my biggest customer, and it changed everything."
- "We had a legal issue, and it took all my mental energy to deal with it."

It doesn't actually matter what the reason is. That's their business. It's your business to be present, available, and the kind of person they can share honestly with once they are ready. You stay top of mind by writing blog posts, articles, and other forms of content, answering the questions your prospects and clients have—even questions they didn't know they had until they read it. And you keep building trust. When a prospect is thinking "Oh, I don't know, I just wanted a little support. This seems way too expensive. I'll just keep on doing my own bookkeeping," and suddenly they receive an article from you titled "The Hidden Costs of Doing Your Own Bookkeeping," they realise you've done this before. They begin to understand they could end up costing themselves far more in the long run; this article you've written explains why and motivates them to get back in touch.

You already know most of their reasons, excuses, concerns, doubts, and fears. When you write about those, you provide them with all they need to get back in touch, at their own pace.

Now, let's look at the writing process itself and the creation of blog posts.

CHAPTER 9
BLOGGING

BY NOW, you've worked out that being an accountant doesn't prevent you from also being a marketer, a creative, a writer.

There are still mental hurdles to overcome. You've written your fair share of emails and then some, but when it comes to blog posts, where do you even start? What does good writing look like? You never learned how to do this when getting your accounting qualifications. What do you even write about? It seems like every accountant has written articles on topics such as cash flow, business structures, management accounts, accounting software and apps, and profitability. Even if you did write blog posts, wouldn't they sound like everyone else's?

You might be tempted to buy content and edit it to fit your firm or publish as is. It could seem faster and more efficient. There are companies who provide this service, and you wonder if it's cheaper to do that than to pay a content writer to write custom blog posts or pay a creative agency for unique content on a monthly basis.

Whether you write blog posts yourself or outsource it, be involved so they reflect you

Blogging is an area I've seen many accountants slowly come to recognise the value of. When I started PF in 2012, it was a massive hurdle to get accountants to write blog posts at all, and most firms wanted PF to write all the content for them. We were (and still are) happy to write custom content based on a firm's style, brand, and experience, but whatever content we create comes from an integrated, collaborative approach. We hold foundational sessions to discuss your audience, style, and tone. We get to know the owners and directors and team. We ask for a list of questions your clients and prospects ask and bullet points or notes of the kinds of things you say often.

Now, when we suggest our Accelerator members write a blog post every week for twelve weeks, most are excited about it—or at least willing to try. Usually, they're experiencing wins and victories before they're even halfway through the sessions. They discover to their surprise they have more blog topics than they ever imagined, and some discover they really enjoy writing. They discover the accountant who is personally involved in their own writing gets the best results. Over the years, we've seen that prove to be true, over and over.

Whether you do all the writing yourself, involve members of your team, or outsource it, you still need to be part of the process. Like all your marketing, your blogging is ultimately a reflection of you, including what you and your team know and the way you explain it when someone meets with you or rings you up with a question. More and more accountants are writing their own blog posts, and they see the impact on their sales calls, answers to their clients' questions, and their time. When they get their whole team involved, the positive impact becomes exponential.

Write blog posts to help people, not simply to sell

One of our clients, the owner of an accounting firm with a small team, discovered the power of involving her team as she made her way through the twelve-week Accelerator coaching group not only once but three times. The first time, the owner participated on her own and followed our suggestion of starting a list of all the questions her clients and prospects were asking. She wrote a few blog posts answering those questions. The second time through, she included all of her team members and began encouraging them to add questions to the list when clients and prospects asked them. She and the team wrote more blog posts. By the third time she went through the Accelerator, writing blogs had become their standard way of answering questions, and she was seeing specific results. Prospects often mentioned specific blog posts in the discovery call and how the helpfulness of a particular blog post was what spurred them on to make the connection with the firm.

When you create consistent content in blog posts, the person reading it realises you've dealt with this before. They get their question answered faster, saving you and your team time. They get in touch faster because they're more motivated, hurrying along the buyer process. Or they qualify themselves out if they're not a fit, saving you the pain, hassle, and stress of taking on a client who is not the kind you want to serve. Like all the content we've talked about in previous chapters, blogging is powerful because it saves you time. It saves your team time. It builds trust. Your prospects make their buying decision faster. And it helps with SEO; your website is made more "findable" by Google as you create consistent, fresh content unique to you. The more you create in the form of blog posts using the words your audience cares about or wonders about (particularly those one thousand words or longer), the more you prove to Google your website is the best search result for this person's question.

Knowing this, it's tempting to write blogs with the sole intention of "getting more business". Although ultimately blogging will be part of your marketing which delivers leads, you do need to be careful with your intent and your mindset when you are writing blog posts. If you approach blogging (or any marketing action) thinking "Will doing this one thing get me business?" your purpose will subconsciously come through in what you create. Instead of a blog post which is helpful, supportive, focused entirely on your reader, it'll read like a sales pitch. Or a description of services. Or a dry table of numbers and percentages. Your writing (like any part of your marketing) needs to be done in a way which gives them value even if they decide not to do business with you yet. (Or at all.)

Everything you create, every blog post you write, is for them. When you approach it in this way, the right person will eventually do business with you. Until then, simply help them and keep helping until they are ready to move forward. Keep this "helping" mentality in mind when writing blog posts. What can you share which will save them time, teach them something new, and guide them along the path they need to be on? What kind of enormous value can you give them which will either answer their question quickly or educate them so your meeting is faster and more enjoyable?

Start with your list of client questions

As you know from chapter 2, the best content comes from the questions your clients ask, an idea made famous by Marcus Sheridan's book *They Ask, You Answer*. The answer is in the title: whatever your clients and prospects ask, create content to answer it. Easy. Done and dusted. (Except, of course, he's written a whole book on it, so go read that once you're done with this one.) Once you've got your list of questions and you've prioritised the ones which help your buyer decide faster, you're all set. You have a blog post topic, and you're ready to write. How do you get started?

Your preparation is similar to every other piece of content we've talked about. Who is it for, what problem do they have (and how does this feel), why are you writing it, and what do you want them to do?

. . .

Blog audience: who are you writing to?

Go back to your audience. Who exactly are you writing to? If your first answer is "prospects," what kind of prospects? What kind of business do they have? What kind of person are they? If you have one specific person or client in mind, that's even better. One of the PF team said, "You could even put a picture of them on your screen to remind you who this is for if that's not too creepy." You could even start with "Hi, Martin" (or whatever the specific person's name is) and write it as if you were creating this blog solely for Martin. In the editing process, cut out what is specific to that one client and hey presto, you've got a blog post applicable for anyone who feels the way Martin did. And remember to only write content for clients you want *more* of.

Once you have an idea who you're writing to, remind yourself why you're writing it at all.

Blog purpose: why are you writing it?

Asking yourself why you are sharing this information in a blog post helps you structure your writing in a way they understand and connect with. You could be writing this post to help in a number of ways:

- To educate them about how a principle or methodology works
- To deliver a how-to with step-by-step instructions
- To answer a specific question many clients and prospects are asking
- To build trust by telling a story or sharing a case study

Whatever your reason for writing this post, deliver enormous value so they either get their question answered and are grateful to you or realise you know what you're talking about, which spurs them on to get in touch. Your primary goal is still to be helpful, and you are also paving the way for more educated, supported clients.

Before you dash off your blog post and publish it, make sure you know exactly what you want them to do after reading this post.

Call to action: What do you want them to do after reading it?

You don't need a direct, obvious call to action at the end of every blog post. You're welcome to have one, but blogging is not a tactic. It's about giving enormous value and setting up the buyer journey so they move through it in the most efficient way.

It's best not to have every blog post end with the exact same call to action. After they've read a few of your posts, the call to action will be invisible because it's so familiar. Many blog posts end with something so vague or repetitive it doesn't mean anything anymore (i.e., "If you have any questions, call us today"). You're giving them permission to do something anyone would do naturally. It's like saying, "Welcome to our website." It's unnecessary and a waste of good website real estate.

Get to the point fast. If they have questions and they like and trust you or are curious, of course they'll ask. They're not waiting for you to say it's okay to do that. And the more specific you are with your buyer journey, the more specific you can be about what they need to do next.

The action might not be something specifically sales-related, like filling in a form or requesting a discovery call; it might simply be sending them to another post or page on your site. Lead them through the journey the way you want them to go. It's always their choice if they follow it. The one thing you want them to do can go anywhere in the post. If you want them to download a guide or register for an event, you don't have to put it at the end. You can include it at the right time in the middle of the blog or wherever it's relevant.

And give them *one* thing you want them to do, not multiple actions. A CTA that reads like this is overkill:

If you have any questions on this blog or on [type of content covered in this blog], call us today on [phone number] or email us at [email address] to discuss your business needs or concerns or request a free consultation [here].

You've given them so many options it takes too much brain energy to figure out which one is best. You've also lacked authority in the client relationship before it even starts by letting them decide how they get in touch. Although the client is the hero, you're still the guide. This is your firm, your brand, your website, your blog post. Based on the journey you already know the client will follow, you decide the action they need to take. That action will help you serve them better. It's not simply about making your life easier, although that's a good thing and helps you be more profitable and efficient. It's about directing them along a path to get them to the answers they need as quickly as possible. After all, you've talked to hundreds or thousands of people like this. You know how the conversation goes, right down to what they are going to ask and in what order. You know what you need to know about them. Craft the call to action so they follow the best path for you and for them.

Once you're clear in your mind about who you're writing to, why you're writing it, and what you want them to do . . . how do you actually do the writing?

How do I write?

The advice from every writer, even going hundreds of years back, is this:

Start writing.

Don't wait for the muse, the motivation, the feeling of creativity. Don't feel like you have to block out hours of your day or else it's not worth starting. Pick a question you've been asked by multiple clients or prospects or pick one of the top questions from your "They ask, you answer" list, put your hands to the keyboard or the pen to paper, and start writing. It might feel like (or actually be) rubbish at first, full of randomness and babble as you struggle to see the words come together. That's okay. This is your shitty first draft. Despite that, remember the first draft is perfect because its only job is to exist. Here's what I do when I don't feel like writing:

Do it anyway. Trying to craft the perfect writing environment or waiting until I feel like writing will only delay things further. I put my fingers above the keyboard, or open the file, or write with a pen on paper, or anything else which will get me going. The goal is not to have the best writing ever of your entire life every time you sit down to write. It's to keep the writing momentum going.

Set a timer. If it's 8:15 a.m. and I know by 9 a.m. the team will be checking into Slack with their priorities for the day, I'll set a timer on my watch or phone and commit to not multitasking, or checking notifications, or doing anything but writing for that time. You might be worried about what happens when the timer goes off and you need to move on to something else. What if you're on a roll and all your brilliant ideas are lost by the next day when you start again? Ann Handley, in her book *Everybody Writes*, taught me a mind-blowing new concept when using a timer for writing. She suggested it's better to stop immediately when the timer goes off, even if you're mid-sentence. The next day, when you start again, you're not having to remind yourself of what the introduction was, what you were writing, and why; you simply pick up mid-sentence and carry on. I tried it and was shocked to discover it works brilliantly well.

Write in small portions. Doing something in one long block of time can be much harder than doing it every single day, week, or month. I've learned I do far better with a little bit every day rather than trying to have a "writing day." Writing is a creative exercise, and it needs flexibility as well as rest, and fresh perspectives, and breaks. For most of us, it's not the sort of thing you can do for eight hours at a stretch without a pause. Even fifteen minutes on the timer will help you make some progress. I went through a period of time working on this book where all I could manage was fifteen minutes a day of writing. Eventually I got it back up to at least an hour, and often longer, but the smallest increment will keep the momentum going.

Drink coffee. Drink water. Get fresh air. When you're stuck or struggling to actually start, help your brain out. Drink coffee, or tea, or hot water with lemon, or get a snack. Do some small thing which will motivate you. Tip: don't spend so long on this that you are merely delaying writing. Get the thing, enjoy it, and start writing. Take a short walk and time it. Use the time in the fresh air to think about what it is you're writing. So often a short fifteen-minute walk has cleared my head and sorted out the confusion I felt when sitting at the screen. I came back ready to write again.

Join a community or accountability group. No matter what you do today, the struggle will appear again tomorrow and all the tomorrows after that. All our PF clients are part of the PF Lab, a community for accountants who create their own content, ask questions, and experiment in marketing. Like you, they want to be better writers and better marketers. Join a community of people who feel like you feel and have the struggles you have. They'll also celebrate with you in your wins!

Make sure you have someone (a person or a group) who will push back sometimes. If you say "I don't feel like writing a blog post today" and the response is "That's cool, mate, neither do I, busy times," that helps you feel nice for a day or two. But eventually it means you'll make excuses or not bother and never get your writing done. Choose a community with a good balance of understanding, drive, and willingness to help you dig into what's preventing you from writing today.

Expect imperfection. Most accountants I talk to are perfectionists. You want to make sure it's right and good with as few mistakes as possible. It's a natural quality for the type of work you do, with numbers which follow rules and patterns. But writing and marketing don't work that way. There are very few, if any, rules to marketing, and it changes all the time. Keep the perfection dream for accounts and taxes, but let go of it when it comes to marketing. Writing a blog post with the wrong title, or a broken link, or a missing paragraph is not the end of the world. When you or someone else notices it, fix it. Otherwise, do the best you can and move on. Not perfect but done.

And finally, for the days when it's not happening no matter what you try . . .

Give yourself grace. Sometimes it's time for a rest. You know yourself the difference between avoidance and exhaustion. One of our PF pillars is rest because, eventually, you will burn out if you never stop. So if you need to, stop. Once you're refreshed, you can start again.

Okay. You've thought about your audience, you know why you're writing, you've started writing, and you have a community to support you. But what if your writing is simply not good? What if this is not your skill, you don't like it, and you feel like you'll never be good at it?

What if I'm not a good writer?

The great news is being a "good writer" may not mean what you think it means. When you think of what you'd consider to be good writing, the more you'll discover you're thinking of other writers, whether it's books or blog posts or other writing you've read and appreciated. You read them and thought, "Oh, they said that so well." All this means is you're thinking of someone *else's* writing.

As with art or creativity, there's no rule about whether writing is good or bad. A painting, photograph, logo design, film, or book you like is not best described as "good." It's best described as something which resonated with you. You appreciated it; it spoke to you. Maybe you didn't like it or even were a little horrified by it, but it helped you to think in a different way. It stirred you or moved you. It gave you things to ponder or caused you to take some kind of action. When someone asks me if I thought a film was good, I try never to say yes or no. I say, "Well, I really loved this about it, and that intrigued me." Or I might say, "It didn't really move me because of this aspect. I probably wouldn't watch it again." The same approach applies to your consideration of yourself as a writer. I'm not going to tell you if you are a good writer or not. Instead, I'll ask: Where is your idea of good writing coming from? Who are you comparing yourself to? Who do you consider to be a good writer? How much writing have you done and for how long? What is hard or difficult about writing for you?

The beautiful news is this: you are a good writer as long as you write so it sounds like you.

When you write about things you care about, what matters or is interesting to you, you're a good writer. When you share things your clients and prospects really need to know, when your intention is to help the reader and you stay true to that intention, it will be a good blog post. Best of all, if your writing is more personal or only for you, then it doesn't matter if it seems like nobody wants to hear it. Write anyway. Write for yourself.

Every time I've dashed off an email or a blog post really from the heart, it gets more replies, more comments, and more engagement than anything else I've sent. Other times I'll write something, thinking, "This is so amazing, so well said, and it's going to get a lot of people to sign up," and then . . . crickets. The intentionality you have behind your writing always comes across, and that's what your reader is looking for.

To maintain this intentionality and authenticity, write in the same way you speak. Everyone has a different style. Don't try to sound like others, "be professional," or impress anyone. Use words you would use in actual conversation. If you're not sure, read what you've just written out loud. Does it sound like you? Does it sound like the sort of thing you would say? If not, say it, and then write that out. Most accountants are worried their writing won't be "professional enough", when, really, most of your clients don't want you to sound like their imagined idea of a stereotypical accountant. They want you to sound like the person they'll speak to when they book a meeting. Even if another team member at your firm has written the words, the brand voice will be the same, prospects and clients will feel the consistency, and this will build trust.

As an accountant and a business owner, writing is a skill you must learn. At the very least, make an effort to learn it. Be willing, be curious, and give it a try. You will never become a better writer by telling yourself "I'm not a good writer" in the same way you'll never lean into your creativity by believing "I'm not creative."

Even if you agree in principle that writing is a good skill and a helpful one to learn, it may be really difficult for you. Perhaps you're dyslexic or the language you're writing in is not your first language. This may indicate your style of writing doesn't start with hands on the keyboard or putting pen to paper. Are you a talker or a writer? This determination will make a big difference in how you approach writing. Think about when a client asks a question which has some complexity to it and ask yourself these questions:

- Would you rather explain aloud what you think (i.e., video, phone call, audio message)? Or would it be easier to type out what they need to know in an email or a series of messages?
- Do you tend to know what you want to say already, or do you think through your fingers? (That latter one is me: I often don't fully know what I want to say until I start typing, and then it starts coming out.)
- Look at the marketing you've done in the past. Do you have more blogs, long emails, direct messages, and

social posts? Or do you have more phone calls, meetings, and audio messages?

- Do you read physical books or listen to audiobooks or podcasts?

This is not a foolproof test; you may simply be listening to audiobooks because it's faster or calling a client because that's what you've always done in the past and what they expect. But what's your preference? Do you enjoy writing even if you feel you aren't good at it? Do you think you could enjoy it if you released yourself from the pressure to be the kind of writer other people are? Have you tried doing it consistently?

If you are a talker or a listener more than a writer or a reader, there are ways to get writing done in a more efficient way. You could record a video or audio and have it transcribed, then edit the content to make a blog post. You could give the audio or transcription to the PF team and have a content writer turn it into a blog post (many of our clients do that on a monthly basis). You could be interviewed by a content writer and do a brain dump of everything you want to say and have them turn it into the writing you need. Because it's yours, it will still be "good writing".

Good writing sounds like you and gets across what you are trying to say. It sounds like what you would say if someone was talking with you or if they were already familiar with who you are. You want the words and tone to match. The best marketing reveals the most real version of you and your firm. Any mismatch, anything fake, any professional-speak or jargon which isn't actually what you and the team would say are going to jar the ear of the reader and cause them to wonder if you're for real. Their doubts will not be overcome. Make your marketing and your blog writing as close to the "live" experience as possible.

. . .

Do you need to block out a full day for writing?

One accountant asked me, "You mentioned you don't do meetings on Mondays. I've been thinking I need to block out a day for creative things so I can focus better. Do you stick to just one day a week, and would you recommend it?" It's a great question, and as with all marketing questions, the answer is . . .

It depends.

Planning your writing time depends on the kind of person you are. I remember working with an accountant and his team on a detailed campaign plan for a live event. We provided them with an organised, prioritised list in detail of everything they needed to create to get the result they wanted, which was triple the number of registered attendees. The actions weren't just things like "write blog posts"; we listed out every blog post with a title and key points. We identified which blog was to be written and in what order, how long each post needed to be, and whether a video needed to be included.

He said, "Okay, great. What I do is just block out a day or two a month, and I'll just burn through these one by one on that day." I asked him if he'd done that before and if it worked for him, and one of his team piped in to say, "Oh yes, that's the only way it works for him. If you try to get it in pieces, you'll never get anything. But if he blocks out time and focuses on it, he'll churn out sixteen videos, two blog posts, and a structure for a Facebook Live."

I found that fascinating because that doesn't work for me *at all*. I've tried it. I remember trying it again after I talked to that client, wondering if I was missing a trick, or was being super unmotivated or was just not disciplined enough. But on the day I'd blocked out, I started later, stared at the screen a lot, created one blog post and a video, felt exhausted, and took a break to work on other types of work. Before I knew it, it was the end of the day, and I had achieved about the same amount as if I had used an hour or two between other work.

For me, having a specific list of content I plan to create and taking ten minutes or a half hour between meetings is one of my most productive methods. I'm more motivated and inspired when I've been talking to a team member, or a client, or an accountant. After we've chatted about what's difficult or what's exciting, come up with new ideas, answered questions, or dug deep into why it's not working, I am *much* more motivated after a call like that to create content. I'm more likely to quickly record a video and be happy with it than to put it on the list and record a week later when I'm tired or didn't sleep well or it's dark in my office or the enthusiasm has faded.

You need to know yourself and be okay with who you are, and this includes when and how you write.

Factor in time for editing, SEO, and all the extras

Writing content for the blog post is a big step. You planned it, drafted it, tidied it up, and it's ready to go! . . . Oh wait. You need some headings and subheadings so it's easier to read. Okay, it's ready now! . . . Actually, hold on a second. It needs to go on your website, and it needs an image to go with it. You'll need to choose tags, categories, and keywords for SEO. Okay, now it's ready to go! . . . Oh wait. Now you need to share it on the socials and in your email newsletter and, and, and . . .

If you plan to do the editing and publishing yourself, you'll need to factor that in to your marketing time too. It takes me only an hour or so to write a blog post once I've prepared the topic and the key points, and that's after blogging weekly for over ten years. But if I were to do all the other bits and pieces, I'd need to factor in at least another hour or two. If the blog was really long or required extra research or review, it could take half a day or longer.

To make sure your content not only gets created but also sees the light of day as a completed and ready-to-read post, have someone who is ready and trained on all the extra tasks relating to your blog post. This includes specific tasks such as the following:

- Edits and tidying: Making sure the whole blog post makes sense, is structured properly, and is readable.
- Headings and subheadings: Reading these like a story in their own right. If you read only the headers on their own, they need to make sense in order.
- Image: Ensuring a good-quality, on-brand image is used with the post. Checking to see if it needs to be edited or resized, confirming you have the rights to use it, and confirming it's on-brand by fitting with your style and colours.
- Drafting: Adding the content to the back end of the website, clicking the tags and categories, adding the featured image, previewing it, and checking to make sure everything works.
- SEO: Reviewing keywords, key phrases, meta data, alt tags, and URL.
- Video: Recording a video to go with this post and making sure this video is in a format allowing it to be embedded into the post.
- Publishing and sharing: Actually publishing the post and sharing it wherever you want it to go (i.e., Facebook, Twitter, Instagram, LinkedIn, email, website page, or all of the above).

I've got an entire creative agency on hand to do these things, but for years, I did it all myself. It took a lot longer then, and now I really, really appreciate all the work that goes into it. I know how to value it because I know it literally saves me two to four hours of time, sometimes even two whole days, and I know what I could be doing with those hours while the team is doing the detail work.

Ultimately, use your writing time for what only you and your team know best. Only you know what you're talking to clients about—their stories, their troubles, their questions and concerns. Only you have the answers, the input, and the success stories to share. Creating a process to get this out of your head and out to the wider world will be the very best use of everyone's time— and it will deliver better results too.

How often do you need to blog?

The more blog posts you create, the more findable you are on the search engines and the more content you have to share with clients and prospects. If you book a meeting with them, the prospect can do more research before they speak to you. So blogging is something you want to do more often rather than less.

Work towards the goal of publishing a new blog post every week. Four blog posts a month means forty-eight blog posts in a year, which is a good solid showing in terms of fresh content for your website. You'll hardly run out of questions—remember, running a thirty-minute brainstorming session with your team will probably give you close to fifty questions, and that's only one session!

When you have a team, get them involved in blogging too. Every single team member doesn't have to be a full-time blog post writer (and, indeed, that's rather distracting from the job you've hired them to do). They can still share questions clients have asked or copy and paste wording they've sent to clients to answer those questions. Some of the team will be interested or willing to write blog posts, and, like some of you, they may be surprised to discover they enjoy writing. If you have twenty-four team members and even a quarter of them commit to writing blog posts twice a year, that's one new blog post going out every month before you write anything yourself.

The more team members you hire, the fewer blog posts they'll need to write, although certain team members who enjoy it can write more if they want to. Invest in their training and learning so they understand why they are blogging and how it helps them in their job. Put them on the Accelerator. The more involved your team are, the more your marketing will reflect the actual experience people have when they work with you and your team. And your team members will see how writing a blog post prevents them having to answer the same question over and over and over. They'll see how these answered questions help attract the very best kind of client—the ones who value their advice, listen to what they say, reply to messages, show up for meetings, and provide what's requested. They'll be reminded that when they work with clients they love, they enjoy their job more.

If writing a new blog post once a week feels overwhelming or discouraging, start with once a month. Once you successfully achieve that goal and you are consistently blogging at least once a month, increase the goal to twice per month and so on. Much of the research I looked into when writing this book suggested you write two to four times per week or more often if you could. That may feel impossible. You might be thinking, "How in the world am I meant to do any accounting work?" But the goal is to share as much fresh content as you need to answer the questions people have before they ask them (or the moment they ask them), and the more you write, the more you'll discover needs to be written.

I've been blogging at least weekly for over fifteen years, and we still get questions which aren't exactly answered in a blog post. When that happens, the new question goes on the list. Sometimes the question was answered many years ago, and it's time to rewrite it. As many of our Accelerator members have said, once you write a blog post or record a video, when a client asks that same question and it only takes you a few seconds to answer it by sending them a link, that's a really, really good feeling. We love saving time—and so do your clients!

"Okay," you're thinking. "Fine. I'll blog once a week. Or even twice a week. Surely I could churn out some three- or five hundred-word blog posts, job done . . . Oh wait. How long does my blog post need to be? What's the ideal blog post length?" My answer to that question is this:

A blog post's ideal length is as long as it needs to be to fully answer the question and no longer.

This could be three hundred, three thousand, or ten thousand words. It could be three words. The point is not to get so caught up with SEO or keywords or what Google is looking for that you forget what you're actually saying. Or what your client is actually wondering. There was a time when keywords were all the rage, and there was a lot of what's called keyword stuffing, which is when people write blog posts with their keyword thrown in as often as possible to get found by Google. Keyword stuffing sounds something like this:

As award-winning accountants and bookkeepers in This City, This Region, This Country, we work with small- to medium-sized businesses in need of accounting, bookkeeping, payroll, management accounts, cash flow planning, profit and growth planning, tax planning, and business advisory. If you are wondering about the cash flow and profits of your small to medium-sized business in This City, you can explore your options by requesting a cash flow forecast or a growth and profit plan from one of our award-winning accountants or bookkeepers. This cash flow forecast will assist you in enhancing your cash flow in This City, This Region, as well as blah, blah, blah, blah . . .

Nobody wants to read that. It isn't really saying anything. Stuffing your website or blog posts with keywords simply tells the person visiting your website you care more about Google and about getting leads than you do about helping them with their very real, very energy-draining problem. Instead, imagine you're writing a blog post about cash flow based on a question a client asked you. Perhaps they mentioned they weren't getting paid on time and cash was low even though sales were improving. You don't need to stuff the blog post with the words "cash flow," "growth," "profits," and "forecasts." You can simply talk about the problem they have. Here's an example:

When you're not getting paid by your customers on time and cash is always low for your [type of] business, it's tempting to think the only way to solve this is by sending letters to your customers requesting payment. That is a short-term solution when you're already in that predicament, and we'll share a few tips for how to send those letters. But cash always being low is a warning light to indicate there are systems you need to change before the customer even starts doing business with you, and we're going to give you three things you can do to help you get paid faster . . .

That sounds more human. More real. I've written it based on no particular firm, so it's still rather generic. If you were to write it, you'd make sure the content sounded like your firm, your brand, and your tone of voice. But it still includes the words "cash," "customers," and "get paid"—words they may actually be searching for. Those are the true keywords.

"Organic SEO" refers to the way Google returns your website in the search results when someone is searching for a particular word or phrase and your site includes content related to that. You haven't paid for Google ads or promoted your content in any way, but it's there organically because every week or month you're creating another blog post, answering the questions your clients ask. Over time as you create more and more, Google begins to recognise your site often has the answer people are looking for and returns your site as one of the search options. However, unlike in the early days when people could simply write lots of words—stuffing the content with keywords so their site would be found by Google—now the algorithm has gotten much, much smarter. The content needs to be relevant. To make sense. When you approach blogging with the mindset we've talked about, you're not doing keyword stuffing; you're sharing helpful information which happens to have the related words in it. This is another reason why it's best to use the exact words and phrases *your* clients are searching for because it helps your content to be found.

Organic search or SEO builds up over a period of months and

years as you continually create content relating to a particular audience or word or phrase. Google's priority is to help the searcher find what they need. This is why your content must also be good, helpful, and relevant. If Google returns your site to a searcher, and the searcher comes to your site, flicks through a few posts, and leaves, Google is going to take note of that and stop including your site in the search results. Or your site might appear less often, further down, or on page two of the search results. And as we all know, the best place to hide a dead body is on page two of Google.

Google does tend to reward (or bring up) blog posts longer than one thousand words as long as the content of the posts are relevant to the business you have and the audience you're writing to. The presumption is blog posts this long actually have something to say and you've put some time and effort into it. Do include keywords, but don't write primarily for SEO. Your audience is not Google or SEO. Say what you want to say in the tone of voice you would say it with the words you would use. Instead of trying to make it Google-friendly, make it friendly to your audience—your very best kind of client. Strive to have a blog post within the eight- to thirteen-hundred word range, but don't obsess over the word count. If you can fully answer the question in three hundred words, you're done. If you've written two thousand and you haven't fully answered it yet, keep writing.

Make sure your blog post is readable

Once your blog post is drafted up, you'll need to edit and structure it for maximum readability. Many people will go to your site and read through your content, but not everyone reads every single word of your one thousand- or three thousand-word post. They read the title, they skim a few of the headers, they get a sense of the content, and they see the call to action. Ideally, they actually take some action! Your audience may be the kind of person who does read every single word, but you don't want to rely on that. Make it really easy for them to get the gist of the story or the answer, and they can go into detail later if they choose.

It's tempting to create headers and subheaders in your blog post which are vague statements like "Three things to consider" or "Your cash flow." But those aren't helping your reader understand what's being said. Your blog headers need to tell a story. To write clearer blog post headers, read them on their own in order. Then imagine the person reading your post *only* read those headers. What story would those tell? Would the reader get the whole picture? Let's use our example above. Say you've written a thousand words about cash flow, but the blog headers read like this:

- Importance of cash flow
- Cash vs. profit
- Your cash flow forecast
- Improving your cash flow management
- Conclusion

When you read them in order, they're simply random words and phrases. Instead, give the answer away in the headers. We don't actually want click-bait titles, and we don't want click-bait headers either. You're not going to be so clever with your title they are desperately crying, "Tell me more! How important *is* my cash flow?" They'll see it as a tactic and will simply leave your site to go find another one that makes more sense faster. Don't make your reader work for the answer; give away the answer as fast as possible, and they can read in more detail if they choose.

Using our example, headers which flow like a story could read like this:

- Don't make business decisions based on your bank balance

- Your cash tells a story, but profit tells a more accurate one
- Fix your immediate cash flow problem by chasing outstanding debts
- Help future cash flow problems by changing your systems and setting boundaries
- Set boundaries: If they're ready to start, they're ready to pay
- Create milestones: Set up automatic payments based on agreed times and deadlines
- Down tools: If they aren't paying, stop working until payment is made
- Put on your own cash flow mask before assisting others

These headers read much more like a story. Even if you didn't read the whole blog post, you'd get a sense of what it's saying. The reader might even get a few ideas without having read the whole post yet. They might think to themselves, "Oh, I remember that customer who kept promising to pay, and I kept working, and the unpaid invoices kept stacking up. That's a good reminder next time to stop working earlier and only pick back up once the invoice is paid." And then they're intrigued to find out exactly how to do that. What to do if the customer complains, or if the house is half painted, or the mortgage is nearly approved. Then they get in touch to talk with you about their unique situation. This is why you give away information and charge for implementation. Give away what they could find anywhere else if they searched even a little; start charging when they need your help applying this information to their particular business.

For your headers to tell a story, they all need to follow the same "tense." For example, "making, telling, fixing, helping" all flow well together. Or "make, tell, fix, help."

Within a blog post, keep sentences short. When I started blogging, I wasn't thinking about my reader. I wrote in long paragraphs with only a few breaks, no headers or subheaders, no bold font, and no short sentences. Over the years, I discovered people don't always fully read blog posts; they skim. So I started keeping my sentences short. The shorter the sentence, the easier it is to read. I also kept paragraphs short so it was easy to move through the content on a phone or when the reader was distracted. Limit yourself to three sentences per paragraph. Get to the point faster. Say what you need to say and no more. That works really well for blog posts, but keep in mind there are different writing styles for different forms of content. In writing this book, I had to relearn the art of long-form content. It feels strange to go back to stories and to a theme running through six thousand words in a chapter and continuing through all thirteen chapters. But a book is not a blog post, so it's written differently.

People aren't sitting quietly in a comfortable armchair with a pipe, leisurely scanning your blog post like it's a newspaper. They're standing on the train station platform, flicking through your blog post on their phone. Or reading it at 9 p.m. once the kids are finally in bed after a long day, glancing at headlines in between shouting at one of the kids to "Get back *in* bed, I won't say it again, and no, you're not getting another drink of water."

People aren't drawn to accounting content by your being mysterious. They're already confused and find financial conversations a mystery. They're not reading more because you've given them some vague concept and hinted at an answer. They're reading more because they're intrigued by a solution to a problem they thought was insurmountable, and they want more detail. They're drawn in when they know exactly what it's about and what it will tell them. If they do read more, it's because they want the research, the extra information, the "how" of your statement. If you say "Follow-up is important for small businesses," it could mean anything to anybody. But if you say "Dentists are losing business by not sending out follow-up notifications," the dentist who is even now making that mistake may be intrigued enough to find out how this is losing them business and what they can do about it.

Give enormous value

Blogging isn't about whether you're a writer or not; it's about writing anyway. It actually doesn't matter if you are a writer, or even whether you want to be a writer or not. Blogging is your opportunity to take the knowledge you have and share it in a way which helps more people find it, read it, think about it, and be ready to talk to you in the most efficient way possible. It means every time a client asks a question, instead of typing out the answer in an email or a text, or ringing them to talk, you simply send them a link to a blog post on your website and say, "Let me know if there's anything that wasn't covered in here."

One of our Accelerator members started blogging every week after joining the group. "I'm a bit of a perfectionist," he said, "so it took me a few hours to actually write the blog post and more hours than I'd like to say to review and edit and get it ready for posting on my website. But once I got the blog post actually published, the very next week a client emailed to ask me that exact question. I clicked reply, said 'here's the answer,' and linked to the blog I had written. Within an hour, the client wrote back and said, 'That's perfect—thanks!' and I'd saved myself at least fifteen to thirty minutes of writing out an answer I'd written before."

It's such a good feeling to answer a question before they've even asked it. They can tell by reading your post you knew this question was coming and you have the answer. The longer you practice this, the faster you respond to clients. You can move through your messages quickly, copying links from your own website, pasting them into the email or message, and hitting send. Job done. No more groaning at the weight of your email inbox, trying to figure out which ones to reply to first, and working your way through them one by one, painstakingly typing out the answer over and over.

Although the written word is powerful for answering questions and sharing ideas, your reader is still missing something— your style, tone of voice, the way you communicate, your personality, and approach. All of this is hinted at in the written word but comes into its own so much more powerfully in another way.

It's time to talk about that one area you've been hoping to avoid: video.

CHAPTER 10
VIDEO

IMAGINE a prospect coming to your website, booking a call, and showing up at your offices for a meeting.

Now imagine they come into your office, and you've put up a big holding wall between you and that prospect. They knock on it, a little confused, and you shout to them from behind it, "Hi! Nice to meet you! Let's chat."

They try to peek round the corner of the wall, but you're not having it. "No, no," you say, "let's leave that there. You don't need to see me. Let's just talk."

Would you blame them for (after trying a few times) getting up and walking away?

This is how many of your prospects feel when they come to your website and there's not a single video of you, or your team, or anything which will help them understand what to expect.

Video helps buyers decide faster

In this age and culture, with the expectations we have about being able to see things and meet people and visit places before we ever get to them, there is no reason not to have video be a significant part of your marketing. Remember, your buyer makes

70 percent of their buying decision before they ever get in touch. If they aren't able to see you, hear your voice, or have any sense of who you are, they may lose interest. They may not bother enquiring at all.

On the flip side, when you do share videos and let them connect with you and your team before they even meet you, the prospect meeting goes far differently. They book the meeting, show up, and when they see you, say, "I feel like we've already met!" or "Oh wait—I forgot we've never met in person yet!"

You'd feel the same way if you met a celebrity in real life. You know their face, their mannerisms, their expressions, their tone. They have no idea who you are, but you feel like they're a friend from how you've connected with them on the screen. Video makes you like a little mini-celebrity in the one area you need to be. And when used well, it definitely makes the sales process easier and faster.

You can use photographs and write great content to help your potential buyer feel comfortable, but video provides the most context, the closest thing to an in-person meet without actually having one yet. Remember the rule about how communication comes across: a large percentage of what you say is communicated via body language (55 percent) and tone of voice (38 percent), which leaves the smallest percentage for the words themselves. Video captures much of the missing 93 percent—your expression, the way you say things, your personality. The "feel" of who you are.

Video helps your buyer decide faster. Always. If you're not recording videos answering your clients' questions, explaining ideas and concepts, and sharing who you are and who your team is, then it is taking way longer to attract amazing prospects. You may be missing out on them altogether.

Most accountants I know would rather face quite a lot of things over recording a video. It feels scary. You don't know what to say. You feel so many other people do it better. You aren't sure how to start. You don't like how you look or sound on video. You don't have the equipment, the lighting, the audio, the editing capabilities. Even if you have these, video feels like it will take so long. You might consider it, or promise yourself you'll start doing more video, but you always return to what feels comfortable. When we avoid things, we're usually confused, unprepared, missing information, or not yet convinced it's worthwhile.

One accountant, Alasdair, noticed an issue common to clients who came to his firm from another accountant. Many of these new clients said their previous accountant sent them hard copies of accounts with tabs, and they didn't know what they were signing. So Alasdair recorded a video to address this, called "Why do accountants post me stuff to sign?" The video is 2:43 minutes long. He recorded it quickly in their temporary offices (the very spirit of not perfect but done). And within the space of a week, there were three new clients who got in touch to talk about working with his firm and signed a proposal because they watched this video.

You'd think that last sentence would have you rushing off to record a video, but it probably doesn't. You're still unsure. Maybe it worked for Alasdair, but would it work for you? Maybe he's recorded loads of video and is really good at it. Or you have already tried video and felt you came across terribly. Nobody contacted you, and there were no new clients rushing to do business with you.

Think again about how your buyer buys and how *you* buy. Whether you're booking a hotel room or buying a house, being able to see it before you make the effort to drive over there makes a big difference. Think about how you feel when you show up to a video meeting with someone you're considering working with. In seconds, you're getting a sense of how the person approaches business and life. Their attitude, facial expressions, the words they use, the way they respond if technology doesn't work—your mind takes it all in very quickly. You think it's a gut feel and maybe it is. But that gut feel isn't random. When you stop to investigate it, you discover it's based on how they showed up, the words they used, the look on their face, and the responses to your questions. You're gathering all this information so you can decide if you'll work well together.

This is what you can and must provide for your buyer. Help them make their decision as fast as they want to. Remember, good marketing divides. If they watch your video and decide not to get in touch (yet or at all), your video has still done its job. Your prequalifying process has saved both you and the prospect time. If they're not the right person for you (or you the right firm for them), wouldn't it be better if they watched your video and decided never to enquire? Wouldn't that release time you could spend on the kind of clients you really love?

Reasons you may feel reluctant to record video

Here are some of the reasons video might be a hard or scary thing to consider and what to remind yourself of as you consider them.

"I'm not good on video." No one is good at video the first time round. I've lost count of the number of people who have been doing video for years who felt extremely embarrassed about their first efforts. This includes me. I don't like looking back at old videos. Sometimes I don't even like looking at current ones. But without our first efforts, all of us who record video regularly wouldn't have made the progress we have. So we're glad for those first videos, and we won't delete them.

"It's going to take a long time to get video right." Yes. It is going to take a long time. Doing video is like anything worth doing: there's no shortcut, no easy way. If you're going to get super fit with rock hard abs, going for a sauntering stroll once a week won't do it. Even if all you want is to be a little healthier, the sauntering stroll is a good start, but you may need more. When it comes to video, you have to try, often multiple times.

There will be lots of takes. Laughter. Embarrassment. Swearing. Tears.

No one records the perfect video the first time round. Even videos which go viral are either capturing a real-life scenario or they're capturing something that has already happened many times before. Practice, practice, practice. Everyone has to go through the process, and with video, there is no better teacher than actually recording video. Think about how small children behave when you pull out your phone. They play with it, make faces, and try different things. What does this button do? What happens if I try this filter? They aren't thinking about who's going to see it, what they're going to say, or how many followers they'll get on YouTube. They're being curious and figuring out how it works, which are at the heart of creativity.

Accountants are recording more video than they used to, but you'll still be an exception when you use video in every part of your marketing. This means you'll have less competition. When your potential buyer comes to an accountancy firm website and sees videos from the owner and team answering the questions they were already wondering, they're not expecting you to be a YouTuber who has been recording weekly videos for eight years. In this situation, they're expecting what most other accountants have on their website (i.e., lots of words, a list of services, an invitation to book a free consultation), or they have a stereotype in their mind of who an accountant is. So when you record and share videos, you're winning already.

"Video worked for that person, but it won't work for me." When you use this excuse, you're trying to be someone other than yourself. If you watch another accountant or any person posting regular videos, it's tempting to think, "But they're really energetic/well spoken/funny/interesting . . . and I'm not." The purpose of video is to help people see who you really are before they even meet you. Would you turn off the camera before an online meeting with a prospect? If they came into your office, would you meet them behind a screen rather than face to face?

Of course not. You are who you are, and pretending to be otherwise is silly. Even if you don't like your own accent, or your nose, or the nervous habits you have (all of those apply to me, by the way), if your prospect becomes a client, they're going to be working with *you*, not fake-video-you. They will hear your accent, see your nose, and connect with you as a human, and the same applies to your team. Your prospect *wants* that. They want the reality, the authenticity, the connection. Even if they come to your website and feel impressed by its messages, they'll still have doubts about whether what you say is for real. About what the experience will actually be like. Video helps convince them this is true—or at least shows it's possible that it's true.

"I'm nervous of what people will say when they see my videos." Someone coming in person to meet you is one thing; video is another. You're thinking, "Okay, I'd meet with one person in my office, but that's only *one person*. A video goes out to the whole wide world! That's like inviting a billion people into my office, and you have to admit that is scary!" Listen. The chances of you going viral to billions of people are very, very slim.

If you haven't been recording video, sharing it regularly on social, embedding it in blog posts, or consistently creating that content we've been talking about this whole book, then there really aren't that many people seeing your videos yet anyway. Only a few people will see your early videos, and most likely at least one of them is your mum or a friend from school days. This will go on for months, if not years.

Persistent marketing is based on building solid long-term relationships with clients who want to work with you for a long time. This takes time and many videos, and most of them will only be seen by the one client you record it for. And that's okay. Better, even. Because this will help you record the video for that one person who truly needs it—rather than trying to record a video for everybody, which means it's for nobody.

It's hard to put videos *out there*, to the whole world. But you're not actually sharing them with the whole world. No one knows who you are yet. You're not a celebrity, you're not known, and you haven't gone viral. With your first video (or first several months of videos), you can start by sharing them in a safe, supportive community. A place of people who know you already and are not judging your video on every tiny aspect but instead are responding to what you're saying. They aren't going to mock you, post hater comments, or something else equally terrifying to you, because they're already familiar with you. You can join the PF Community, which is full of accountants like yourself, or you can create a community for your clients who already know and love you for who you are.

Most people who don't know you will simply ignore your video or not comment. True hater comments are a result of sharing edgy or controversial topics or for people who have a massive following. Every accountant I've known who has started recording video and nervously shared something honest, authentic, or something they felt wasn't that great ended up getting encouragement and support from their clients and those who care about them. You're starting somewhere, and even when you're nervous, you're still you.

"I don't have time for video." You tell yourself (or you tell me), "I want to record more video, but I don't have time." You've also used this excuse for every other part of marketing you're less comfortable with. You don't have time for blogging. You don't have time to go through the Accelerator coaching group. You don't have time to write a book. But time is never the problem. We always have time for what we decide is important and worthwhile as well as what we are comfortable doing.

American author H. Jackson Brown Jr. once said, "Don't say you don't have enough time. You have exactly the same number of hours per day that were given to Helen Keller, Pasteur, Michelangelo, Mother Teresa, Leonardo da Vinci, Thomas Jefferson, and Albert Einstein."

"Well, I'm no Einstein," you think. "I'm not exactly Mother

Teresa." And that may be true, but they didn't have one extra minute more than you do. DaVinci wasn't a great artist because he had so much time. It's not about the time; it's who you are and how you use the time given to you. It's how you *want* to use it. It's what matters to you. And if you want to work with the very best clients, the ones you love, video will shortcut that process for you.

"I don't have the right video equipment." Do you have a phone? Good. You're all set. Equipment isn't what makes someone good at what they do; it's a support to help them do what they do better. As I mentioned before, my expensive camera equipment didn't make me a great wedding photographer; it was my eye, how I used my creativity, what I saw, and what I shared. You're not a better writer because you have a house by the sea with a desk at a huge picture window looking out to the big sky. You're not a better accountant because you have fancy offices with a gym, a pool table, and coffee machines in a big kitchen. You're not a better parent because you have the latest baby swing, pram, or custom-built cot. The best equipment can be really helpful, and once you've started, it can even help you keep going. But it isn't what makes you good.

Buying equipment is not going to solve your doubts and fears about video. Matter of fact, in my experience, buying equipment can delay your progress further because when you finally *do* buy it, the equipment sits there in the corner of your office, judging you, and you feel even worse and put it off even longer. You feel bad because you've realised that wasn't what was holding you back. The only way to start is to start.

"I don't know what to say on video." This reason is a good one. It's still not a good excuse, but it is a reason to stop and sort out what you're missing so you can move forward with video. There are a few ways to defeat this, and they depend on the type of person you are. One is to simply start talking with a camera pointed right at your face. You don't even have to press record yet. You'll figure out what to say by saying it, and in the process, you will figure out very quickly whether you're getting your point across or not. I've done this hundreds of times. Opened my video software or the camera on my phone, clicked record, and said, "Hi, I'm Karen Reyburn. I'm the . . . [long blank pause]." Other times, I've started sharing our pillars and values and suddenly blanked on what they were: "Our four pillars are creativity, integrity . . . wait, integrity? Service? Hang on."

I know what the pillars are. I say them all the time! But having a camera pointed at my face, even a small one on my phone, can seem to wipe them right out. When I'm presenting or speaking, I'll practice literally thousands of times to help the words be so familiar I could say them in my sleep. That way, when I stand on a stage or have a video camera pointed at my face, I can default to what I've memorised or said thousands of times already. A similar approach applies to video; it feels more comfortable and natural to say what you've said a hundred times before. Try saying something over and over before you even start recording. It makes the actual process of recording much easier.

You can also use the content from your blog posts. This is a great way to start recording video because not only do you have content to say but you've also written it (or it's been written for you based on what you say all the time) and it's been structured with headings and an introduction and a close. Structure and planning are some of the most challenging parts of video, but the practice you've built by creating blog posts has you covered. If you've been blogging once a month as I suggested in the previous chapter, you've already got twelve video topics to record. As you increase your consistent blog posts, you'll have even more video topics. Start with those to help you get more comfortable.

"I tried video, and it didn't work for me." Perhaps you've tried a few videos. You recorded one, posted it to YouTube, and . . . nothing. No clicks, no comments, no three new clients in a week. "Clearly video doesn't work," you decided. You went back to what you were doing before. Remember, you're playing the long game. Video is only one part of your integrated web of marketing.

Also, one video doesn't work on its own; it works because, in addition to videos, you've updated your branding to reflect your firm better. You've built a website and made sure the messages talk to the right kind of clients. Posted regularly on social so people get a sense of who you are. You've written blog posts answering their questions.

If video isn't working for you, it's likely you haven't stuck at it long enough or there are other foundational marketing elements you need to address. You can begin by sending videos to individual prospects and clients so you can get some small wins. They don't have to go out to what you consider "the whole world."

One of the ways to move past this is by doing a 100-day challenge. We run them regularly through the PF Lab, and it involves working on video every day for a hundred days and sharing your videos on a social media platform. You may record the full hundred videos; you may only record sixty. Or six. But you're consistently working on video every day. Your videos could be about anything. You could be talking to the screen. You could capture your children or dog running around at the beach. It could be a walk-through of your offices. The point is not to get clients, become an expert, or go viral; it's to get more comfortable on video. Anything you do for one hundred days you will get better at, even if you don't think you're making any progress. You get better at it because it's easier, faster, more familiar. If you drive, think about when you started driving and the difference between then and now. If you have children, think about how you felt the first few days with your first child and how you feel now helping three of them navigate daily life. You get into patterns from doing things day after day until it becomes habit.

One hundred days is long. And hard. You'll get to day seven and think it's not working. You'll get to day thirty and think,

"I'm less than one-third of the way through: it'll never happen." You'll get to day fifty and want to start changing the rules. The reason you need one hundred days is to build familiarity so when opportunities arise in your business and life, it's natural for you to record a video and be more focused on the message than on the method.

You could record a two-minute video from your kitchen and change someone's perspective or even their life because of what they learned. Or you could prepare a perfectly scripted, perfectly shot twenty-minute video which affects or appeals to no one. Be like a child and play with video until you understand how it works. Then bring in the message, the content, what it is you want to say.

The message matters most

When the message in your video is right, it doesn't matter where you are or how "professional" it is. As I've mentioned before, accountants can get obsessed with marketing needing to be "professional", whether it's your website content, the photographs of you and your team, blog posts, videos, or social media. "People will think we aren't good at what we do," you worry. "If I post pictures of my dog, they won't respect me as much as if I record a video sharing the new tax regulations." You expect photographs for the website which are carefully crafted—people with folded arms, serious faces, and in business clothing. You might even carefully cover up tattoos or remove piercings to preserve the professional vibe.

But "professional", when defined this way, can come across to prospects as "boring." Stuffy. Filled with jargon that's confusing to people who are not accountants. Full of numbers and data and lacking personality and humanity. The standard "We are ABC Accountants, we are great, we have been around for eight hundred years . . ." could seem like you're trying too hard; at best you'll just look like an old, traditional accountancy firm (which I'm guessing is not what you want).

This sort of image also means holding back on transparency. You don't want to admit you're sick or tired or, even worse, sick and tired of being sick and tired. You worry about sharing you've been a bit depressed. Even if you do share it, you find it more acceptable to do so when it's all over, after the hard part, after you've triumphed. This, you think, will make sure you are still coming across as professional and can handle, well, anything. It says to anyone watching, "Yes, I had this struggle in my life, and it was hard, but I made it through, whilst at the same time building an accountancy firm and raising several children and building a new home myself and growing all my own food in an organic garden." Sharing the good things, the positive news, is the highlight reel. It protects your image.

The problem with that approach is this: it's not human. It's not real. It doesn't connect with people where they are. Video connects with the people you may one day work with, and it meets them where they are right now. They want to know you're real, not this imaginary perfect person whose image you've built up.

It's also tempting to think video for your accounting firm needs a professional videographer, and they bring in heavy equipment, drones, and a team of videographers to capture your offices, your city, and your team. Maybe the team dances about and sings in harmony, or you have interviews with each team member sitting in a corner with perfect lighting and a plant to the side, and there's a line underneath saying, "Team Member John, Accountant" or "Brian, Firm Owner since 1984."

This kind of thinking can cause you to hold back on doing any video because you're not ready for a professional videographer or for your team to dance about the offices and sing. That's okay. I'm here to confirm you don't ever have to sing if you don't want to and it doesn't fit with your brand. Before you hire choreographers and videographers or build brand new offices for your first video, think about the content and purpose of your videos.

With video, as with all other content, it's the message which matters most

What matters more than what you're wearing or where you're sitting is what you're saying. So let's talk about your message now. What will you actually talk about?

Video is merely one of many formats to get your message out to clients and prospects. Whether you record a video, write a blog post, share a social post, or create a website page or a guide or a podcast episode, you're still getting a specific message across. You could use what you've learned from chapter 2 ("Issues") or chapter 9 ("Blogging") to create a huge list of topics. You could take one of those subjects and create content using all of the methods we've talked about so far, including video, letting your clients choose how and when they engage with that content.

If you're still looking for ideas, here is a list of topics which easily lend themselves to video:

- *A welcome video for new clients*: I'd suggest starting with a personal welcome video for each new client. Your team could do the welcome videos as well, with the team member responsible for the client recording the welcome. A general welcome is harder and will take longer.
- *Onboarding videos:* This could be a whole series of videos, including a welcome, what to do on day one, the first three things you need them to do before you get started, training videos, and even a one-month review video.
- *Our process/our way:* Explain how you do things at your firm, ideally with the cornerstone asset we talked

about in chapter 3. You could start with one summary video and build on it with more detailed videos.

- *FAQS for clients or prospects:* Record videos answering the individual questions a new client, long-time client, or new prospect might have. Then, when the person asks that same question, you've got a video to hand. Keep these videos very specific, and build up an FAQ library that will save hours (even months) of time!

- *Training videos:* Make a list of all the things you train clients to do. This could include how to use certain elements of their accounting software, how to submit receipts and expenses, how to approve payroll, or a hundred other small tasks. Each video can be as long as it needs to be to answer the question, whether it's 30 seconds or 30 minutes. Again, you're building a library to make your clients' lives easier.

- *Video reviews for the team:* Instead of endless meetings with the whole team or individuals within the team, record review videos every time you do a review of any work a team member does. Train the team to do it with each other too. Even if the review is being done in person at the office, you can still record it. That way, you're building a team training library which can be accessed by every new team member, saving everyone time and keeping the training process consistent.

- *Proposal videos:* Include a video with every proposal you send out. No exceptions. Even if a prospect says, "Send over the proposal, and I'll sign it instantly," you lose nothing by recording a two-minute video saying how excited you are to start working with them or giving them a reminder of how this will help solve the problem they mentioned. If they're even slightly unsure (or very unsure), your video makes them more likely to sign the proposal. Or at least sign it faster since they don't need to come back to you many times with more and more questions. If they do have more questions, you can send them the FAQ videos you've already created!

Once you get started, you'll get into the habit and find yourself doing multiple videos every day for different people. A video for a team member, a video for a client, a proposal video, or a live video on social. It will become a habit, it will be comfortable, and it will help the buyer move along at a faster speed.

Purpose: Why are you recording this video?

Your audience expects video everywhere. There are demo videos, funny cat videos, speaker reel videos, vlogs, masterclasses, and more. But the best videos are relevant to a topic, an issue, or a niche. Before you start recording a video, ask yourself why you are recording it at all. Is it because you believe "a video is a good thing to have" for your accounting firm? Is it because other accountants are recording video and you think you need to get on that bandwagon? Is it because an accountant mentioned they had three new clients because of their video on TikTok and you suddenly realised you might be missing a trick?

Stop and remind yourself of the purpose of video. It's for your client, your prospect. Start preparing for your video by considering who it's for, what questions you'll answer, where the video will be posted, what other videos you'll create, and what you want people to do after watching it. Let's look at these in more detail now.

Who will watch it: Is this video primarily for prospects who are wondering what kind of firm you are? For clients to get to know you better? Imagine the perfect client—the one you got recently that you absolutely love and wish you had more of. Think about what you want to say to that one specific person and craft the video for them.

The questions it will answer: When you make a list of questions, you might actually find that you need five different videos to answer them. You might need ten. Or a hundred. The point is not to showcase how great you are and what you say about yourself. It's to answer your prospect's questions or give them something to think about and help them realise they may need your help.

Where the video(s) will be posted: Knowing where and how the video will be used tells you more about what kind of video it's going to be. Will it be in the background of a website page with movement and colour but no sound? Is it a case study to be embedded on your "Work with us" page? Are they a series of training videos which need to be watched in order?

This also helps you understand what level of quality is required. Whether a phone video will do or whether you need to hire a videographer. Remember, a phone can produce a seriously high-quality video. The platform you use to share the video will also inform whether it needs to be shot in portrait or landscape and how long it needs to be. Every social media platform has minimum and maximum lengths, so consider these ahead of time to make sure you're able to upload the video you've worked on so long. If you've recorded the perfect video which is three minutes and twenty seconds long and the platform you need to upload it on has a limit of three minutes, you'll either need to do some editing or record the video all over again. A few minutes of preparation save a lot of hassle later.

What other videos you will create: Recording individual videos to stand alone is a good way to start and practice. Over time, you can begin to think about how these videos will fit together. Think about how this one video fits into the bigger picture of your marketing. For example, you might record a welcome video for new clients followed by smaller onboarding videos to explain each step of the process.

What they will do next after watching it: When you know what you want someone to do after watching your video, you can tell them either in the video itself or in your closing statement. Say it at the end or share a link so they can click through to the next step. Keep it very specific. For example, if you say "Book your workshop today at [link]," they can decide if they're ready to book the workshop. If you say "If you have any questions, email us at [address] or call us on [number] or visit our offices at [address]," they have to think about the action they want to take. Giving too many options encourages them to choose none of them.

The order of importance in video

When it comes to actually recording your video, focus your attention in this order:

1. The message
2. The audio
3. The visual quality
4. The captions

Message: You've already identified some of the messages you need to get across for your firm. Even bullet points or a few short statements help you structure a good video. You don't have to script your entire video, and I'd suggest this will only hold you back in the early days because you'll be so focused on saying it perfectly you'll forget what it is you're actually saying. It won't sound natural or personable. To get started with the message of your video, plan your first sentence, your core concepts, and your closing sentence.

Write down your opening sentence. If you don't, you'll likely begin with "Hi, I'm [name] from [name of firm], and I wanted to talk to you today about *x*," and you'll ramble for a good thirty seconds before you start getting to the point. People don't have a long attention span, and they aren't opening your video with all the time in the world to slowly listen to you. As with a blog post, get to the point fast. Give away the ending. Making a strong statement draws people in and causes them to be more curious. Your goal in the first five seconds is to get them to listen to the next fifteen seconds.

Practice saying the opening sentence out loud. If you write down the most perfect opening sentence ever, say it aloud, and realise it doesn't sound right or doesn't sound like you or it rambles, try again until you get it right.

Write out one to three core concepts you'll be covering. You don't have to always have three points as if it's a carefully practiced speech. Many speeches could often be improved by having only one point instead of three, four, or five which all happen to start with the same letter. It feels clever to say "I'd like to talk to you today about Planning, Perseverance, and Protection," but it's likely so clever no one will remember it.

Prepare talking points and concepts, not carefully crafted statements. If your video is about how a forecast will help their business, your points could be the following: a story about a business owner who didn't prepare a forecast and what happened, a screenshare of what a forecast looks like, and two things a forecast needs to include. You may start recording your video and realise it's too much for one video; instead of one video with three points, it makes more sense to record three videos, one for each point. The more focused you can be in one video, the better. This is personally a hard area for me; I have so many things I want to say that my video starts with one core concept and ends up covering four or five different aspects of that concept when it would be far better for me to split it into four or five smaller videos.

Write down your closing sentence. Again, if you don't do this, you'll finish with something rambling and vague like "Well, thanks for listening, and if you have any questions, talk to me or one of my team, and it was really nice to share these things with you, and we'll talk soon." In speeches and in video, people remember what you started with and what you ended with.

When you write down your closing sentence, you help your brain, which has gone blank in the last few seconds of the video and doesn't know what to say.

Talk naturally from your core concepts. Hit record, say your opening sentence. If it's still not working for you, say it again until it feels natural. Then start talking about your first core concept. After that, move into your second and however many you have until you're done. Finish with your closing sentence.

You don't have to follow this process with every single video you ever record; in fact, you don't have to follow it at all. But it's good practice to get into the habit of knowing how you're going to start so you don't waste their time. And knowing how you're going to end gives your audience one action to take or one thought to hold onto once the video is over.

Audio: Regardless of visual quality, always make sure you can be clearly heard. Even if the lighting could be improved, it's better to have a video with a great message which can be heard clearly. Oddly enough, although a video feels like it's about the visuals, audio is still the more important factor to consider first. If they aren't hearing the message, it doesn't matter how nice it looks. And if the audio is crackly, or quiet, or keeps cutting out, no one will hear the message you worked so hard on. I love it when people look back on their early days of recording videos and laugh at how they recorded themselves walking through a windy forest or sitting in their car with traffic buzzing past. If your audience isn't able to hear the message, they'll give up and watch something else.

Make sure you have a good microphone or you're in a place which isn't distracting in terms of sound. If you're planning on having more people in the video than just yourself, be sure their voices can be heard as well. Use the video equipment list in the Accountant Marketer workbook. Equipment doesn't have to be big or costly to work; a small lapel mic which connects to your phone can be enough. Remember, focusing on the equipment can be an excuse to get out of actually recording the video. Get something small that works for now, and you can always get something better later once you're comfortable with video.

Visual quality: You are recording a video, after all. So when you're clear on your message and have made sure your voice will be heard, look at the lighting and visual quality of the video. Natural light is the simplest solution, and you don't have to be a videographer to figure out how standing in this corner is darker than standing over there by a window. Or how standing with the window behind you may show you as a silhouette, whereas turning round to face the window solves the problem, and you or your subject can be seen clearly.

Again, play with it like a child would. What happens if I stand here? What if I lift the camera a little or bring it down? What if I stand it on this little tripod or make my own mini tripod with a stack of books? What if I turn this light on or off? If you're really not sure, ask a colleague or family member to point out which one is better.

You could also create a space in your office or home with good lighting, a tripod, a ring light, and a simple white background. Then whenever you need to record a video, go to that space, set up your phone or camera, and press record. It will take a little while to set up the first few times, but after a while, it will simply be how you do things. When you want to capture what a team member or a client has shared, you can be ready to record video at any moment. The hard work has been done already, and you can focus on what you want to say and share.

Captions: Most people watch videos on silent for a while before they turn on the audio, and it doesn't always help to instruct the viewer to "turn on sound." They may be watching it in a public place, or somewhere quiet. They may be flicking through their phone while doing three or four other things. They may have hearing difficulties. Let them decide when and if they want to turn on the audio and listen to you talking. Adding captions helps them decide how interesting the video topic is and when they want to engage. It also helps those who struggle to hear audio for whatever reason. Imagine how much content you'd miss out on in your life if you could only watch videos with captions. The same goes for adding image descriptions when you upload an image to a social site or a website. It takes only a few seconds and helps so many people.

Captions are standard on most social platforms now. You can click a button, and your words are instantly transcribed. Make sure to do that for most if not all of your videos. If you're recording a video on your computer or phone and need to add captions later, there are online services which will do this quickly and at a low cost.

Small, practical ways to get started with video

The best video coach is you doing video. Press record, share, and do it again and again. Most of what you need to work through is a mindset issue. Your desire to "do video properly" will hold you back at the start.

If you're avoiding video because you want it to be perfect, you're expecting too much too early. You're not likely to immediately have top-quality audio, crisp video, perfect surroundings, spot-on delivery by you and anyone else in the video, with new prospects contacting you immediately afterwards.

Like anything else on earth, you have to start small, learn as you go, be persistent, and fail along the way. After all, failure can be the fun part with video. Don't we all love a good blooper reel? To have a laugh when someone else mixed up their words, or dropped the phone, or the tripod fell over? Be a person first and a business owner next. Prepare yourself for some failure and focus on the learnings. It's not about celebrating failure but celebrating what you've learned. Being real gets you more views, more engagement, better relationships, and better marketing. Every time.

Start small, start safe. Say to yourself, "I will not get this perfect, and that's okay."

A great example is a Facebook live by a friend of mine who was a speaker at a marketing conference with me. On the Saturday morning after the conference, he decided to shoot a live video talking about what he learned from it and helping others know what to do with what they learned. He shot it in his kitchen, and a few minutes into the first live video, the whole thing shut down, and he had to end it and start a new one. The second one starts with him laughing his head off, explaining what happened, and then sharing his learnings from the conference. When I went back to listen to the first one, I noticed in the second one he was more personable as well as sharper, crisper, and more direct with his points about the conference. The failure of the live video made his second video much better.

You can also get comfortable with video by using expiring video "stories." If you're not familiar with stories, they're built into social media platforms to give you an opportunity to share photos and video which disappear after twenty-four hours. You can set it up so these photos and videos are saved automatically on your phone in case you want to use them for anything later, but no one else will be accessing them after a day, so you're safe. This is your chance to learn video, figure out how it works, play with it, try things, fail, have a laugh, and give it a go. Chances are you have about four followers, and none of them will be watching you live, so it's not as if you are under any pressure. I've got thousands of followers, and I still only get a few people watching me live. But it's great practice, and I learn something new every time I do it. Often, I record my live sessions on Instagram, and as long as they're less than ten minutes long, I can upload them to other places to share.

Join a safe community where you can share your early videos. The PF Lab is a community of accountants who are exploring and experimenting with marketing, including video. We only allow accountants in this group, so not only will everyone else understand how you feel but many of them are as terrified (if not more so) of video than you are. Join the group, record an intro video on your phone, and share it. No edits, no retakes, no fixing. It will take you two to three minutes, and you'll feel relieved and wonder what took you so long. You'll also get comments from other accountants saying how great it is to meet you and how they want to be doing video too.

Not every video has to be a carefully crafted three-minute message. When you look at anyone who is sharing video regularly, you'll see they aren't merely recording videos of themselves sitting at a desk or in an office explaining facts. As entrepreneur and internet personality Gary Vee says, "Document, don't create." Video is your opportunity to document things like your day, your office, meetings with clients, chats with the team, events you attend, people you meet, and ideas you've had.

If you really need a little motivation, buy some basic video equipment. No, equipment is still not going to solve all your problems. But if you need something fun to get you excited about video instead of dreading it, buy a small microphone, a ring light, and a tripod to connect to your phone. Make sure you actually use them when they are delivered to you instead of setting the box aside in a corner and telling yourself you'll do it tomorrow.

Above all, focus on helping your clients, not on getting sales from video. If your goal with video is to get more business, the stress level becomes incredibly high. You worry about lighting, and backgrounds, and the impression you're giving. When your goal is to be genuinely helpful to your clients and prospects and to share this in a way that reaches more people faster, it changes everything. Capture a quick video of something you saw which reminded you of a business or accounting concept useful for your clients. Grab footage of a party you're holding, or a few seconds of your team's online Zoom get-together. Record yourself sharing an idea you had that day or the story of a client you worked with who had a great victory. Focus on the message rather than the money.

. . .

Video editing: What to do with your video once it's recorded

Simply recording the video is the first step. Being prepared for what kind of video it needs to be, who's going to watch it, what you'll say, what the call to action will be, and where it's going online will help you know how long it needs to be, and whether it will be portrait or landscape.

But say you've done all that, and you have a three-, ten-, or thirty-minute video. Now what? Maybe you've got a lot of ums and ahs, a few glitches where you stumbled over your words, and a section where you mentioned an event you're running which dates the video. Can you do some simple editing so the video is still useable? Or do you need to rerecord and let that original video go?

Video editing is a skill, and it often takes far longer than you imagine until you try it. Most social media platforms allow you to do basic editing (or even quite complex editing if you experiment long enough!), so you can start there. You may feel like this is an extreme waste of time; maybe it is, maybe it isn't. It depends on what interests you, how you want to stir up your creativity, and how it will help you understand how videos are used. I do a minimal amount of video editing myself, clipping out small sections, fixing the start and end of a video so it doesn't begin with silence or a blank face for a few seconds, and adding captions. But when it comes to "proper" video editing, I have the PF team work on it. Video editing is well worth paying for when the core video content is good. When your core content is focused on a message which will last far longer than a few days on the socials, it's worth investing in a video editor to help you do it right.

More often than not, what you're doing with video as an accountant is learning *how* to shoot video. This includes becoming comfortable with it and figuring out those "filler" words you say and working on replacing them. Sometimes it's best to simply leave silence instead of those repetitive words. A lot of this comes down to making new habits: Reaching for your phone to record a video rather than sending a one-to-one email or message. Getting used to seeing yourself on video. Inviting your team to learn video too. Trying different kinds of videos—not simply staring at the lens and talking but capturing a variety of live footage, interviews, or different perspectives. Trying your hand at basic video editing. Even if you have someone else edit your videos now or later, you'll still be learning how to value the work that goes into video editing.

To get started with basic video editing, use your phone, a free video editing software, or paid video editing software. Let's look at the options available to you.

Use your phone: Even the default photo/video app on your phone has some basic video editing capabilities such as cropping out the start and end of the video. Play with the app. See what it does. Even if you clip out the wrong portion, you can always undo it and try again. If you're really worried about losing a particularly good video, duplicate it and edit the copy. Record a test video to see what your phone is capable of in terms of editing.

Use a free video editing software: Use the tried and tested brands. Adobe usually has some good free apps, and Canva allows some editing as well. If you do an online search or look in your phone's app store and come across an app you know nothing about, check with a few people or with us at PF first. We'll give you some suggestions.

Use a paid video editing software: I've been using Camtasia for many years; it's got more capabilities than I tend to use, but it allows me to clip out sections right down to the 0.01 of a second. I can also change lighting and audio, export in different formats, and segment out portions to use for different purposes. It's simple enough to use, and I keep learning new things every time I use it. You can also use Canva Professional for most of the same kinds of edits.

The apps I mention change often, so check in with us in the PF Lab for the latest and simplest video editing tools. Part of experimenting is being willing to try new things, and we're in a time when equipment and apps are getting better every day! Simple video editing will give you and your team something to get started with, and it also helps you value the cost of a good videographer and video editor once you're ready to make that investment.

You must record video content yourself—you and your team. There is no one who can be you, in place of you. No one else is going to give the impression you will when someone meets with you, whether in person or online, and it will take so much longer to build trust without them knowing who you are. But once you've recorded the core content, you can do a little video editing yourself, and once you've gotten into the habit of doing this regularly, you can hire video editors. You'll value it more because you know how hard it is to do and how much time, expertise, and skill it takes. Sort of like how your clients feel when they try their hand at bookkeeping, payroll, and running accounting reports and then finally hand it over to you. What a relief. They managed it—sort of—but it's hard, and it's not what they want to spend hours and hours doing.

If you really want to simplify the video process, here's a handy guide.

How to record video: a ten-point guide

1. Think of that question everyone keeps asking you.
2. Pull out your phone (or an app like Loom).
3. Press the record button.
4. Start talking.
5. Say everything you need to say on the subject, and then stop.
6. Press stop.

7. Choose the social platform you use the most (or hate the least).
8. Click the share button.
9. Upload your video and add a few words about it.
10. Press post.

You are done. Congratulations. You've achieved what you've been avoiding or fearing or worrying about for years. Now bask in the gratitude of the clients and people who needed an answer to that question and have been helped by it. Repeat as necessary.

Conclusion: Use video to invite people into a story

When you use video to explain your services, to show your way of doing things, and to answer questions, the prospect feels they know you and are far more likely to start the conversation. After all, that's all you're asking them to do: say yes to the next step. Say yes to the form, the meeting, the proposal, or the client relationship. You're the celebrity they need, and they're excited to finally meet you.

The whole of your marketing is a story. As you create videos for the people and businesses you work with, you're inviting them to be part of that story. And as you create these videos alongside other content, including blog posts and website pages and PDF guides, you start to think, "Okay, I've got some actual content now. I'm creating and publishing it. But how do I get people to actually *see* it?"

Time to look at the content you'll be sharing on social media.

CHAPTER 11
SOCIAL MEDIA

ANYONE WHO FOLLOWS me on any of the social media platforms will recognise my five personal pillars: coffee, walking, whisky, soul, and magic.

The platform which currently shows this best is Instagram because it's visual. You don't post anything on Insta without a photo or a video. Our human life is all about story, and I love the way you can share little pieces of your day, and over time, people come to understand what you care about and who you love. When you see what I share and post, you'll see these pillars, and over time you'll discover more. Not just coffee: black coffee. Walking, yes; running, no. Scottish whisky, ideally from the Tobermory Distillery or within the Auchentoshan range. The magic of Harry Potter as well as everyday miracles and mystery.

Social media helps clients get to know you with no pressure

When I started using Instagram in earnest, there were very few accountants following me. Few were even on Insta at all. Most accountants were and still are on LinkedIn; they feel more comfortable there. As a social media platform, LinkedIn seems more professional, a place where you can talk about work and get business. Accountants don't see it as a place for sharing videos of kids in the snow, morning coffee, or new running shoes.

As I kept being consistent on Instagram, I noticed something interesting. The accountants who started to explore working with PF or signed up for the Accelerator group began setting up accounts on Instagram too. Primarily it was the ones curious about the creative element, who saw the potential of sharing photos and videos about their life and connecting with others who owned businesses in their area or even worldwide.

The point here is not to make you use Instagram (you don't). And this is not to say LinkedIn isn't useful (it is).

Social media is your opportunity to help future clients begin to get to know you—the real you, the firm, the team, clients, locations, and personal pillars—so they can get a sense of whether you're their kind of people. This can happen on whatever platform you use. You may share articles, blog posts, videos, website pages, downloadable guides, or stories. Perhaps you'll share about a client you met with today who had a problem you were able to work through. Maybe a team member solved what felt like a crisis to one of your clients.

People still do business with people. Yes, your firm itself has a brand. But your brand is ultimately a reflection of the work you and your team (the people) do with clients (also people). And it's also a reflection of who you are as humans. Conversations with clients don't usually leap directly into, "Okay, so you owe this much in tax." You ask how they are doing, or they share something about their family. You meet up with some clients for a beer or a coffee because you like them and enjoy their company.

Your firm is not like every other firm. Just as every human being is unique, so too every accounting firm is unique. Your buyer is trying to discover what you're really like, not merely what you say you're like, so they can make their decision based on reality. And the buyer is not sure yet. They have expectations of accountants already. Those expectations may be good or bad. They may not realise it's possible for an accountant like you to exist, someone who can answer their questions and be a support in their life. Someone they can collaborate with to build the life they want.

Every part of your marketing, including your presence on social media, helps reassure the buyer before they meet anyone from your firm. Social, especially, allows your prospect to connect with no pressure. If they aren't ready for a discovery call or a proposal, they can see how you do business. Because it shows far more than a website page or a few testimonials, social is a place where they can begin to sense a pattern, a way of living and working. Marketing content isn't you *telling* people who you are; it's an opportunity to consistently *show* them who you are over a period of time. Social is also an opportunity to start exploring what the business relationship could look like.

Confidence: It comes with practice

Remember the one hundred-day challenge we talked about with video and how the best video coach is you doing more video? The same applies to social media posting. You can read about social media, watch videos, join courses and masterclasses, and watch others doing it. But one of the best teachers will still be the practice of doing it yourself. When I talk with accountants about what holds them back with social media, their concerns are very similar to their fears around video:

- "What's the point of sharing things which are small and personal?"
- "Do I have to share personal things or photographs of my children?"
- "What if I don't have anything to say?"
- "This isn't in my comfort zone!"
- "I don't have the smallest idea what I'm doing!"

Whether in social media, video, or any other area of marketing, it's fear which is often the real problem. It's not usually about the equipment. The hashtags. The tips and tricks. Those come in handy once you start practicing, but the only way out is through. You're not going to shortcut learning how to use social media by skipping it or by delegating (actually abdicating) to someone else. Handing social media to someone who you believe "knows social media" isn't enough, because what is posted on social is a representation of your brand. Even if you aren't the one clicking "publish," social posts are a part of marketing which is ultimately your responsibility. Those who take care of your social posting need to be connected with you and the team members in the firm so your posts are a genuine reflection of your brand. This way, the people who read these posts can feel they know who you all are, what you stand for, and how you do business and life. This also means there's no mismatch when they do meet you.

To start building confidence in social, learn about it first so you understand how it works in connection with the rest of your marketing. Then use it yourself on a regular basis (preferably daily), and as you begin to see results from it, you'll be inspired to do more.

You may think the best place to begin is to simply start. To just use it and see where that goes. But those who take that approach with social media often give up or get discouraged because they don't know what they're doing or they're looking at it in isolation. All your marketing elements work together. Social doesn't stand alone. Writing blog posts, updating your website, rebranding, hiring new team members, and moving offices are (and need to be) tied in with social media.

Using it yourself will help you understand what you're actually delegating if and when you take that step. If you don't understand it and don't care, it's hard for you to value the work a team member is doing for your firm on social. It will feel unimportant and less valuable. You'll press for instant results (i.e., did their video go viral or did they get a lot of likes and followers?), and your team member could feel frustrated because of the pressure and because that's not how social works.

Your personal involvement in each part of marketing helps your overall marketing to be better. This doesn't mean you need to do all the marketing all the time. It means you need to understand what's involved, how hard it is, what the complexities are, and how these elements come together *so that* you can delegate it. When we work with accountants on their social media, we're not holding one strategy call and then posting on their socials the next day. We spend time understanding your goals, your brand, your website, and your marketing plan. We ask a lot of questions, then listen for words and phrases you use. We meet with your team to gather ideas and to understand their daily work. And we always encourage owners to take responsibility in this area and at least try. This way, delegating your social media is not because you're avoiding it, see it as a waste of space, or can't be bothered. It's because you've invested the time, see its value, and are using your time well.

Personal account, business account, or both?

It can be confusing for business owners to decide how to use social and from what perspective. Do you need personal social accounts as well as accounts for the firm? Do only the owners have personal accounts? Do team members have a connection to the firm's social? Do you use a business profile and keep the content purely business focused?

If you're a smaller firm, start with personal accounts. The smaller the company, the more important it is to focus on your personal profiles. After all, even if you have one or two part-time team members, the business is mostly you, and that's who they're connecting with. They'll feel a bit of a disconnect if you only use an official business account, which isn't as human. It's like having a website that says "we" all throughout the content when it's really only the one owner. You can create your official business accounts on social media, but as a smaller firm, you don't need to do too much with them right now. You can worry about that later if you decide to start hiring and building a team.

For medium to larger firms, you'll need the business profiles as your core, while personal accounts for you and the team members can support and supplement those. No matter how hard you try with business accounts, they're always going to have a more corporate, less personal feel. Someone commenting on a post doesn't know the human who wrote it, and they have no idea who's going to reply, if anyone. Sending a message to "the firm" feels rather clinical until they get a reply and start talking with someone. Use the business accounts to let people get a feel for everyone and everything which makes up the firm. Share photographs and video. Consider having each team member use their initials when replying to messages so the prospect knows the human they're connecting with (not the generic "firm"). Then, from your own personal accounts, you and individual team members can share articles you personally wrote, videos you recorded, or individual perspectives on a trending topic.

When it comes to personal accounts, I'm passionate about my social accounts being *mine*. When you message me on any of the socials with my name (karenlreyburn), you're talking to me personally. It's discouraging to me when someone has a social account with their own name, but you discover later you're actually communicating with their assistant, a team member, or an outsourced social media person who doesn't even work there. It's your choice how you manage this, and my way is not the only way. But if your social accounts aren't truly you, I'd suggest being transparent about it. Say "this account is monitored by me and the whole team" so people know.

Conversation: Actually talk to people

The most important thing you do on social is not the posts you share, what you say, how many of them you share, or how clever you are. It's your ability to listen.

When you're starting out with social (or even if you've been doing it for some time!), you feel pressure to be seen, to get followers and likes, to get results of some kind. You focus almost exclusively on what you're going to say, how many views your latest video had, and how popular you are or how valuable you're shown to be. But the purpose of social media is to be . . . social. So before you create a calendar of social media content, automate all the posting, and leave someone else to manage it, think about what you're going to do with all these online connections you are building. Start by connecting with others and focusing on them more than yourself. It's a great way to remember social media is not a one-way conversation.

Start by following people and businesses in your ideal audience category. If you work with creatives, or authors, or dentists, follow as many of those as you can find. Read what they have to say. Be interested in them. You can also connect with groups of people you want to work with. Look for your ideal audience in groups which focus on what they're interested in, whether that's marketing for authors or a local or national group of dentists. If the group is public or looks like you may be able to join, jump in. Listen. See what people are posting.

At this point, it's critical not to sell. Building traction on social media doesn't mean proclaiming your services. As you connect with these other people and businesses, you don't even need to comment. Just listen. Pay attention to what they're talking about. What frustrates them? What excites and motivates them? Notice who they appreciate and how they feel. Look at the results they're getting or not getting, and listen to the questions they're asking.

After you have been listening for a while, engage a little bit. Like some posts and comments. Go wild and use an emoji. If it's a public post, share their content with a comment about why you like it or are curious about it. At this stage, you're not thinking about making a sale from your one share. You're doing this to learn and to be helpful.

Once you've been doing this for a while, begin commenting, asking questions, and engaging with people. Why did they ask this? Do they have a recommendation on that? Again, you're not yet selling or promoting your services. The *only* thing you're doing is being visible, caring about what they think and do, and being curious or helpful. If someone asks a question you've answered with a blog post, a video, or some other content, you can reply with that, but don't blast people with your content. Share it because you're seeking to help and understand. Ask a few questions first before you fire in with your solution or your answer. You could even say, "We've recorded a video on that. Would you like me to share?" If they never reply, you haven't bothered them with something they don't want or need yet. If they say yes, you have permission, and they're more ready to read or listen to it.

Finally, once you've been doing this for a few months, it's time to start sharing your thoughts, your posts, and your videos. Let's look at the 80:20 rule.

Sharing content: Use the 80:20 rule

The 80:20 rule protects you from making social media all about you. When people come to your social platforms, think about how it looks if every single post is some version of the following:

- "Here are the services we offer."
- "Did you know accountants can do x?"
- "Sign up for our guide/event/workshop today."

Worst of all is when these are WRITTEN IN ALL CAPS LIKE THIS. THAT'S INTERNET SHOUTING. Don't do it.

As with all marketing, social media is not for you. It's for those who are reading and those engaging with you as a human. The 80:20 rule means you share content in this way:

- **80 percent nonpromotional content:** Helpful, educational, supportive content in the form of articles, videos, or stories. They could be yours; they could be someone else's. These posts are not actively selling something, but they're connecting you to your audience.
- **20 percent promotional content:** This is where you tell people about something they can sign up for or buy, whether it's a finance workshop, a discovery call, an event you're running, or a pack of tax resources.

When you look at the last few posts you've shared and realise they're all about *your* firm and *your* services and *you you you*, the 80:20 rule reminds you to be social. Think about others. Content marketing works because instead of leaping in to promoting yourself or your services before someone knows you yet, you're being helpful with what you know and sharing it. The beautiful thing is, you don't actually need to promote yourself. You don't need to cold call or push your services on people who don't want them. This relieves you from the burden of feeling salesy. Sure, you tell people what you're doing (i.e., here's an event, an offer, a service), but you share it because you really care about your clients and their results. If you don't have anything to say and you don't know who you're talking to, using social media for your firm won't do you any good anyway.

This is why we're looking at social towards the end of this book. All the work you've done on understanding your audience, building your cornerstone and brand, helping your website messages express these, and being clear about who you are and who you work with—*that* is what helps your social media to have impact. You're not merely selling services. You're revealing who you are and allowing people to connect with you at their own pace.

Consistency: Be present on social

By this point in the book and mostly likely in the life of your firm, you've either started creating content or you've been doing it for some time. Day after day, week after week, month after month. You've written blog posts, updated your website, produced a few PDF guides, but you're not sure anyone knows it's there. If you do share it on social, you get a few likes, but it's hard to tell what's working and what's being seen. Some of it is getting seen, but much of it doesn't seem to be. How will your perfect clients find you, the ones you'd love to work with and who'd love to work with you just as much except they don't know you exist? How can they know about all this amazing content you've been creating?

Social media is like roaring white-water rapids. It's continual. It's endless. It swirls about and feels overwhelming. If we're in the midst of the rapids, we almost get pulled under, and if we stand at the side of the river and watch, it's still hard to make anything out. That is, unless the same little blue inflatable tube goes swirling by over and over, or maybe it gets stuck in the rocks for a moment. Your audience is overwhelmed by the presence of so much content. You need to be saying the same sort of things to the same sort of people over and over until they begin to see the pattern. Your little inflatable tube begins to be noticed. "There's the blue one!"

Consistency (combined with tracking, which we'll cover in the final chapter) will help your audience find you. Once you're connected, use social media to get to know the humans who will buy from you rather than focusing on whether you made a sale from one post.

. . .

Involve the whole team

At the very beginning of this book, we talked about the Concentric Circles of Team Involvement and the power of involving your entire team in marketing. Whether you have one or many team members, get them involved with social media too. The more involved they are, the more accurate it is, the better reach you get, and the easier it is for people to recognise patterns. Your firm's values are not to be mere words on a website page; they're meant to be lived out by you and your team.

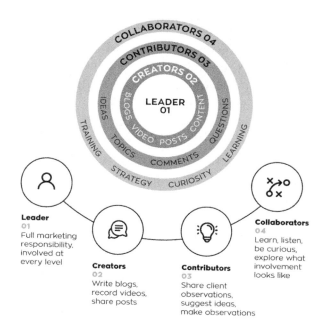

Leader
01
Full marketing responsibility, involved at every level

Creators
02
Write blogs, record videos, share posts

Contributors
03
Share client observations, suggest ideas, make observations

Collaborators
04
Learn, listen, be curious, explore what involvement looks like

Remember, not every person in the team will have the same kind of involvement in social media, but every team member will have some involvement. Most team members will be a Contributor or Collaborator, and some will be open to being Creators. And all of the team will follow your leadership: If you as the leader are not doing anything on social, it's unlikely they'll be enthusiastic about it. As you pay more attention to it, learn how it works, and explore how it helps the firm, they will too.

Involving your team in social media is not as simple as asking them to post once in a while. One of the worst things you could do would be to tell your team to post or to share the company's posts with no direction, no training, and no idea what they're doing or why. They'll either copy other accounting firms (which means they're not on-brand for your firm, but for someone else's), do what works for them personally (which may not work for your firm at all), or be salesy and spammy with their posts, even unintentionally (which is not how social media works best). They need to understand why they're being involved. You want the team members who are participating to be clear about how you want them to be involved, what kinds of things to share, who your audience is, how to talk with them, and what connection and community look like.

Here's how you can begin to support your team in their involvement in your firm's social:

Be clear about the firm's tone of voice. The brand book we talked about in chapter 4 will help with this. You are welcome to create a social media book for your firm which outlines the types of things you share and say or don't say. Be very clear about how team members can be themselves and still represent the firm. It's good for them to share things according to their own personality (you want that) whilst still reflecting the firm's core messages and values across the board. Don't merely create this book and hand it round to the team, commanding them to follow it whether they like it or not. Involve them in the process and help them feel ownership of it. This will build confidence for what they'll share on social. When what your team shares reflects what's in your brand book, then your marketing is real. If it doesn't match, you have more branding work to do because you may have a false belief in your brand which isn't being reflected by the people who live it out every day. You don't need to have a brand book to start posting on social, but the bigger the team you have, the more critical it is for all of you to be consistent.

Decide together what social media accounts they'll post from. Help them work through what is best for them and best for the firm. With some of the firms we work with, team members have a personal social media account on which they share both personal and firm content. They might post their own weekend plans as well as thoughts from a recent accounting conference. It's their choice. Some people personally love Instagram but would rather not use it to connect with clients. Some almost never use Twitter, and they choose that account to share accounting content. Some use every single social media platform for both personal and firm posting.

Whatever they choose, have conversations about it. Discuss it in team members' regular check-ins. Talk about it as a team, and work together to create individual targets and goals for socials. Review the analytics together so they can see what they've contributed to. Some team members will be uncomfortable connecting their personal life to the firm's business life. They may want a clearer dividing line between the two. As you understand their feelings about it, consider other solutions which will result in the same success and still allow the team member to have the life they want to have.

Invest actual cash in their marketing skills. This is one of the most effective ways to help team members be part of your social media and all your marketing. Look for ways to help educate them about *why* they are doing this. How does this help them? How does it make their job easier? Let them discover, as you have, how content marketing saves them time and brings more of the best kind of clients they get to work with. They'll see how good content marketing divides, sending away the hard, difficult ones who would have made their working life (and the rest of their life) miserable. Help them realise how being involved in marketing actually makes their job and life better.

It's taken you months or years to begin to see this impact on your own life; it will take them time too.

Buy the entire team a copy of this book. Encourage them to read it, think about it, and share their perspectives on it. Buy other marketing books. Listen to podcasts on creativity. Hold regular sessions to gather the questions clients and prospects are asking so the team can feel part of the firm's marketing. Invite one or two team members to join you in going through the Accelerator coaching group. Talk with them about how these principles apply to your firm after each session.

The more you involve your team, the better your marketing is. Every time. It's more authentic, it's more accurate, and it's more enjoyable. Investing actual cash in your people shows you value them and their input because when you're ready to really do something, you're ready to pay.

Share the social numbers so they can see the impact of their involvement. We create a marketing Co-pilot report for our monthly clients so they have a summary of all the marketing numbers for their firm. It's like monthly management accounts for marketing. For each client, we gather the numbers related to their social media accounts as well as website analytics, proposal numbers, client and prospect numbers, sales, net profit percentages, and email data. There are core numbers every firm needs to be tracking, but every Co-pilot report varies depending on each firm's unique marketing goals. As your firm goals begin to change (and they will), the numbers you'll track adjust as well.

Sharing a Co-pilot report with the team shows them the impact of their involvement (or lack thereof) on the firm's overall marketing, including social media. When it comes to social, a favourite statistic of team members is seeing which social media post was the most popular that month. They can literally see the impact of something they created out of their own head or contributed to.

No one marketing effort stands alone. Integrated marketing means you may have had a flurry of activity on one particular social platform or a lot of views on a particular video, but you don't put all your hope into that one piece of data. You look at all the marketing numbers together, see how they integrate, and make decisions for the firm based on the bigger picture. You're not blown about by every wind of data, distracted by the success of one popular blog post. That could send you off on a tangent and prevent you from achieving the goals you said were so important. Track the numbers, look at patterns, go back to your goals, share them with the team, and talk about what they mean.

Now let's look at some of the practical questions about the platforms themselves.

Which social media platforms will you use?

You will be tempted to follow one of two directions when looking at what social media platforms to use for your firm:

1. You'll be tempted to use the one you personally like the best.
2. You'll be tempted to use them all indiscriminately to get more reach.

Since your social media is not for you, choosing what platform to use is also not primarily about what you like or where you want to hang out or feel comfortable. Think about the type of people you want to work with most and look at where they spend their time. What platforms do they use? Where do most conversations happen? It isn't about blasting out content like confetti; it's about placing your content where the people who will appreciate it can read it.

LinkedIn and Twitter may feel more "professional" to you. Yes, there are fewer personal posts and more business-related topics on LinkedIn, especially. You may also feel like you get a lot of engagement on these platforms because other accountants are liking or commenting on your posts. However, unless other accountants are your ideal client, you need to pay attention to the platform being used by the kind of clients you want, even if it's one you don't feel very comfortable with right now. Otherwise, you're falling into the trap of feeling really good about yourself and not making progress of the kind you want.

It's okay to use a platform you personally enjoy, even if your ideal audience isn't there in droves yet. Remember what I discovered when I started using Instagram. I wanted to stretch myself, try something new, and learn different ways of sharing content besides linking to a blog post. Instagram is very visual, it's harder to include links to content, and it feels more personal. I kept using that as my core social because I liked it, and, as I shared before, I was surprised to discover the kind of accountants we love at PF were using it too.

It's still true. Often, those who use Insta tend to believe in their own creativity, enjoy connecting personal life and business, and love experimenting and new things. Some joined because it was new, some because they were disillusioned with the over-professionalised, over-salesy platforms full of the humble brag, the self-praise, the "and then I realised" sort of posts which only share hard things once the tough part is over. We know that's not how life and business happen. Social media is about meeting people where they are right now, not where they were one time in the distant past when they had the three toughest years of their life and never told anyone until they figured out how to break through.

You don't have to share the details of the toughest times of your life. It's okay to keep some things private, and I certainly believe in staying positive even when things seem dark. You'll know as an accountant when to share a mistake and when to simply fix it internally and move on. But the more you share the good and bad together, the triumphs and the fails, the wins and the losses, the confusions and the clarity, the more you connect with real human people. And those are people you'll be working with one day, people who will be more likely to share all of those things with you as you work together.

To figure out what platform your audience is on, do a little research. Nothing fancy, no six-hundred-page strategic report. Just go onto each platform and do a few searches with words and hashtags. If you work with dentists, look for dentists. Look for groups, networks, comments, posts, and pages. Are these your kind of people? Do they share the sort of things you find interesting? Look at the numbers. Are there more on this platform than that other one? Are there fewer on this one but they're more your type of client? Once you start to notice a platform where more of them are hanging out, having conversations, or connecting with each other, you hang out there too. Based on where they are spending time, try out a new platform. When you do, be like a child:

Be curious. What does this button do? How does that filter work? How many hashtags do people tend to use on this platform? What happens if you do this or that?

Try stuff. Press the button. Post something new or different, something you wouldn't normally post. See who responds, if anyone notices, or if you get more views or less.

Get things wrong. You're going to be tempted to do social perfectly or not at all. This doesn't work. The whole point of social is to give it a shot—be human, be real.

Let the team do this too. Let them be curious, try stuff, and get things wrong. Remember, this requires being a place of psychological safety.

There is an argument for your firm having a presence on all the socials, at least the Big Four: Facebook, Instagram, Twitter, LinkedIn. Simply being on them is not a guarantee of success, of course. You could post every day on all four platforms and get nowhere, especially if your content is boring or you don't have an audience in mind.

Begin with the platform preferred by the kind of clients you love to work with. This will be the one where you get the best kind of conversations with the kind of people you enjoy talking to. It's not about more but better. Just because you get a lot of leads from LinkedIn doesn't mean they're the best kind of clients who stay with you the longest. Do you get leads which turn into proposals leading to clients who stay with you for only six months and then leave? Look at the long game. Look at the lifetime value of the clients you have and how you built relationship with them. It wasn't built only on day one but on all the other days following. Look for patterns.

Wherever they are, be there. All the work you've been doing up to this point helps you know who you are and what you want to share. Understanding how social media platforms work and change affects how you get seen: the hashtags, the video formats, the type and length of posts, the best way to tag people, and the kind of images that fit your brand and the platform.

Remember the platforms change *all* the time. Every social platform is changing and adjusting itself constantly to reach its own goals. Instagram is not there to help you get business. Facebook doesn't really care if you work with people you love. They will do whatever the numbers tell them to do, even if you don't like it. Even if it means accounts with more followers are helped and small personal accounts are harmed. You're an accountant who really cares about your clients, and you want to work with people whose values and life match yours. The social platforms are products, and they're there to help themselves. Pay attention to the little details which will improve your visibility, and don't rely on them to stay the same. Be willing to adjust and adapt the way you use a platform. And no matter what those products do, stay focused on your own values and your own community. If you can use their platform to build community with real humans who work with you or may want to work with you in future, do it. If there's a better way, do that. Social doesn't get you business —you do.

. . .

Social media connects you to future team members too

In chapter 0, we talked about how marketing is not only for reaching potential new clients. The same applies to social media. What you share and where you share it affects the decision potential team members will make about applying to work with you and the relationship they'll have with you if you do hire them. Your social media posts help them understand who your firm really is and what it will be like when they join you. Show them what a day in the life of your firm or a particular team member is like. Remember what we learned in the website chapter: show, don't tell. Have other team members record videos. Show the content your team members have created and talk about the kind of clients you work with.

You create content for your prospects based on the questions they ask and what they want to know. Do the same for your ideal team member. What are they like? What kind of a person are they? What do they care about or want to know? What questions do they have about the hiring process or your firm? Answer those in blog posts, on website pages, in video, and on social media. That way, instead of replying to thousands of applicants with answers and emails, you can send a link to a piece of content which not only answers their question but also helps you discover what kind of a person they are. Are they willing to look around, research, and make an effort to get to know your website and social media accounts? Are they expecting you to do everything for them and make their life easy? Or are they ready to contribute and support the work of the firm?

People who are considering working for you will absolutely check you and the firm out on all the social platforms. They'll notice what you say and don't. How you post, who posts, and how that matches (or doesn't) with what you express on your website. I've lost count of the number of people who have applied to work with PF and said in the interview process, "It seems like you really live out your values. They're not only words on a website page." They say it cautiously and carefully because they've been burned before. But as they come to the end of our quite extensive seven-stage hiring process, they are beginning to see we are serious about our values. We do live by them. We do hire and fire by them. We talk about them, incorporate them into our daily language, we mention them in social posts, and we record videos reflecting them. Social, like all your marketing, is an opportunity for any prospective client or team member to see patterns of who you all are as a firm. And what they see will help them decide whether they move forward quickly or at all.

Automating social media doesn't solve all your problems

Automating social media, like any other automation, isn't going to do your marketing for you. That idea feels like the ultimate dream. Your posts are created ahead of time, crafted perfectly with images and hashtags and content, and go out on a drip feed without you having to notice or think about it. Social posts appear like magic on every platform, people see and engage with them, and you don't have to do anything. Sounds nice, but it's unrealistic, and it's not really what social media is for.

You can still use automation. It can be a good way to ensure consistency of posting. But don't look to automated social posting to solve all your social or marketing problems. You can only automate what you are already doing really well. Automation doesn't tell you what to say or how the system needs to run. When we talked about automating your onboarding system, we recognised it's not about crafting the perfect system straight away. You make slight adjustments to your system with each new client. The same approach applies to social media automation. Automating social posts won't do all the work for you; it doesn't tell you what to post or how to reply to someone else's post. It doesn't have conversations for you. It simply streamlines the process once you've already tried and tested social and have seen what works and what doesn't. It allows you to have the conversations you want to have.

Social is about actually connecting you with humans. Even if you perfectly automate every post you want to share, you still need to reply to comments, ask more questions, follow their account, and engage with their content too. That's how you actually use social as a back-and-forth conversation. It's like a tennis match. I don't know a great deal about tennis, but I do know if one person hits the ball over the net repeatedly, and the other person stands there and drops them into a bucket on the other side, there's no game. If you're serving your social media posts and they're landing in the corner, no one is going to gather around in excitement to see what happens next. There's no game. It's not social.

When it comes to automation tools for social media, it really doesn't matter which one you use. Accountants, especially, can get caught in a cycle of attempted perfection, starting out with one software and getting distracted by another. When you're nearly ready to use one software, an article comes out about the greatest social media automation of all time, and you turn from what you were doing to try this new one instead. It's the "squirrel!" approach, and it doesn't work. No tool will work perfectly for anyone.

No matter which tool you choose, it will do what it's designed for, and it will handle some things really well. It will also be weak in other areas or be missing entire features you wished for. Think about all those hours you spend trying to find the perfect app. Those hours could be used to prepare better content. You could be talking with the actual people you're trying to connect with, or training your team to post on behalf of the firm or on their own, or learning more about it yourself. Do a little research and find a few apps which seem to have most of the features you want. Then pick one, start using it, and keep using it consistently. Make it work for you with a few adjustments or find a way to connect other apps together.

ROI: How do I get a return on my social media efforts?

The ultimate ROI question. Why bother with social media if it's not delivering leads? We'll talk about tracking and ROI in the last chapter. But, as with every other element of marketing, we're back to the reminder that social media (like every other element of marketing) is only one element within the marketing web. Instead of relying solely on social to bring in leads by itself, pay attention to how it ties in with all your other marketing. Instead of asking how many leads you got from Facebook or from Twitter, track all your numbers and consider them in an integrated way.

Once you start tracking *all* the numbers, you can look for patterns. You might say, "Oh look, we were really active on Twitter for that event a few months ago, and the number of proposals we put out in the three months following increased. Is that connected?" This way, rather than simply saying Twitter works, Facebook ads are useless, or email is or isn't worthwhile, you can look at the integrated numbers and make better marketing decisions.

Ads on social platforms can sound really appealing for the quick win. Our experience for accountants is that ads are usually tried too soon. You're turning to ads to solve a problem you've identified as "getting more leads." And while ads can be an excellent way to gain visibility, build awareness, and bring in leads and sales, they don't work in isolation from the content you're sharing and all the other marketing you're doing.

And what if you don't really need more leads? What if you need better ones? What if, instead of getting double the amount of leads—many of which are the wrong kind, not ready to work with you, not ready to pay, not looking for you specifically but just any random accountant—you got fewer leads of the right kind for you? That means going back to your audience. Your goals, your brand, and your cornerstone. This is why we're talking about social media now rather than at the beginning. If you approach social without having worked through the questions within chapters 1 through 10, you've got some work to do.

I suggest waiting until you have been posting and sharing consistently for one to two years before you even consider social ads.

When social campaigns or ads seem to fail, it's often because the proper foundations aren't set. It's like building a website and suddenly wondering what words you're going to put on it. A website isn't going to be effective because you picked a nice-looking layout and then stuffed some words into the sections. It's going to have an impact when it's been crafted around your buyer's journey, including their problems, their issues, and your stories and solutions. Similarly, a social media campaign won't work if you decide to run some ads simply by picking an image and some words to go in the ad. It's got to be built around your overall purpose and connect with every other part of your marketing.

You might have gone through the same thing with SEO to help your website be found. SEO isn't a magic trick to get more leads. Both SEO and ads can support all your marketing, but if you put all the pressure of your marketing upon them, they will eventually collapse, even if they seem to work well for a time. What are you SEOing? What goes in the ads? The content you've created is your best support.

The best thing you can do with your time and investment is to create a library of good content, share it organically, and track your analytics to see what's most popular. Social ads are not an easy win. Ads of any kind, particularly Facebook ads, are extremely comprehensive and can require expert support. We've seen so many accountants spend time and money on ads and get frustrated with the results or lack thereof because it's too much pressure. Too salesy. Trust must be built first. A funnel must be clearly identified. Use the Buyer Progression Model. And then try and test, over and over, until you identify what works and what doesn't.

The what-ifs of social media for accountants

Even if you feel ready to make some effort on social media, you have your own doubts and fears. In the same way your prospects have things they aren't sure of in relation to finding a new accountant, you have things you're not sure about in relation to helping them find you.

What if I'm nervous or confused about social media? Being nervous and confused is part of anything new. Remember your first day at your first job? Being a parent for the first time? Starting a new relationship? It's okay to be unsure. The key is to admit this is the real problem, whether with social media or any other area of marketing. You're not avoiding social because it doesn't work or because there aren't enough case studies of success. It's unknown territory for you, and the way to feel more comfortable is to start moving into that territory rather than standing on the edges looking in. Learn about it. Use it. Start tracking all the numbers. Encourage the team to use it. Get a few small results, and look at where those came from. When you see how social doesn't stand alone and how writing blog posts, recording video, updating your website, and rebranding are all tied in, you begin to get more comfortable with it.

What if I'm boring? I don't have anything interesting to share. This circles back to the "I'm an accountant, not a creative" lie. You've believed for too long you are boring, and you have been staring at yourself and your own imagined inadequacies instead of looking at your clients and the amazing results you've helped them achieve. You are interesting, and helpful, and creative. You are. And you know it's true because your clients like you, appreciate you, and are grateful for the work you do for them. If you're wondering how to share on social and make it interesting, you're focusing too much on yourself. Practice sharing exactly who *you* and your firm actually are without worrying about how interesting they may find you. It's not about giving the shiny, pretty version all the time, and it's definitely not about presenting a stuffy "professional" viewpoint. You don't want everything tied up neatly and delivered safely so not one person could ever be offended. Talk about some personal things. Share real photographs. Give an opinion. Be interested in other people. See what others are sharing on social, and do something similar with your own spin on it.

Fear will still be involved in all of those items. You'll be afraid to have too strong of an opinion; after all, what if someone disagrees? What if it doesn't seem professional to share a personal photo? What if a new idea doesn't work? Part of leaning into your creativity is accepting there will be some fear involved. I'm not going to pretend that the greater the fear, the greater the creativity; that's not how it works. But if you've never once felt a little worry before pressing the share button, it's possible you're not being creative. You're simply being safe.

What if I'm too busy and forget to post regularly? Maybe you've done some social, but it's been pretty ad hoc. You do it now and then or get a burst of enthusiasm that quickly fades away. How do you keep it up day after day? Being involved personally in your own social is good (and I'd argue critical), but it's not enough. Having a system of posting on a regular basis, either daily or a few times weekly, helps keep the visibility going without relying entirely on you. This means having someone either inside or outside the firm who does this for you. That way, you have consistency even if you're busy, confused, sick, or forgetful. And when you do post or your team does, it's a nice top-up to what's already being done. Create a social content calendar (there are templates available in the PF Lab) and spend a few hours writing out posts you'll share later. You can use the social platform itself or an automation tool to prepare these ahead of time. Just be sure to double-check the posts before they go out. What seemed really relevant on Monday might not come across the same by the time it goes out on Friday. And be alert to what's going on in the world and how your scheduled posts could conflict with that.

What if it doesn't work? Social media is useful and helpful for thousands of businesses, including accountants. The question is not whether it works but how it works for you. When we ask Accelerator members to share what they learned and got from social, they discovered, to their surprise, that social was a helpful part of their integrated marketing. One member, George, said he was getting more leads than he normally would at that time of year, and when he reviewed the elements which had changed, he noticed it was the changes made to the website and their social media activity. It felt like a good payback for the marketing actions he was doing, specifically in relation to social. Another member, Vanessa, said what helped her the most was being reminded it's okay to just be yourself in marketing—not to worry about what to say, how to say it, and how to edit everything you put out. "We began making our marketing more conversational," she said, "specifically on social media. As a result, our new clients have been telling us they chose us as their accountant because they found us to be friendly and helpful, and they liked our social media posts."

When your approach to social is focused on your clients and their needs, on engagement and connection, you get more than new leads. You get confidence, new skills, and a clearer understanding of the people you connect with.

Finally, be aware of the invisible followers. They see your videos and posts, understand who you and your firm are, consider working with you . . . and you don't even know they exist. They haven't commented, or liked, or reshared, or done anything to reveal they are there. But one day, when they're ready, they'll be in touch because they've done their homework and they know who you are. There are so many more people who are seeing what you're sharing than you realise, and they don't appear in your numbers. When they do finally sign up, notice what they say about your marketing and your social. Keep going for those invisible followers too.

Conclusion

You don't have to use Instagram as an accountant. You don't have to use LinkedIn. But social media isn't about what you like or prefer; it's about being present so you're findable by the right kind of people. Social platforms rise and fall with the wind, and it's not about being loyal to a platform or even using it in a particular way. It's being present where your future buyer is also present. Be ready for conversation and for connection so they can buy the moment they are ready.

And now you're ready for the last and final piece of the puzzle, the twelfth piece: your marketing campaigns.

CHAPTER 12
CAMPAIGNS

In the film *Karate Kid* (the original one from 1984), a young, energetic kid goes to Mr. Miyagi, ready to learn karate.

The kid, Daniel, imagines great things from his training. He'll be wearing a *gi* and learning kicks and strikes. It might take a few sessions, but he'll soon be ready to defend himself against the school bullies the next time they come after him. Instead, when he shows up at Mr. Miyagi's home, he is given a sponge and pointed in the direction of some old cars to wash and then wax. Days later, he's given a paintbrush and a fence to whitewash. Later still, he's given a sander and a wooden floor to sand.

To give Daniel credit, he does these things. Faithfully, consistently. Up, down. Side, side. Wax on, wax off. But after a while, he gets really frustrated. This is going nowhere! He came to learn karate, and he's doing household chores! What a waste of time! When does the real karate start? And then Mr. Miyagi shows him the strength of the small patterns he's been building, hour after hour, day after day.

Up, down. Side, side. Wax on, wax off.

Suddenly Daniel is blocking a punch and stopping a hand about to strike him. He's doing karate. And he didn't even know he could.

. . .

These marketing elements have been teaching you how to build a campaign

The marketing elements we've been discussing in this book feel a little like household chores. You're making lists of the questions clients ask. Writing blog posts. Recording videos. Posting on social. It feels disconnected. These are such small, almost insignificant things. When are you going to blow everyone away with your amazing marketing skills? When will the prospects begin appearing out of nowhere on a drip feed? When will forms be filled in on your website over a weekend or random strangers sign up for your webinars or live events? When does the real marketing start?

Congratulations, small grasshopper. The little elements of working on your audience, blogging, writing emails, posting on social . . . these are your patterns.

Up, down. Blog post, video.

Side, side. Social post, email.

Wax on, wax off. Website page, resources.

When it comes to building a marketing campaign, there is nothing new I need to share; you have all the elements now. A marketing campaign is made up of the previous eleven elements. Whether it's a few days or a few weeks long—or something you're sharing over a longer period of time—no matter the size or type of campaign, you consider each of the elements in order. And voila! You have a campaign.

Let's say you have a particular service you know is useful for your clients, like management accounts. You know it will help them understand their numbers, grow their business, and get the profit they want. You want more clients to know this service exists and to sign up for it. Whenever you've mentioned it in passing, some clients have been interested, and others don't seem to think they need it. When you considered a marketing campaign for this service in the past, you started with the service itself. It's about management reporting. It costs this much. It gives clients these things each month. You figure you need to prepare some emails and a website page.

Now you know better. Wax on, wax off.

Start with Chapter 1: Audience.

You ask yourself exactly who this campaign is for, what they are like, and what they care about. You think about your clients, particularly that one whose profits fluctuate every month and who never seems to know how business will go. They have hundreds of unpaid invoices sitting in someone else's bank account. They figure that's the way business works, and they feel embarrassed to chase the money because they've never had to do that before. They keep buying what they aren't yet able to afford, and there goes their profit again. Meanwhile, they'd love to hire more employees, but they keep doing the work them-selves, and they're exhausted.

Oh look, you've naturally moved to Chapter 2: Issues.

You're considering what this person, this audience, is facing. The wrongs which need righted, and what's really troubling them. In their minds, it's not management accounts they need; they need to know where their money is coming from and where it's going and when so they can plan for the life and business they dream of.

Documenting the answers to each of the eleven elements in order *is* your marketing campaign. A marketing campaign is

a series of focused marketing efforts

on the same topic

with one clear call to action

for a defined period of time.

Let's build a campaign now.

Example marketing campaign: Management accounts service

A marketing campaign might feel like it must include a series of emails or social media ads. But a campaign (like all marketing) doesn't begin with the platform or tools you use; it begins with the people you want to reach and the problems they are facing, problems you are able to solve. You could build a campaign lasting exactly one day. Or one month. Or a year. The length will depend on your call to action, specifically what you want them to do and how you help them see the need for it.

Above all, keep your audience in mind. Despite the fact you are running this campaign to get people to download your guide or help the right kind of clients find you, the campaign is not for you. It's for them. They are the reason and focus.

Back to the management accounts. Yes, you want more clients to sign up for this service. But the campaign isn't about the service per se; it's about why they need it and the value they'll receive. You could run a campaign to promote an event for clients so they understand growth and profit better. You could promote downloads of a PDF guide which explains what business owners need to understand about growth and profits so they sign up for management accounts to learn how.

As we review the first eleven elements of marketing in this chapter, let's use the management accounts campaign as our example. Following this, I'll show how you can apply this same campaign principle to literally anything you want to share, feature, or promote.

Before we begin looking at your audience for this example campaign, take a moment to step back to a question you must answer in order for your campaign to be successful: What is the *one thing* you want them to *do*?

The "call to action" sounds obvious. You want them to sign up for management accounts services. Easy. Next question, please. Wax on, wax off.

Hold fire there, tiger. The way you answer this will change your entire campaign. To help you determine what your one campaign action is, answer the following questions:

What is the one action you ultimately want them to take? If you want them to sign up for management accounts, what are the steps of the buyer progression model they will follow along the way? They could download a growth and profit PDF guide, have a discovery call, or sign up for a growth and profit strategy session. They may choose to work with you monthly on getting management accounts, strategic support, and forecasts. It's tempting to answer, "Yes, all of these, please. Whatever they want," but that doesn't help you build a successful campaign.

A good marketing campaign divides. It draws in the right people for you and sends away the ones who aren't a fit. It asks people to make one initial decision and leads them on a journey to the one action you believe is the best. If your ultimate action for the event is someone signing a proposal for monthly services, let's look at the timeline of actions they take which will lead them to sign up:

- Be aware of your growth and profit guide
- Download the guide
- Get and read the emails and follow-up (which mention a discovery call)
- Register for a discovery call
- Attend the call
- Book a growth and profit strategy session
- Attend strategy session
- Agree to a proposal meeting
- Attend proposal meeting and review together
- Sign proposal to work with you monthly

This "funnel" of people who are genuinely interested will get smaller and smaller as you get towards the end. Some people will be aware of your guide and never download it. Some will download it and never read it or notice what's next. That's okay. You know that's how marketing works. You don't expect every person who is aware of your guide to sign up for a monthly retainer; after all, it's unlikely every single person will be your ideal client. Your marketing campaign is doing its job and dividing out those who are your people and those who aren't.

Some will move fast. They may never see the guide at all but move directly to a call with you. Some will move more slowly, absorbing information and building relationship over a period of months or years. Either way, you've got all the pieces to let them decide at the speed they want to.

They still, always, have a choice. They can choose not to download your guide. They could ignore your emails and posts, or they could sign up and never read the guide. But it's not your job to decide what they will do; it's to present them with the very best option and explain why it matters so much. Knowing the ultimate action you want them to take helps your marketing campaign be specific and get exactly what you are asking for. Some people will take that ultimate action; some won't. But if you're vague, far fewer people will take that action because they don't know what they're supposed to do.

Thinking about the ultimate action you want them to take is already changing how you think about promoting your growth and profit guide. What name will you give it? Is "Growth and Profit Guide" enough to help them understand what they get from it and who it's for? Does it need to be more specific? Will your audience actually download and read a guide, or would a video be a better introductory piece of content?

You're already moving into the marketing campaign elements, so let's start building it in order.

1. Audience: Know *exactly* who your campaign is for

For most campaigns you run as an accountant, you want to include your clients. If you don't have any yet, you're running it for the kind of clients you want to have. Be clear who exactly this is for. It's a nice idea for the guide to be open to "everyone," but content for everyone could end up being for no one. A good marketing campaign divides. So who is your guide for?

Consider what kind of people it's written for. Will they own a certain type of business? Are they part of an industry, a niche? You could start by saying it's for literally all types of clients: free-lancers, limited companies, personal tax returns, and jointly-owned businesses. Then you can think about the ultimate goal of your campaign (the monthly management accounts). You realise pretty quickly some of these people will not be the best fit for the kind of monthly retainer you most want to sell, so they aren't the ideal audience for this campaign. This brings you down to, say, owners of limited companies.

The next question: *All* limited companies? Or is there a particular type of person or company who would most benefit from this kind of service you're offering? Let's say you realise the owners you most enjoy working with, who you've helped get the best results for, and who stay with you the longest and bring your firm the most profit are owners of digital creative agencies whose sales are at least £1M per year. Maybe it's even more specific: female owners of this kind of agency. Or people who have owned their agency for at least five years. Or those who have at least ten employees. It's your call, depending on who you're best placed to serve. But the more you know about who *exactly* you want to work with regularly, the more you can craft content which appeals to them.

Compare these two messages:

- "Growth and Profit Guide for Business Owners"
- "Growing but Not Profitable: An Intensive Plan for Agency Owners Who Are Tired of the Grind"

The first is generic; it could apply to anybody, and therefore it isn't wildly appealing to the people you most want to attend. The second is specific, applies only to a particular audience, and will be far more likely to attract only those people. Yes, it does mean you'd get fewer (if any) downloads from those who aren't agency owners. But which is better? Having four hundred people download your guide, maybe four of which will be your ideal audience, or having only four people download it but all of whom are exactly who you want to speak to *and* who request the strategy call after?

Now we know exactly who we wish to reach and ultimately work with, we move to the problems they are facing.

2. Issues: Know the problems this campaign solves for them

Thinking about the problems this audience faces helps you create the content you need for your campaign. You'll know what goes in your guide, the videos you'll record, and the emails you'll send. You might start by saying their agency is growing but not profitable (hence our very specific guide name). But the root problem—the issue behind the issue—is your reason to reach these people in the first place. It will give you focused wording and will help you point to the solution.

Your ideal business owner might have an agency with high sales but isn't making a good profit. There are multiple reasons behind this. Perhaps their team isn't efficient or is overservicing. Their prices are too low. You dig into the reason behind the reason, thinking about things like:

- The team's heavy workload, which comes from . . .
- The team overservicing clients to make sure they're happy and stay with the agency . . .
- Which results in pressure to get more business and hire more people . . .
- Who overservice, too, like the rest of the team . . .
- Which results in a more overworked team who aren't sure how much time to spend on any given project . . .
- And no one knows which clients or projects are profitable.

The core problem is not a need to hire or get more sales. Project profitability is not being monitored, and it's not clear who is taking responsibility for that. The solution to help them track this profitability and connect it to business success is building this into their management accounts and reporting. That means working with you on a monthly basis.

Look at the feelings your client and their team are experiencing. They're worried, busy, overwhelmed, and rushed. They feel like it will never get better. They're not sure where to begin or what to try. Meanwhile, they're frustrated with the team and taking it out on them, and all of this results in resenting new business instead of being excited about it.

Considering these things will help you explain how your solution solves these issues. It could also cause you to question what the best first step is. Do they need a monthly service to review their management accounts with you? Or do they need a review of their pricing and projects first?

Your decision depends on the clients you work with and want to work with. Focus on them and no one else.

3. Cornerstone: Identify the asset which will form the basis for your campaign

Your firm cornerstone is based on your values, your way, and your client journey. For a campaign, build an asset (or use an existing asset) focused on the issues your audience is having. Like a cornerstone, it sits at the heart and holds the campaign together. Often, the best asset is a graphic image (i.e., a map, diagram, path), and then the "stackable content" element comes into play. You have one asset and share messages from this asset in social media posts, a series of emails, a website page, videos, and blog posts.

Each of these stackable content pieces support and add value to the asset itself. If your asset is a graphic showing the correlation between growth and profit for creative agencies over a ten-year period, you could write a blog post explaining in detail what happens in years one to three, years four to six, and years seven to ten. If your graphic highlights the challenges arising in a particular year, you could create an individual social post for each challenge.

Whatever you create, your campaign asset and its supporting content need to give *enormous* value. Give away information (the guide), and if they need implementation (time with you to work on how this applies to their business specifically), they book a discovery call. The asset intrigues them enough to take a small action and still leaves enough questions about how it applies to their business to encourage them to take another action when they're ready. In your asset, show them what is possible. Give them either a taste of success or help them get more clarity on the problem. Either way, they'll realise this is not your first rodeo and will be intrigued to find out more.

Think about the growth and profit guide you are creating in light of what we've covered here. What can you share which will help them see the real problem they are facing, which is not an inefficient team but a lack of financial maturity? What image or graphic reflects this progression, and how can you help them see where they are in it? The best way to start this asset is to simply sketch or draw it out with pen and paper, on a tablet, or on a whiteboard. Think about the stage they're in first and then which one comes after that. Consider how they build the financial strength to get to the place of healthy profit. As you do this, your initial "Growth and Profit" guide title begins to sound rather vague. Think about your audience again, not in general terms but as one specific person you know who runs a creative agency and has this problem. What would help her to understand where she is and where she's going? And where can she go with your help? Sketching these lines is the rough draft; you can make it beautiful in the branding and design sections.

4. Brand: Make sure everything in your campaign is on-brand

Every action in your campaign must reflect your firm's

brand. This doesn't merely mean the right colours, fonts, and styles. It means being confident all the following are true:

Audience: The people you're talking to will become the very best clients for your firm. The guide is for them and only them. It gives them practical help straight away and encourages them to take further action by booking a call with you.

Design: The core asset has been professionally designed along your brand guidelines.

Tone of voice: The words you use fit your style, the way you and your team speak, and the "personality" of your firm. The title matches this too. If you have a positive, optimistic brand, you'll want to say things like "Your growth is encouraging. Now use it to build profits" instead of "Fourteen things you shouldn't be doing in your agency."

Feelings: You've considered how they will feel and brought those feelings and emotions into your marketing. If they are feeling worried, exhausted, overworked, and frustrated, they might not feel like downloading a forty-two-page PDF guide. Think about that when writing your content.

Values: Look at your entire campaign in light of your firm's documented pillars or values. If your values include family, freedom, and curiosity, make sure to refer to these in your guide. Talk about how the decisions they'll make affect their family and the freedom to make their own choices. Encourage them to be curious and ask questions.

Now it's time to turn to the campaign items to be designed so all these brand elements are felt. Design is an extension of your brand.

5. Design: Be clear about what needs to be designed for your campaign

Depending on the complexity of your campaign, some elements may be professionally designed, and others you can put together yourself. Remember, good design doesn't make people say, "Wow, that's been designed so well! It looks really good!" Instead, it helps people connect with the message and take action. Your designer needs to understand all twelve elements of your campaign and how they hold together. For our example campaign, you may need one or two of these:

"Financial strength" graphic: Take your sketch and bring it to life with a designer. Remember, simple is clear. The more complex it is, the harder it is for your prospect to understand it quickly. You can supplement it with other content so they learn more in pieces.

PDF guide: Include the financial strength graphic in this guide. Explain more about each stage of the journey, describing the risks of going off the path and the successes they'll have when they build their agency's financial strength. Have this guide designed to match your graphic using your firm's branding guidelines.

Videos: Record a few short videos talking through the key points of the guide. You've already got your script in the content of the guide. Break it up into three or four short videos so they can read the guide or listen to you talking it through.

Social media images: Have your designer create a series of images reflecting the core problems from the graphic or pulling out quotes from your guide. Talk more about who the guide is for and what's in it than about the fact you have a guide. You're not promoting the guide as much as you are sharing the issues and problems your audience is facing, and the guide is presented as a next step to help them.

6. Website: Create a website page as the foundation to your campaign

Regardless of the size of the campaign, it would be rare to have a marketing campaign without a core website page at its heart. In this example, create a page explaining what's in the PDF guide, who it's for, and what happens once they download it. Here are some elements you could include on your guide page:

Header: "When your agency is busy but never seems to catch up: A guide for agency owners who want to discover their missing profitability"

Call to action: Download now

Main message: "You and your team are making sales and delivering great work, but you're not as profitable as you know you could be."

Other messages could include a "This is for you if" list based on the issues we looked at earlier:

- You're the owner of an agency making £500K–£5M in sales.
- You have a team of at least ten people.
- You're growing every year, but profits have gone stagnant.
- You feel exhausted and don't have time to work on the business.
- You are pulled into project work more often than you'd like.
- You experience a "feast or famine" seasonality in your agency.

Results: Share stories from existing clients working with you who are getting management accounts monthly and any related successes.

Quotes and stories: Pull out a few of the best statements or ideas from the guide. Don't go for the clickbait approach. Give away the best parts to help them feel more comfortable about downloading it.

Video: Create a short video sharing where these issues come from, how you know what they're feeling, and what this guide will help them understand. Within the video, encourage them to download the guide.

Create a thank-you page which will appear once they download the guide. This page can include the guide itself, and you could even include the next step (the discovery call) after the guide. Be careful of sharing too many actions for your thank-you page, or they could feel overwhelmed and take no action at all.

Your page becomes the core of your campaign, bringing together the other campaign elements. It talks to your audience about the issues they're facing, provides a link to your corner-stone piece of content, and includes design and branding to fit your firm. It will also be the core for the next several steps, all of which point back to your website page and your asset.

7. Email: Write the emails you will be sending

If you have an email list already, pause and think before you start firing out emails to all three hundred, three thousand, or three hundred thousand people on it. Who *really* needs to receive these emails? Even if you've identified clients and prospects, you may still need to categorise agency owners or non-agency owners. Now is a good time to do that. This way, you can send an invite for your new guide as well as send out follow-up emails and know who was interested, who never saw it, who clicked the link, who signed up, and other data. This will help for future content too.

While you're doing that, start preparing the content for your emails. It's tempting to spend ages making the email look nice and just have the text say "We have a great new guide. Here is the link to download it." But that kind of content is all about you. Go back to your audience and their issues. Prepare a series of emails to introduce the reason for the PDF guide and what's in it.

It's helpful to have your website page and your guide created first because those provide content you can use for your emails. Here's a suggestion of the timing and content you could include over a one-month period:

Day 1: "Experiencing this issue in your agency?" Mention issues or feelings they have. Explain the guide is coming soon.

Day 5: Choose an issue from the PDF guide and include a video about it.

Day 7: Guide now available! Remember these issues? Download guide now.

Day 10: Numbers you need to know which will turn your profits around.

Day 15: Book a discovery call to apply the points from this guide to your business.

Day 20: Story of a client who implemented this (include specific results—i.e., their profits increased by $x\%$, which allowed them to do y).

Day 30: Know someone else who has these issues too? Download the guide and share it with another agency owner now.

Not everyone will see all your emails, and some won't see them at all, which is why you will share your guide in ways other than email.

8. Follow-up: Plan how you will follow up leads to your campaign

At least 50 percent of the effort into your campaign needs to go into follow-up. Think about it. Why go through the effort and pain of all this work— strategising, preparing content, creating website pages, getting the PDF guide and social posts designed, and recording videos—if you're not going to make the most of each person who has shown interest?

Prepare your follow-up before you kick off your campaign. Once it starts, it will either be wildly successful and you'll have lots of leads, or it will go slowly and you'll feel discouraged and need to adjust things for a while. Follow-up isn't sending a few emails the day or two after they download the guide; it's a steady stream of contact so they don't forget about you.

Follow a similar structure to the "guide is available" emails you already created, and think about how they'll feel and what you want them to do next once they've downloaded it. You can prepare emails for different categories of people:

- Downloaded guide and booked discovery call
- Only downloaded guide
- Expressed interest but did not download guide

The content and call to action of these emails will vary depending on the people you send them to. If there are only a few people, send personal emails and include a personalised video. Keep promoting the guide in a variety of ways, and remember you're playing the long game.

9. Blogging: Identify what blog content will drive people to your campaign

Blogging is a double win; the content you create in blog posts relates specifically to your short-term campaign and remains longer-term content which can be referred back to in the future. Writing a blog post about the PDF guide you're providing may seem like duplicate content, but everyone absorbs content differently. Here's an example of blog post topics useful for our example campaign and beyond:

- How overservicing is costing your agency profits (and how easy of a trap it is to fall into)
- When your agency is busy, hiring more people may not be the answer
- Tracking profitability by project: A how-to guide
- Why getting more clients could be making your cash problem worse, not better

The titles are based on the issues you identified. As you write, you may find the content you thought would fit into one blog post is actually three separate posts with different topics.

Your call to action in the blog post will drive the reader to download the guide. Remember, the CTA doesn't have to be at the end. Those who want to download the resource will. Those who don't want to will skip it, find help from your post, and take action themselves. They may come back later.

As your campaign continues, you can write blog posts about the issues and questions raised during the discovery calls you hold. This includes any subjects you hadn't thought about or hadn't worded in a particular way. Only use content from those who are your kind of people—the kind of clients you want to have.

10. Video: Plan the videos you'll record to help your buyer understand and sign up

Creating video follows a similar pattern as blog posts and other content. Some videos will be about the issues they face, some will be about the PDF guide itself, and some will tell success stories from clients who are getting this service now. Before you press record, stop to think about the purpose of the video, who it's for, its length, and where it will be posted.

A one-minute "guide available now" video is a lot different than a ten-minute "think about these things in your agency" video. You could record what you feel is the greatest video *ever* and discover it's thirty seconds too long to fit on the social platform you wanted to share it on, so you have to spend time editing it, have someone edit for you, or even rerecord the video. The more time you prepare, the better your videos are.

You don't have to share the entire guide before they download it, but the more you share, the more likely they are to take action. Think about your own motivations. Why do we keep going to concerts when we know exactly what song they're going to sing and we know the words? What motivates us to read a book when the author has shared most of the key points on a podcast? We want to know more, go deeper, and maybe even meet the author or others who loved this content. Share as much as you like about what's in the guide and why you created it. If someone gets so much from the guide that they do all the work themselves and have no desire to connect with your firm or get help, they weren't your people anyway and would never have become a client. Or they'd have been quite a difficult client because they only wanted free information they could apply on their own.

11. Social media: Share your campaign with the world

Everything you create within your campaign (i.e., website pages, blog posts, videos) can be shared on social media to reach the audience you've identified earlier on. In our example, you could share social posts mentioning creative agencies, creatives, and agency owners particularly. Use hashtags relevant to their industry or needs. Tag agency owners or groups you know personally when it's relevant to them. Follow agencies or groups, and share their content too.

You could create a private social group for clients and share more detailed content there, or run an online or in-person session to discuss it further. Don't rely on your mass emails or social posts to reach everyone. People may see the content and wish to sign up, but then they get distracted or busy.

Use everything you learned from the social media chapter to apply to your guide specifically. Write out content for your social posts ahead of time. Keep the content of your posts focused on your audience even when you're tempted to say things like "Our growth and profit guide is available now for download" or "New guide available for agency owners." Those statements are focused on you and getting downloads for your PDF guide, which isn't helpful for your audience. Create posts about them— their issues, their feelings, and the solutions you'll be talking about.

This is also why social media is number eleven of the twelve elements; once you've created content for emails, blog posts, and video, you've got 90 percent of what you need to share good-quality social posts about your guide. You don't really need to write much at all. You simply need to take the content you've already created and adapt it for the right length and style of social posts. Include imagery you've created in the design stage of your campaign.

Once your prepared social posts are ready, combine them with off-the-cuff posts by yourself and the team. Sometimes random, last-minute posts get the most engagement and interest, although this could be the cumulative result of the posts you've been sending in advance. If a client mentions how useful the guide was, share their comments (with their permission, of course). If you have a meeting with a client on these issues, tell a little about it and mention the guide: "Met with a client today who realised their most profitable product wasn't what they thought because . . ."

As you post on social, you'll be wondering whether it's doing any good. Or whether your entire campaign (which is the twelfth marketing element) is doing any good. It's time to talk about bonus element thirteen, tracking.

13. Tracking: Seeing the results of your campaign

While we'll talk about the overall tracking you need to be doing for all the marketing your firm is doing in the next chapter, you'll also track numbers for your specific campaign. Even if an individual campaign does not seem as successful as you hoped, it can still contribute to your firm's overall marketing success. Perhaps forty people downloaded your guide, ten requested a discovery call, five showed up, and one signed up for monthly management accounts. But how do you know what's going on with the other thirty-nine? Some aren't ready. Some need more information. Some will refer you to others. It's a long-term ROI game you're playing. Trying to figure out if this one thing worked instantly or not is a recipe for disappointment because you're only looking at one angle. Work out your own buyer cycle. If, on average, it takes them six to twelve months to sign up with your firm, you may still have a whole year of marketing to do before they're fully ready.

In our example, you could record some of these numbers. Some will be easy to find, and others will take time to gather. This is why tracking your marketing numbers consistently in all areas of marketing is so valuable. When you run a specific campaign, you don't have to dig for the numbers; they're already there.

- Number of asset downloads
- Social media likes, shares, comments, posts
- Registrations of interest (for this or other content)
- Video views
- Blog posts written
- Emails sent (including open rate, click rate, actions taken)
- Website analytics (visitors to page, bounce rate, percentage who took action)
- Discovery calls booked
- Proposals created (number and value)
- Proposals accepted

In one sense, no marketing campaign is ever worthless. Even if no one downloaded your guide at all, you can look at what you did and when you did it—and learn how to adapt it so it's more successful next time. If your campaign brings all the wrong kinds of leads, it has worth in helping you understand what you need to change.

Other kinds of marketing campaigns

We've successfully applied all twelve of the content marketing elements to one example: an individual monthly management accounts service and guide campaign. Congratulations!

I'd let you sit for a moment and bask in the glory of this campaign we created together, but as I'm sure you've realised, this is merely one campaign of many.

Even the shortest campaign will at least briefly consider the other eleven elements. You could be throwing around an idea in a team meet and decide to feature a new app and tell all your clients about it. Before you all say "Yeah, great idea. Let's send that email," stop and check yourself and your campaign for just a moment. Who exactly is this app for? What kinds of issues are clients having which this app will solve? How will it do that? Is there an asset you have already developed which relates to it, or could you sketch one out very quickly? You could build a miniature campaign using these elements in minutes, and it will be far more effective than something focused on you, your firm, and your service. A campaign is not for you.

Here are several campaign examples. Each one shares what you'll be tempted to focus on and what to do instead. Turn your gaze outward to the client (or future client) experiencing the campaign.

Niche or industry focus campaign

Temptation: Worry you'll alienate all your other clients (the ones who aren't in that niche or industry)

Instead: Start small, start safe. Focus on this niche in a small way with a website page, an event, a few blog posts, or videos, and see how it goes. Those it doesn't relate to will simply not see it.

Asset campaign (guide, course, training, book)

Temptation: Presume others will see your campaign and instantly recognise how amazing it is and want it, because *you* have been working on it for ages and you're proud of it and know how valuable it is.

Instead: Remember it took you weeks or months or even years to build this. It could take them an equal amount of time to begin to see how valuable it is, how it relates to them, and how it helps them. Be consistent, be patient, and keep going.

Hiring campaign

Temptation: Only kick this campaign off when you desperately need to hire someone, and then stop when you find the right person.

Instead: Always be hiring. Have a continual campaign which keeps your firm top of mind, and build smaller individual campaigns for specific roles. Start them before they're needed; you'll be glad you did.

You can build a campaign yourself using your workbook or join the Accelerator coaching group to connect with other accountants like you. You can also get reviews of your campaign content.

Conclusion

You are ready, small grasshopper.

Yes, there is more learning ahead. You know now you are creative, and you are leaning into it. You have the core elements, and you will build on them over the years. Platforms, tools, and apps will change. You, your accounting firm, the people in it, and the people you serve will change. There is more to learn about your own creativity, involving your team, and turning your content into assets.

But you have what you need to begin. The Karate Kid had wax on, wax off. Up, down. Side, side.

You have these principles to guide you:

- It's not about you.
- Start small, start safe.
- Good marketing divides.
- Not perfect but done.
- The twelve elements.

There are people out there who would love working with you if they knew you existed, and they need to know you exist. Their life will be better, and so will yours. Their business will be better, and so will yours. It has begun. You are an Accountant Marketer.

Go be who you are.

CHAPTER 13
ROI, TRACKING, AND BUDGETS

THE MAKING of Scottish whisky takes time. The minimum length of time for it to mature is three years, and most distilleries let it mature much longer—ten, fifteen, twenty-five, or even fifty years. This is part of its charm, and anything less wouldn't be good whisky. And like good whisky, good content marketing takes time to see results.

"The right way is the long way"

Even before it's put into casks to mature, every distillery has a process which varies depending on their history and passions about the whisky they create. The still, which is basically like a massive copper pot, purifies (or "distils") the whisky, and again, every distillery has slightly different types of stills and ways they use them.

One of my favourite distilleries is Glengoyne, which proudly proclaims they have the slowest stills in Scotland. "The right way is the long way" is painted on the doors of their distillery, and the unique flavour of their whisky comes from this approach. Throughout the distillery and in their marketing, this brand says: We are slower on purpose. For good. To create a different kind of whisky.

As you consider your brand, you get to choose. You can choose the kind of firm you'll be, the values you will live up to, and the people you will serve. You can even decide the pace at which you want to move and how much you want to invest to help your firm get where you're going. But just as whisky has a minimum maturing time, so does content marketing.

If you want to be at the place where your consistent content marketing delivers what feels like a magical drip feed of the leads and clients you want and all your twelve elements of marketing are working seamlessly together, you will need to be consistent for at least three years. The right way is the long way for you too.

The work you put in now bears fruit many years ahead. Knowing that can be hard. At first, it seems much more appealing to hurry. Rush. Get the quick wins. Use ads and promotions, discounts and offers. Get noticed. Go viral. Hurry, hurry, hurry.

But the firms who get that drip feed, the best kind of clients coming regularly to them, are the ones who follow the process consistently, day after day, year after year. Their clients aren't even sure where they heard of them; if they were asked, they'd say "This firm seems to be everywhere!" or "I've been following them for years, and now I'm ready." You'll still get results and victories in the early days; many of our Accelerator members have wins to share within a few weeks of joining the group. But the right marketing way is the long way, and knowing this changes how you approach the way you track your marketing numbers.

So how do you track your marketing numbers? Which numbers do you track? And how do you know it's working?

· · ·

Identify your marketing goals so you know what's working

First, start with your goals. It is literally impossible to know if your marketing is working if you don't actually know what "working" means. "Oh, I know my goal," you say. "I want more clients." You may need or want more clients, but it's still about better, not more. Marketing's job is to relieve the pressure of having to sell, push, and find new leads. You want *them* to find you. Each accountant's goals, or those of the firm, will vary as much as each individual accountant or accounting firm varies. If your goal is to get more visibility, you'll have different marketing actions than a firm whose goal is to get rid of the small tax return clients and only take on businesses with £1M or more in sales.

If your goal is to reach more people, you'll create and share more content and keep it personal. You'll record and share videos daily, join communities of the audience you want, and offer to create guest content for companies who serve your ideal audience. If you need to reach more people fast, you have to invest a lot more, especially in terms of your time, learning, and experimentation.

If your goal is to convert leads faster, create content answering every question a prospect could ask. Record videos walking them through these issues, where they come from, and how you help solve them. Create case studies (including videos featuring your clients) to showcase what results look like. Share the numbers in a results page or blog.

If your goal is to build your team by hiring good people, show future team members what it's truly like at your firm so it all matches and there are no surprises. Build a hiring process. Design it in a series of assets. Record more video from the entire team. Attend job fairs. Be more present on social media where the best team members can find you.

If you're happy with the number of clients you have but your goal is to increase your average transaction value by serving them in more and deeper ways, your marketing actions will focus on existing clients over new prospects. Build website pages for your services which focus on the problems solved, not the service name. Create a client community group. Run events exclusively for clients. Offer one-to-one training and mentoring for clients. Involve the team in creating great content which helps clients understand their numbers better.

Keep track of the core marketing numbers

Once you know what your goals are, there are a bare minimum of marketing numbers you need to be tracking beyond number of leads and new clients this month. Track these on at least a monthly basis and more often if you're accelerating growth. Ideally, you'll be tracking these numbers for three to six months, looking for initial patterns which begin to appear, and in the following months, you'll explore those emerging patterns more deeply. We've organised these by the twelve elements, but as you'll see, some of them cross over into multiple categories because marketing is integrated.

There are many more numbers detailed in the Accountant Marketer workbook, so for the purposes of this book, I've chosen only one to three numbers per marketing element so you can get started:

Audience

- Number of clients
- Average transaction value
- Number of enquiries
- Discovery calls booked, attended, missed

Issues:

- Number of blog posts written
- Number of videos recorded

Cornerstone and Assets:

- Number of assets
- Number of downloads

Branding:

- Team happiness rate
- Client happiness rating
- Google/Facebook reviews (and ratings)

Design:

- Assets/pages designed

Website analytics

- Number of new visitors
- Average bounce rate across site
- Average time on page

Emails

- Number of names in database (prospects, clients, specific lists)
- CTA clicked

Follow up:

- Number of proposals created
- Percentage conversion rate (number of proposals accepted divided by number sent out)

Blog posts:

- Longest read time
- Number of views on most popular blog post

Videos:

- Number created
- Views on social platforms (see next section)

Social media:

- Track these for both company and personal accounts on all the platforms you use:
- Number of followers
- Retweets/shares
- Impressions for the month

Campaigns:

- Downloads/sign-ups
- For each campaign, you can track individual numbers from all the previous categories and aggregate them to see results.

How to track and measure your results

The simplest way to track these is within a collaborative Google Sheet. There's a template in the Accountant Marketer workbook you can use to start.

Simply tracking all the numbers we've listed above is not enough to see if your marketing is working.

Question everything and check back against your defined goals. Is that brilliant new marketing idea really that brilliant, or is it a distraction from what you identified at the start of the year as your primary focus? Do you have shiny thing syndrome and are simply bored of the consistent, steady, reliable approach which works in the long run? What do you have to stop doing in order to have time to do this new thing? What will that cost you in terms of what you'll need to give up and the impact it could have over time?

Break down goals into smaller goals. Every marketing action, every marketing number, exists to help you achieve your goals or your one wildly important goal. Breaking down that one goal into smaller achievements and checking how the integrated numbers contribute to those achievements will help you see if you are getting results. This will be true even if you have fewer leads, hardly any asset downloads, or no event registrants that month. Stay focused on the long game. Review and adjust to see if the numbers move one way or the other, and keep going.

Look for patterns over at least six months. As accountants, you'll have easy access to your own financial numbers from a variety of apps and software. Track on a monthly basis (at least), and get perspective and guidance on what to do with these numbers. Otherwise, you'll be flung about by every wind of analytics and get frustrated because you're changing tack every few days. The longer you're tracking, the more patterns you can see. You'll consider seasons and world events. Challenges within your firm and team. Personal life events. As you consider your patterns, question everything.

Sometimes, no matter what you do, it seems like it's just not working. This could be a result of situations with the team and hiring, a flurry of clients leaving for reasons you couldn't foresee, or a national or global event which impacts businesses. It could even be because there is something you're going through personally, and it's affecting your attention or mindset. When this happens (and it will), check whether your goals have changed.

Make sure you're continuing to track all the numbers on a

monthly, if not weekly, basis. If that practice has trailed off, pick it up again. Consider whether it's time to involve the team. Pay attention to whether you've slipped back into old habits of taking on any client rather than focusing on clients you love. Marketing to the kind of clients you don't enjoy working with is soul-destroying. It may be time to reevaluate your audience.

And check in with yourself. Are you going through anything personally right now? The mental, emotional, physical, and financial impact of heavy personal situations affects your marketing. Often marketing is the first thing to be impacted negatively because it involves steadily doing what delivers in the long run, and you don't have instant results to fire you up again. When you're motivated, inspired, and healthy, you'll have ideas and enthusiasm, and your marketing will deliver. When you're weary, grieving, or sick, your marketing will suffer. This may not be your fault, but it is your responsibility to take some kind of action towards it, even if that action is to share the marketing load. It could be with a team member or the whole team, with PF, or with a business partner. Do what you need to do to heal on your own time. Healing isn't something which can be rushed, and adding marketing pressure will only cause it to take longer.

Whatever the reason is, address it. And whatever you do, don't stop tracking those numbers! Once the issue is resolved, you'll wish you had the numbers which reveal the patterns you need to know about over time.

What if you get more leads than you can handle?

Another fear you might have is what to do if your results are far better than you hoped. You might be reading this and think: "Okay, let's say I do all the marketing things and track the numbers and discover it works *too well*? What if I get so many leads I literally cannot handle them? What if I don't want to hire, or what if I do but I know good hiring takes time? I better not get started. I better slow down, be careful, and take my time because my firm isn't ready. My team isn't ready. My systems aren't ready."

First, you will never be completely ready. There's never a perfect time to get all the leads, or have a social post go viral, or become a world-class renowned author overnight (the more copies of this book you share with others, though, the faster that will happen for me, thanks). Secondly, it really is rare for super-fast, instant, and viral results to kick in. The kind of marketing you're doing is for the long game. You'd rather have it done right than done rushed. It's far more likely you'll start steadily getting new leads, and by the time you have too many, you'll have invested in all the other areas of your firm which will allow you to handle them.

Getting too many leads may be a nice problem to have, but it is still a problem. You don't want to sign so many new clients the team aren't able to serve them well, and you destroy much of what you were working for. However, the answer to that problem is *not* to back off on marketing. It isn't. You need to always be marketing, even in (and especially in) your busiest times. You need to keep the momentum going because you never know when you're going to need to call on that momentum, to draw down on it and apply it to your firm. Here's how you do that: create a waiting list.

A waiting list isn't merely a form someone fills in to say they want to work with you sometime in the future, and they sit around while you serve everyone else. It's an entire process, a way to market to people who are ready and willing to become clients. Sign them up for small things. Give them things to do while they're waiting. Create a course or a series of resources they can learn from. Send them blog posts, videos, and content you and the team have created. Prepare them to become the very best client ever, and when you're ready to sign them up, they're ready to go too. Your waiting list could include a website page to explain why you have a waiting list and what they can do while they're on it. It could also include an asset or graphic to show the process. A pricing page or content to explain how pricing works so they can get all the information they need before you start working together. FAQ pages.

If you're worried people might see you have a waiting list, get disgruntled, and leave, you are absolutely right. Some people will do that. But ask yourself: Are those really the kind of clients you want to work with? Do you want clients who have urgent issues, need you to respond instantly, and when they say jump, you ask how high? No, no, a thousand times no. You want the clients who respect the process, who would rather have it right than have it rushed. Set up a waiting list and explain how this will benefit them. Remind them they don't need to panic, and show them why with the educational content you've been creating for years. The right clients will appreciate it.

Marketing budgets: How much do you invest and when?

You still need to invest actual cash in your marketing, and it can be hard to know where to invest that, and when, and in what (or whom). Even people who've been following us for years, who think well of PF and of me personally, love our values and team, appreciate the marketing map and the stories of all the other accountants who have seen great success . . . they may still have doubts, fears, and concerns.

This may be you. Maybe you've had bad experiences. You've invested money and felt like you may as well have stood at the top of a mountain and flung it to the wind. You've read books and followed the process or methodology or paid for the Groundbreaking Forward-Thinking Progressive Modern Blueprint Knowledge Model (GFTPMBKM), and you got nothing. Or not as much as you hoped. You've watched other accountants follow similar processes and have success like you never dreamed of, and you feel frustrated.

You're still tempted to go for the quick win even though you have a sneaking suspicion it doesn't work or doesn't last. I trust you've seen in this book how the long-term approach has the best impact over time, why focusing on the clients you love matters most, and why the right way is the long way. But it's still hard. And you're still unsure. That's completely fair. Your doubts and fears are valid. So let's talk about marketing budgets.

Only work with the right agency and people for you. "Great," you're probably thinking, "I knew it. I got all the way through this super helpful book, and now we get to the sale. Time to put lots of money into PF. Time to pay the piper."

I mean, you can put lots of money into PF if you want to. But we'll only take it if it's the right amount for you, spent in the right places, focused on the right priorities for you. And only as long as you're willing to collaborate with us in your marketing. If any of those aren't true, we don't actually want your money. It wouldn't help you, you wouldn't enjoy the process, and you wouldn't get results either. We want to see accountants use their marketing money well and get to work with the kind of clients they love.

Whoever you work with, make sure you love working with them and respect their approach, their methodology, their values, and their people. All of those are part of the service you receive when you collaborate on your marketing. It is never as simple as paying someone some money and getting some money back. Like the conversations you have with your clients, this is relational, not merely transactional. Life is too valuable and too beautiful to simply trade money around.

Have you heard of the good-fast-cheap rule? When it comes to the three qualities of good, fast, and cheap, you may only ever have two out of three at the most, and this absolutely applies to marketing. When marketing is good and fast, it won't be cheap.

If it's fast and cheap, it likely won't be good. And sometimes, with the very best marketing, you only get one.

Good only (not cheap or fast): The complete rebrand. You have got to be all in with this kind of project, willing to dig deep and go slow if you need to. A branding project needs creative space, rest, and time to think. Better done right than rushed.

Fast only (not good or cheap): You find someone who throws together a website for you in a week or a month. You thought they knew what they were doing, but there were a lot of things they missed, and it ended up costing you about ten times more than you planned in the long run. As the saying goes, if you think hiring a professional is expensive, try hiring an amateur.

Cheap only (not good or fast): You "just want" whatever it is—a graphic designed, some video editing, or a new website page built. You hire a freelancer you've never heard of because you're not sure how to value it, and you don't think it's that important. Not only do they do a sort of okay job at best but it also takes way longer than you planned. All that money you saved doesn't do you much good when you end up waiting months for it because they got busy or never replied to your messages asking about the status.

Okay. On to budget.

How did you decide on your budget? The question is not "how much is your budget?" but "Where did that budget number come from?"

Sometimes you don't know how to answer that question because it's really hard to say. You don't know what you don't know. But I know what it feels like not to want to throw out a number in case the company latches onto it. You know the feeling when you request a quote from a company and they ask, "What is your budget for this?" You have that instant fear reaction, thinking, "I know why they're asking this. They want to know the number in my head so they can meet it or go a little above or below it. If I say £10,000, they'll give me a quote for £9,995. They're just trying to get as much money as they can."

Sadly, some businesses do work like that. It happened to me when I got a quote from an agency who asked my budget. I said I didn't know because this was all new to me, but I had done enough research to know it would have to be in the £8 to £10K range. The quote came in at (I kid you not) £9,999. It felt suspicious and made it hard to truly value the quote and the service.

You've seen this yourself when quoting services from your accounting firm. Many people who get a proposal from you have either had a bad experience with their former accountant or no experience at all. They don't know what to expect or how much it's supposed to cost or what they get for the money they spend. Even if you asked them what their budget was, it's probably too low because they don't understand where that money goes, and why, and what they get from it. The fees your clients need to spend on accounting will vary by their type of business, the state of their bookkeeping, their business model, and their understanding of the value you will help deliver as they work with you.

A rough percentage for your marketing budget is 3–10% of your revenue. As a percentage of sales, work towards the goal of spending 3 to 10 percent of your firm's turnover, or annual revenue, on marketing. You'll be closer to the higher end of the scale in the early days when you need to invest more in foundational elements like a new brand or a custom-built website. Over the years it will vary depending on what you do in-house and what you outsource. You may even decide to build an internal marketing team. The firms we work with who have followed the marketing map, created content consistently for at least three years, and are in that dream place of getting a drip feed of leads and clients they want will have a marketing spend within the 3 to 10 percent range, and some spend more.

If your jaw has dropped to the floor (or you've dropped this book) as you consider this number, think about your business model. Think about the average length of time a client stays with your firm, and the value of investing in one really good client you and the team love and who is profitable to you. Accountants, you have an incredible business model which is amazing and worth investing in because you're building client relationships which last for the long run.

Invest not only your cash, but your team's time. Your marketing budget isn't merely about money. Yes, it's about the cash you put in, but it's also about the time investment you're willing to spend and your commitment to the journey for the long haul. You can spend less cash, but you'll need to invest more time.

One of the patterns we've seen is the more an accountancy firm's whole team is involved in marketing, the better results they have. This is true even (or especially) during difficult times. In 2020, one of the toughest and most challenging years we all faced around the world, every single client we had on monthly retainer was seeing increased numbers.

Increased website visitors.

Increased social media followers and engagement.

Increased average fees.

Increased sales and profits.

Increases, increases, increases.

That was because all those accountants who were already doing the work consistently stepped up to the content plate. They wrote more blog posts themselves. Sent emails. Ran webinars. Posted on social. Recorded videos. Went live and shared the video recordings. They stopped worrying about content being perfect and just got it out there. Not perfect but done. At the same time, because we knew them so well, we were able to support them with design, editing, copywriting, publishing, and all the things. Teamwork. Partnership. That's how marketing is done well. Their foundational consistency got a big boost by their personal efforts, and they saw the numbers ratcheting up. Every firm, without exception.

Interestingly, we've seen some firms invest at a pretty high level (with us or elsewhere) but struggle to see results when they are not personally invested in their own marketing. So it's not all about the money. Remember your whisky lesson. It can take three years for the proper drip feed of content marketing to really pay off.

You can start small and safe. If the amount quoted to you for any aspect of marketing feels so far beyond what you're expecting you cannot for the life of you figure out how or why you'd spend it, there are questions you can ask yourself about that sticker shock. Often when we say something isn't in our budget, what we really mean is "I don't understand how it will be worth that and how it will pay itself back" or "I didn't have a budget in mind, but that feels high." Again, it's not about the money. Yes, you need to actually get help with your marketing, but it's okay if it's in a small way to start. Start small, start safe. Better to invest a small amount and do some prep work than throw money at it and get frustrated because it's overwhelming. I've included some specific suggestions in the next section on how to start small and safe.

Are you comparing apples to other apples, or to oranges? It's possible your sticker shock comes from an experience you've had in the past. You could be comparing the quote you got for a marketing service to another kind of service altogether. Maybe you always used templates for building websites, and it's new to consider a custom-built site based on your clients' journey. Or you could be comparing what seems like the exact same service when the companies are actually very different. A quote from a freelancer building a website for you in their free time is going to massively differ from a quote received from a marketing agency involving content writers, designers, developers, and an entire team. The number in your head might even be two, five, or twenty years old. It's now fifteen years later, and prices have changed.

When you quote a prospective client for accounting services, you want them to understand what these services will actually *do* for them. They need to understand the long-term value they'll receive from the relationship you'll build. The same applies to marketing. If you begrudgingly admit you need a new website but aren't seeing its connection to your brand, your hiring, your prequalifying, and your onboarding, you may struggle with whatever number you're given because this is a grudge buy. You're not excited, inspired, and enthusiastic about how this will help you be a better firm, showing the best of you to the very best clients for you. It's just a box to tick, so the value will never be much higher than the vague number in your head.

Foundational and stackable assets are worth the cost. Some marketing projects can feel really expensive because they're foundational. They set the tone for other marketing which will stack on top of it, beyond the item itself. Branding and websites fall within this category; it's really hard (if not impossible) to track the full return on the amount you spend on a good brand for your accounting firm or on a custom-built website. Tracking your numbers across the whole firm for three years might begin to show that to you, and getting that one big lead you've been dreaming of might do the same. But you know there are no guarantees.

The principle here is stackable content. One piece of content, one designed item, or even a new full rebrand does not exist in a silo. It forms yet another part of your entire marketing message, repeated over and over, day after day, in both small and great ways. When you realise it's not about paying this particular amount for getting a PDF guide designed but, rather, about investing in another part of your whole marketing picture, that one spend begins to take on more value. That PDF guide will go on your website. Portions of it will be shared on your social media over the years. You'll record a video summarising what the guide says. You may turn all the content into blog posts or, vice versa, take good blog posts and turn them into a guide. It all stacks together, interlocking so the prospect gets a picture over time.

You're in it for the long term. This is not about an instant return on spending hundreds or thousands on one marketing item. This is about contributing another high-quality marketing item to your firm's story.

Good results require consistency. It's also why consistently working with the same agency and the same people who have known you since the rebrand or since the website build day in and day out, month in and month out, will help your marketing investment be more effective over time.

When we've been working with a firm for five years and they have a huge opportunity and need a PDF guide, or a slide deck, or social images created urgently, we know them and their firm so well we can move fast. We are already familiar with their brand, colours, style, tone, and team. We have all the brand files. We've got the PDF guides or slide decks we've created in the past with them and can adapt quickly based on the new information.

If you're continually changing the people or agencies who help you with various kinds of marketing, you're going to feel really frustrated (and so will they), especially if you're using multiple people or agencies who aren't talking to each other. It's not cohesive. Everyone is sitting in their own little rooms, separate from each other, and no one is really talking to you and the team on a daily basis. You won't get good marketing done, and you won't see good results because it's not collaborative and consistent.

What's the cost of *not* investing in marketing? Finally, as you consider your marketing investment, ask yourself the cost of *not* doing this now. We've seen people get a new website page created which is put together so well with the right messaging and the right calls to action that people who are looking for that particular service sign up within minutes. Think about how many people are coming to your website or your other marketing and saying, "Ehhhh, I'll decide later." Does your marketing cause them to hesitate or to hurry up? If it causes them to hesitate, you're losing business—and probably from the very best kind of clients, too. The kind you really like and wish you had more of. Many of you have clients who are not living up to your values, and they're frustrating and difficult, and the team grits their teeth a bit when they get in touch. You need to replace those clients. That's a big cost. Think about what it's costing you to wait.

How to start small, start safe with your marketing investment

Okay, you get it. Invest for the long term. But what if you're in the position where you've lost clients, they've gone out of business, or you decided not to pursue a niche anymore and you literally do not have that money right now? If that's genuinely the case, there are some things you can invest a little bit in to start.

Whether it's a little time, a little money, or both, there are things you can do to start small, start safe. That way, by the time you do start your marketing project, you've got some prep work done so you're a more informed accountant when it comes to marketing. Also more willing, more ready, and more excited! Here are some things you can start doing today:

Read good business and marketing books. You're already reading this one, so I'll share some others I'd suggest you begin with.

- *They Ask You Answer: A Revolutionary Approach to Inbound Sales, Content Marketing, and Today's Digital Consumer, Revised and Updated* by Marcus Sheridan
- *Rising Strong: How the Ability to Reset Transforms the Way We Live, Love, Parent, and Lead* by Brené Brown
- *Steal Like an Artist: 10 Things Nobody Told You About Being Creative* by Austin Kleon
- *Oversubscribed: How to Get People Lined Up to Do Business with You* by Daniel Priestley

- *Building a Story Brand: Clarify Your Message So Customers Will Listen* by Donald Miller
- *Atomic Habits: An Easy & Proven Way to Build Good Habits & Break Bad Ones* by James Clear

The content of these books fits with what you're reading here and gives you insights from a different perspective.

Write. Write blog posts, write social posts, and write content for guides. Even if these aren't perfect and even if your writing feels boring or stale. Just start. You will learn as you go. Write even when you're not in the mood.

Record videos. These can be one-to-one videos for a particular client, or short training videos for clients, or thoughts on something useful for your clients. Use free screen recording software. If the video is great and you want to use it elsewhere, you can download it. If it's a one-time video and that's it, you've still gotten some practice.

Get free marketing training from the PF Vault. This includes articles as well as tutorial videos, checklists, downloads, and practical marketing help with the thousands of questions we've been asked by accountants for a decade or more. You can also follow PF on the socials. We are regularly sharing marketing ideas, training, and links to other resources and other companies who will help as you build your accounting firm and your own skills. You're also welcome to follow my own personal social accounts, which are usually @karenlreyburn.

So there you have it. ROI, tracking, and marketing budgets. WHEW. Those are often the first questions we get asked at PF, but as you can see, they rely on everything which came before. Without the previous twelve chapters, your approach towards ROI, tracking your numbers, and how much to invest will simply be based on your past approach or mindset. This book has been all about changing your perspective on marketing so you can change your results.

. . .

Conclusion

There's not much more to say. Now it's on to the doing. I'll leave you with three short statements which I live by in my own marketing and my own life:

1. Just get started.
2. Just keep going.
3. Stay creative, stay kind.

KAREN L. REYBURN

ACCOUNTANT MARKETER AT A GLANCE

A quick summary of the concepts which will help you become a better Accountant Marketer

Not perfect but done
It's a matter of iterations, not perfection. Get it out there.

You are creative, too
Exercise the qualities of problem solving and curiosity, which you already have.

Start small, start safe
When in doubt, try something small and test it with a few people first.

Good marketing divides
Its job is to bring in those who are a fit for you and send away those who are not.

Just get started
The perfect conditions will never be there. Leap in.

Just keep going
When you're tempted to give up, remember you may be closer to the end than you realise.

The right way is the long way
Good things take time. Be willing to see it through.

Give away information, charge for implementation
Be free and generous with information they could find anywhere. Once they need to apply this information to their circumstances, start charging.

It's relational, not transactional
You're connecting with humans. Take the time to build relationship, not just make sales.

Anyone means no one
Marketing for "everyone" is marketing which applies to no one.

Question everything
What? Why? Where? Who? Does it matter? What if we…? How might we…?

Not perfect but good
Be proud of what you do share.

ACKNOWLEDGMENTS

I always knew I'd write (at least one) book. I thought I knew it would be hard, and long, and I'd have moments of wondering if it would ever get published. Turns out there was more of that than I expected.

There was also more excitement and motivation than I expected. The process as well as the end result has brought me more confidence in myself, and in the value of what I have to share with the world. It's not only accountants who wonder how to get across the value they provide: every human wonders this and doubts this and faces this.

The people who impacted me along the way and helped me get over the line are:

Every team member of my agency PF, who helped me see the gathering of knowledge and structure and stories were a book, not a PDF guide. Thank you for telling me I was not allowed to make it a PDF guide, you wouldn't stand for it, and you'd fight me on it if need be. You saw the potential of it long before anyone else, and you had my back on the days when I wasn't sure if it was ever going to become a reality.

Every member of the Accountant Marketer Prelaunch team, including those who read the very first original draft which was far too long. Thanks for helping me figure out what sections were repetitive or didn't focus on the intended reader. Through you I was reminded this book is not for me: it's for my readers. Thanks to Alasdair McGill, Alexander Malmstrom, Amy Walker,

Andy Sullivan, Cheryl Sharp, Chris Jones, Colin Comerford, Emma Fox, Georgi Rollings, James Abbott, Karen Kennedy, Kat Wellum-Kent, Nickie Sheehan, Patrick Scotchmer, and Scott Johnson. Thank you for being part of the enthusiasm (and bringing extra enthusiasm when mine flagged) before we shared it all with the world.

Every accountant I've ever had the privilege of working with. Some are in the prelaunch team and others are named in this book, but many more are known to me as some of the kindest, loyal, creative, and interesting people I know. You all defeat the stereotype every single day.

Paul Barnes, who was one of the first PF clients ever, and who has been my company's accountant through the hard and the good, the weak and the strong. On multiple occasions your invaluable advice protected me from going off in directions I really didn't want to go, yet you always provide advice in a way that makes it clear the ultimate decision rests with me. I'd also like to thank David Arden and the whole MAP team, who have together seen me through so many phases of a changing business. David, you have remained calm and patient when my emotions are running wild. Thanks for reminding me to listen to my gut and pay attention to the numbers, because the combination works.

James Ashford, founder of GoProposal and someone I had the privilege of working with in the early days. So many phone calls, good questions, ideas, events, and stories. Thanks for creating not only a product to help so many accountants worldwide serve their clients better, but also for creating a community of accountants who love to learn, ask questions, be curious, and try things.

Marcus Sheridan, author of *They Ask You Answer*, has impacted my business and so many accountants worldwide with this very simple concept of creating content relating to what your clients want to hear about. I'm grateful for your book and everything I've learned from you personally - and from your own content - along the way.

My very first accounting professor Dr. Nancy Wilburn, who was so enthusiastic about accountancy that I absorbed that too. You made it clear you believed accounting was a good direction for me to go in, whilst leaving me to make my own decision on it, and you celebrated enthusiastically when I did go that direction. Thanks for being one of the first people to show me the impact accountants can have on the (and their) world.

My incredible family, who have borne with my decision to move across the ocean and live in another country with grace, understanding, humour, and love. The dedication is for my Dad, who is no longer with us; I'd also like to thank my Mum, who is an example of the #justkeepgoing principle, and who listens and empathises and also cheers me on. My oldest sister Janice, who is there for me any time I need her, day or night, and with whom I have decades of photographs and memories and travels and laughter - so, so much laughter. Thank you for your faith and for being an example to me of someone who never gives up. My sister Laura, who runs marathons and manages to be tough as nails as well as soft and gracious. Pin, who brings me laughter on a daily basis and with whom I have endless inside jokes which could never be explained, and which I sometimes forget where they even came from (but you never forget). You believe fiercely in the right and the good, and I love you for it. Velvet, who became and remained family, and not in the typical way. There is nothing typical about you. And my brothers in law: DJ, you are one of the most patient and gracious people I know, and you appreciate both the beauty and the bizarre. I love the way you love people. Scott, you are generosity itself, and the eternal optimist. And my remarkable nieces and nephews who are leaning into the potential I always knew you had: Zach, Luke, Jake, Marcus, Audrey, Jude, Marin, Anika. Thank you for being and bringing joy into my life.

And finally you, the reader. By investing in this book you are investing in yourself, and in the potential you have to help others see the value you bring to their business and life. I believe great accountants quite literally save lives. You certainly save businesses, and if business is anything at heart, it is and must remain human.

ABOUT THE AUTHOR

Photo by The Profitable Firm (PF)

Karen L. Reyburn is a qualified accountant (CPA) and creative agency owner who has worked with accountants for over twenty years. She founded the creative agency The Profitable Firm (PF) in 2012 to exclusively serve accountants all over the world. She is a speaker for accountants and entrepreneurs in addition to giving presentations on topics such as creativity, rest, and female business ownership. She is a dual British-American citizen living in Scotland and is fueled by daily walks in the Scottish country-side, and copious amounts of strong black coffee.

GET ACCOUNTABILITY AND SUPPORT IN THE ACCELERATOR COACHING GROUP

JOIN THE NEXT GROUP

Audience · Issues · Cornerstone · Branding

Design · Website · Email · Follow-up

Blogging · Video · Social · Campaigns

Since 2016, over four hundred accountants have learned and applied the principles summarised in this book by being part of Accelerator coaching groups.

Join live sessions led by Karen and the PF team; submit content for review and feedback; and receive additional training videos, checklists, and resources.

Convert your marketing ideas from notes into reality by joining Accelerator.

GET ALL THE DETAILS AT

wearepf.com/accelerator

LOOK FORWARD TO MEETING YOU SOON!

Printed in Great Britain
by Amazon

40251768R00198